SKIP WILLIAMSON

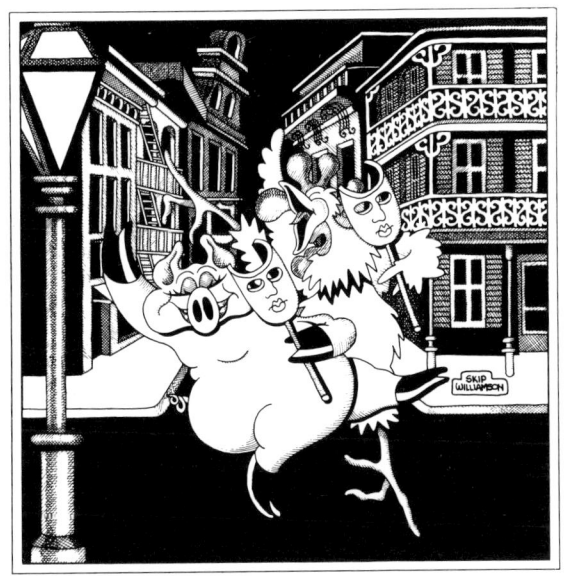

THE SCUM ALSO RISES

AN ANTHOLOGY OF COMIC ART BY SKIP WILLIAMSON

For Richard Baily and Tim Blickhan who,
no matter how much they may attempt to disassociate themselves,
must shoulder their share of the blame.

FANTAGRAPHICS BOOKS
1800 Bridgegate Street, Suite #101
Westlake Village, CA 91361

Editorial coordination by Gary Groth.
Design and art direction by Doug Erb.
Interior color separations by Palace Press.
Cover color separations executed by Skip Williamson.
Cover negatives shot by Port Publications.
Production assistance by Mark Thompson and Charles Lieurance.
Typesetting by Inez M. Gorell and Everett Nielsen.
Gary Groth and Kim Thompson, Publishers.

First Fantagraphics Books edition: November, 1988.
1   3   5   7   9   10   8   6   4   2

ISBN: 0-930193-67-9

Printed in Singapore through Palace Press.

CONTENTS

FOREWORD

I wonder if guys who clean out septic tanks run into a lot of youngsters who want to do the same when they grow up. I'm always running into people who want to draw cartoons, even if they don't know who I am or what I do. I mean, a guy could get killed for doing this, and the odds of making a decent wage drawing cartoons is a long shot at a tiny target. If enterprise is what these people have in mind, then better to clean out septic tanks.

Youthful zeal being what it is, the callow cartoonist is fit with blinders, and there's no sense lecturing on the pitfalls and dangers. I say let these young minions go willy-nilly about their foolhardy business and after 20, 25 years or so, perhaps they'll stand as wretched examples to another generation of misguided youth, rapidographs at the ready.

On the other hand, why not lecture a little invective advice?

Extremism in the pursuit of cartooning is no vice. The comic strip artist especially needs the resolve of a capricious point of view in order to seem to justify his narrow personal reality. A talent, an ability to draw, is a place to start but certainly not a necessity.

A quick look at the comics page of any daily newspaper is proof of that. Likewise, draftsmanship doesn't always equate comic art, a fact verified by any number of Marvel, DC or similar comic book titles.

A command of the language, the ability to turn a phrase cleverly toward your own ends isn't a bad tool. If you can sarcastically unearth the raw nerve of abhorrent human nature by the way of nearsighted satire, it's possible to catch the public eye. In final desperation, the pimply aspirant can poke around in his own dark, reprehensible self and reveal his most neurotic abominations. If nothing else, it saves throwing money you don't have into the fat coffers of the psychiatric profession. Then, if what you turn out is garbled swill and is recognized as such, at least you have the comfort of numbers. After all, there's much more garbled swill on the comic pages than not.

But if that which oozes from the most odious recesses of your inkwell is hailed a newfound genius, if the intellectual liberals rail on and chase their tales in polysyllabic rant over your plainly irresponsible anarchistic scratches, then, like the wretched rabble before you, you will most certainly reach for the tantalizing bait of peer recognition. You will, sure as shootin' in Beirut, be lured into the gaping maw of Life as a Cartoonist. The trap will snap shut with such diabolonian ferocity that you and the lives of your kin will be laid waste. You will be the shame of your neighborhood and will be left broken and bleeding, the bastard child of the Art Community. But what the heck, it's a living.

But who am I to lecture? My past is littered with more than a quarter of a century of paper. There have been nihilistic diatribes, unflattering caricatures, paintings, gags, arguments advocating drug usage by underaged adolescent females, blind political rants, quick indecipherable sketches, invitations to anarchy, and odds and ends too demeritorious to mention. It's as if some colossal mutant beaver waddled through whole timberlands ingesting whole wildwood and excreting scraps of paper festooned with loathsome cartoonery. This book is a collection of some of that and probably a lot of shit you haven't seen.

Skip Williamson, 1988

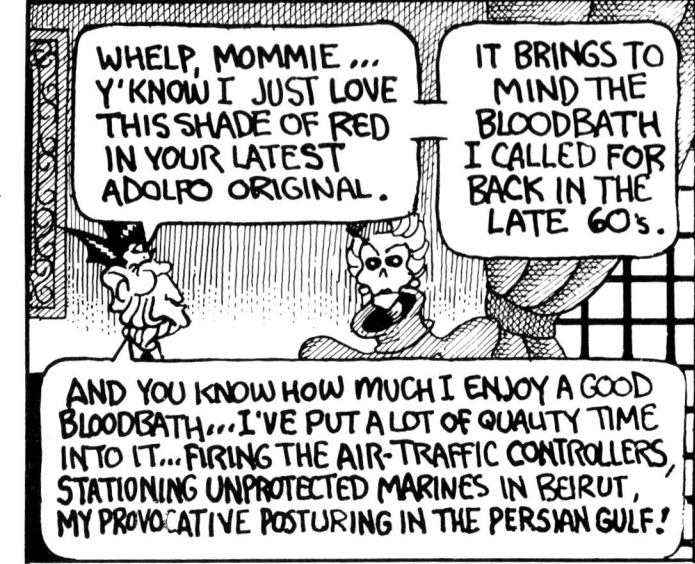

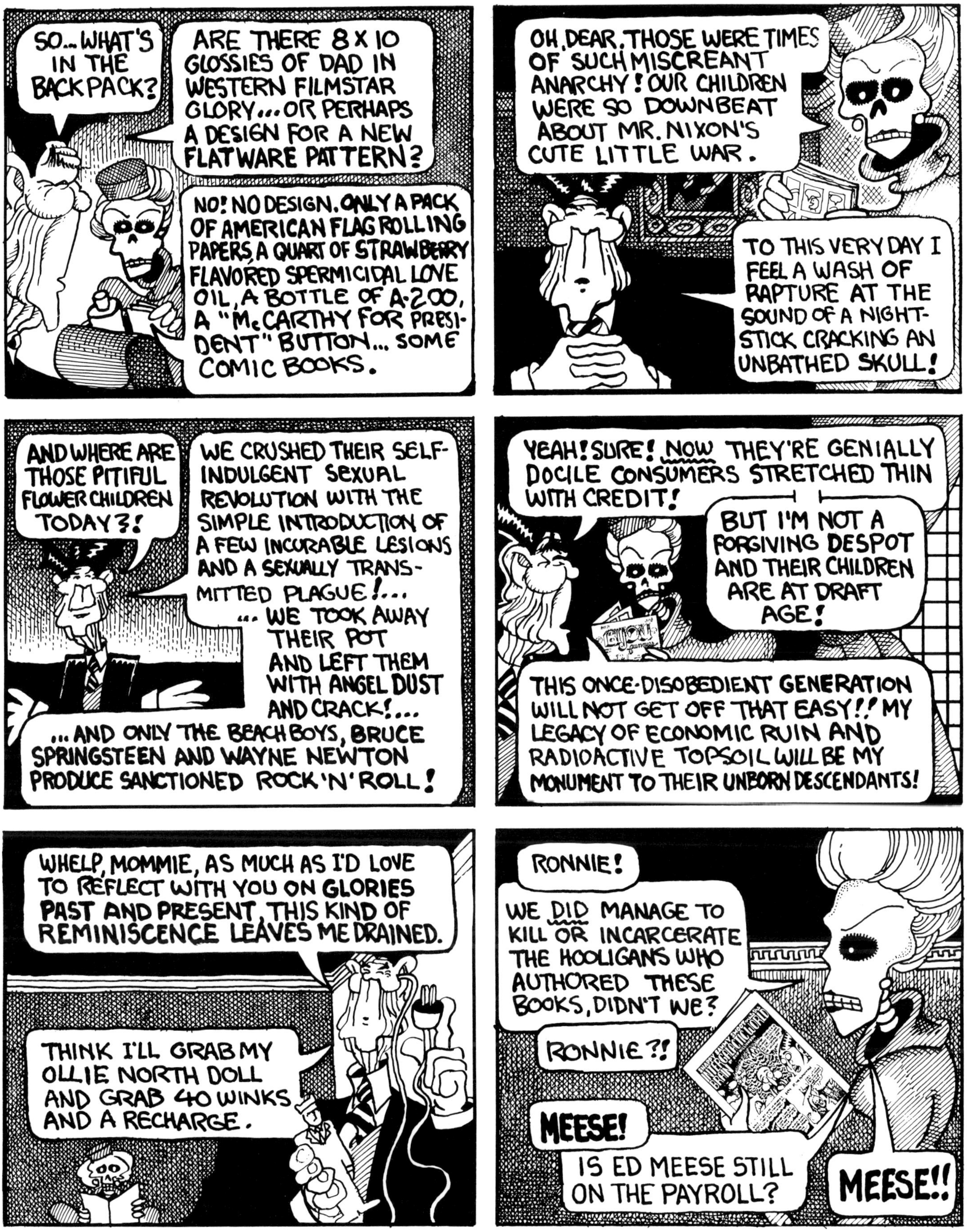
SO... WHAT'S IN THE BACKPACK?
ARE THERE 8 X 10 GLOSSIES OF DAD IN WESTERN FILMSTAR GLORY... OR PERHAPS A DESIGN FOR A NEW FLATWARE PATTERN?
NO! NO DESIGN. ONLY A PACK OF AMERICAN FLAG ROLLING PAPERS, A QUART OF STRAWBERRY FLAVORED SPERMICIDAL LOVE OIL, A BOTTLE OF A-200, A "McCARTHY FOR PRESIDENT" BUTTON... SOME COMIC BOOKS.
OH, DEAR. THOSE WERE TIMES OF SUCH MISCREANT ANARCHY! OUR CHILDREN WERE SO DOWNBEAT ABOUT MR. NIXON'S CUTE LITTLE WAR.
TO THIS VERY DAY I FEEL A WASH OF RAPTURE AT THE SOUND OF A NIGHT-STICK CRACKING AN UNBATHED SKULL!
AND WHERE ARE THOSE PITIFUL FLOWER CHILDREN TODAY?!
WE CRUSHED THEIR SELF-INDULGENT SEXUAL REVOLUTION WITH THE SIMPLE INTRODUCTION OF A FEW INCURABLE LESIONS AND A SEXUALLY TRANSMITTED PLAGUE!...
...WE TOOK AWAY THEIR POT AND LEFT THEM WITH ANGEL DUST AND CRACK!...
...AND ONLY THE BEACH BOYS, BRUCE SPRINGSTEEN AND WAYNE NEWTON PRODUCE SANCTIONED ROCK 'N' ROLL!
YEAH! SURE! NOW THEY'RE GENIALLY DOCILE CONSUMERS STRETCHED THIN WITH CREDIT!
BUT I'M NOT A FORGIVING DESPOT AND THEIR CHILDREN ARE AT DRAFT AGE!
THIS ONCE-DISOBEDIENT GENERATION WILL NOT GET OFF THAT EASY!!! MY LEGACY OF ECONOMIC RUIN AND RADIOACTIVE TOPSOIL WILL BE MY MONUMENT TO THEIR UNBORN DESCENDANTS!
WHELP, MOMMIE, AS MUCH AS I'D LOVE TO REFLECT WITH YOU ON GLORIES PAST AND PRESENT, THIS KIND OF REMINISCENCE LEAVES ME DRAINED.
THINK I'LL GRAB MY OLLIE NORTH DOLL AND GRAB 40 WINKS AND A RECHARGE.
RONNIE!
WE DID MANAGE TO KILL OR INCARCERATE THE HOOLIGANS WHO AUTHORED THESE BOOKS, DIDN'T WE?
RONNIE?!
MEESE!
IS ED MEESE STILL ON THE PAYROLL?
MEESE!!

SNAPPY SAMMY SMOOT visits the INTERGALACTIC WORLD BRAIN

BY SKIP WILLIAMSON

> GOSH!...THIS L.S.D IS ALMOST AS EXCITING AS THE TIME I WENT TO PITTSBURGH FOR THE WEEKEND!

> GOLLY...IT SEZ HERE IN READER'S DIGEST THAT L.S.D CAN MAKE YOU SEE A LOT OF PRETTY COLORS!

> MAYBE I CAN GET SOME FROM FILTHY FREDDIE, THE LOCAL PUSHER...

> HE'S ALWAYS DOWN AT THE GRADE SCHOOL PLAYGROUND TRYING TO GET SOME KIDS "HOOKED!"

LATER... AT THE PLAYGROUND

> HEY...LITTLE KID! YA' WANNA BUY FIVE CENTS WORTH OF HEROIN?

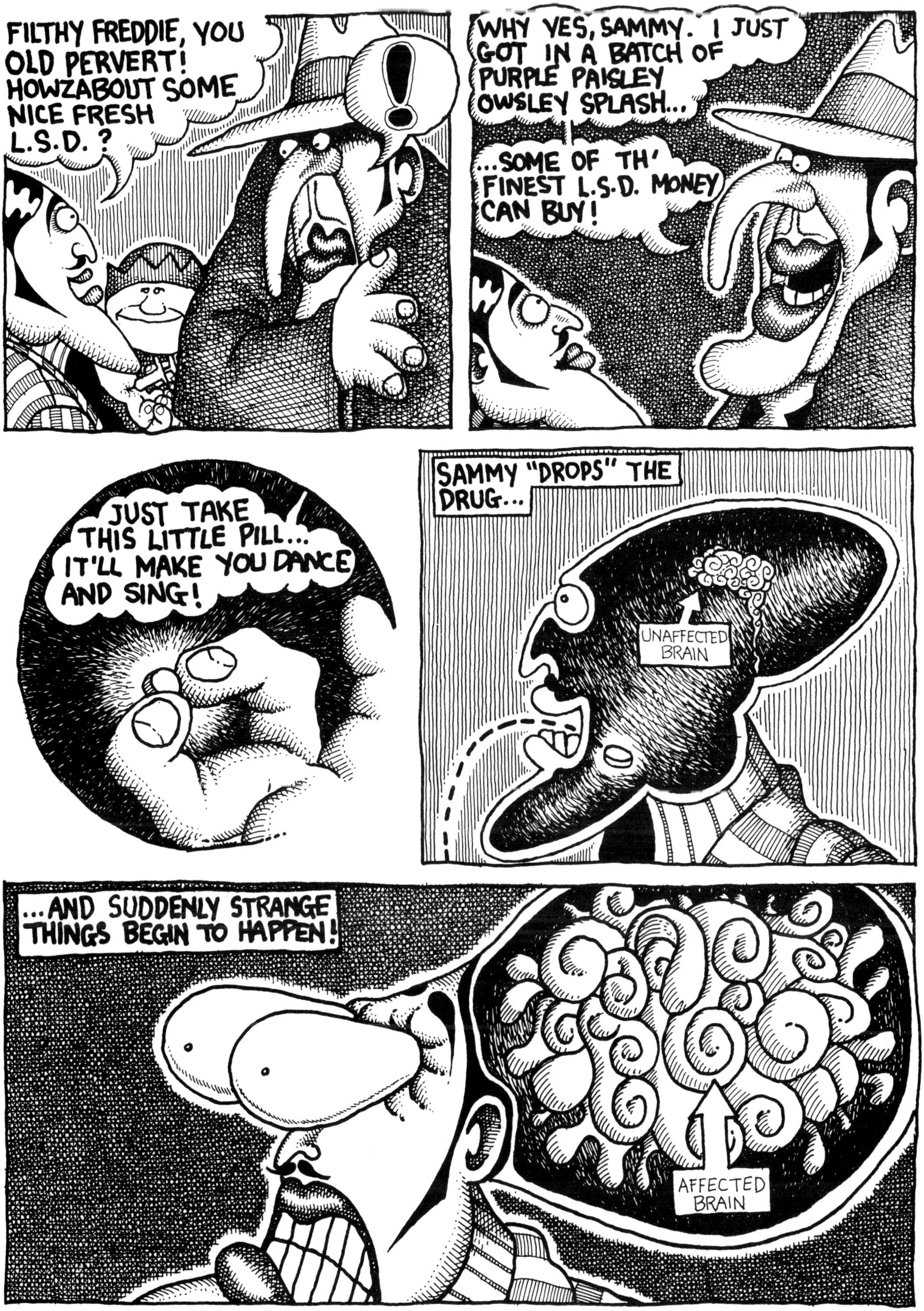
FILTHY FREDDIE, YOU OLD PERVERT! HOWZABOUT SOME NICE FRESH L.S.D. ?
!
WHY YES, SAMMY. I JUST GOT IN A BATCH OF PURPLE PAISLEY OWSLEY SPLASH...
...SOME OF TH' FINEST L.S.D. MONEY CAN BUY!
JUST TAKE THIS LITTLE PILL... IT'LL MAKE YOU DANCE AND SING!
SAMMY "DROPS" THE DRUG...
UNAFFECTED BRAIN
...AND SUDDENLY STRANGE THINGS BEGIN TO HAPPEN!
AFFECTED BRAIN

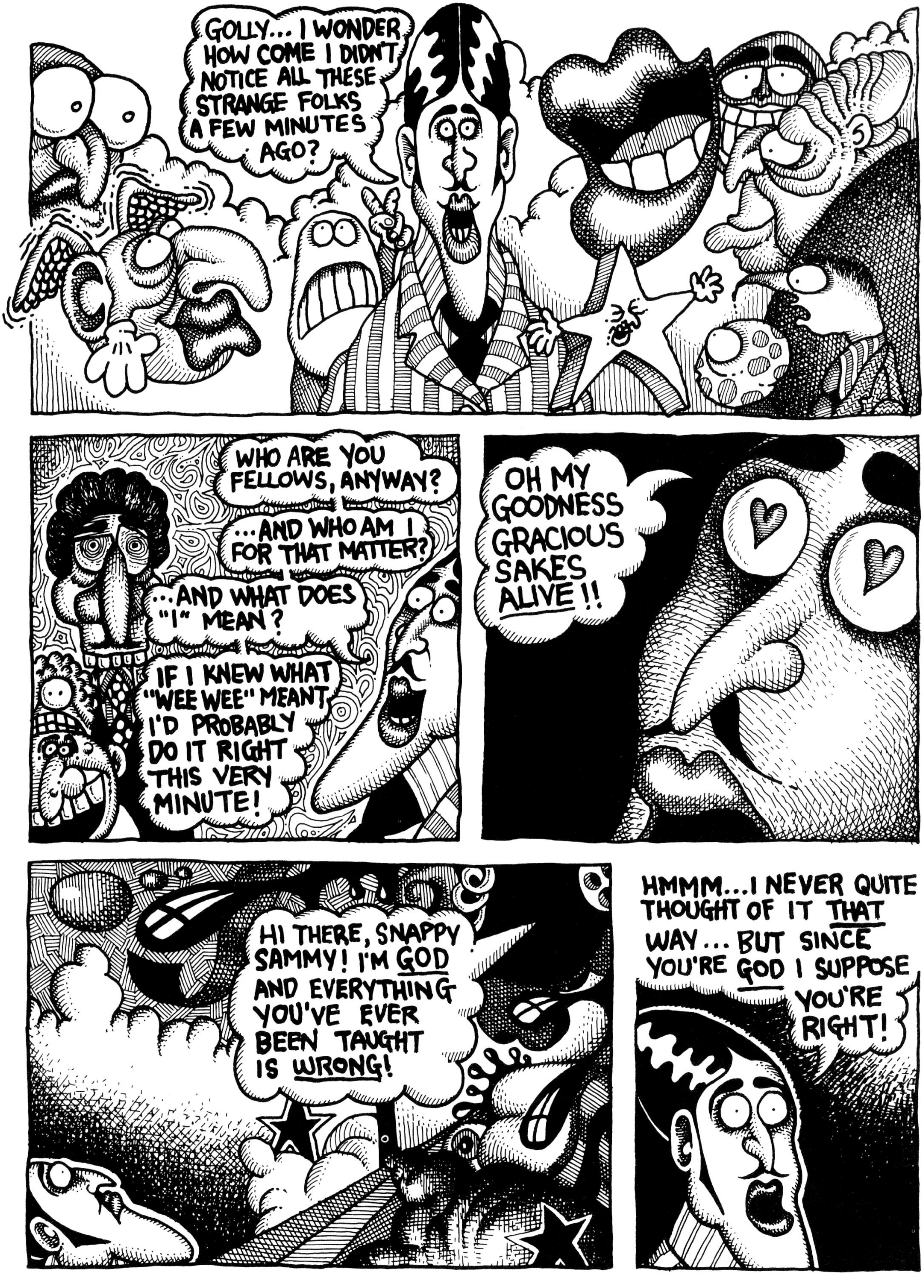
GOLLY... I WONDER HOW COME I DIDN'T NOTICE ALL THESE STRANGE FOLKS A FEW MINUTES AGO?
WHO ARE YOU FELLOWS, ANYWAY?
...AND WHO AM I FOR THAT MATTER?
...AND WHAT DOES "I" MEAN?
IF I KNEW WHAT "WEE WEE" MEANT I'D PROBABLY DO IT RIGHT THIS VERY MINUTE!
OH MY GOODNESS GRACIOUS SAKES ALIVE!!
HI THERE, SNAPPY SAMMY! I'M GOD AND EVERYTHING YOU'VE EVER BEEN TAUGHT IS WRONG!
HMMM...I NEVER QUITE THOUGHT OF IT THAT WAY... BUT SINCE YOU'RE GOD I SUPPOSE YOU'RE RIGHT!

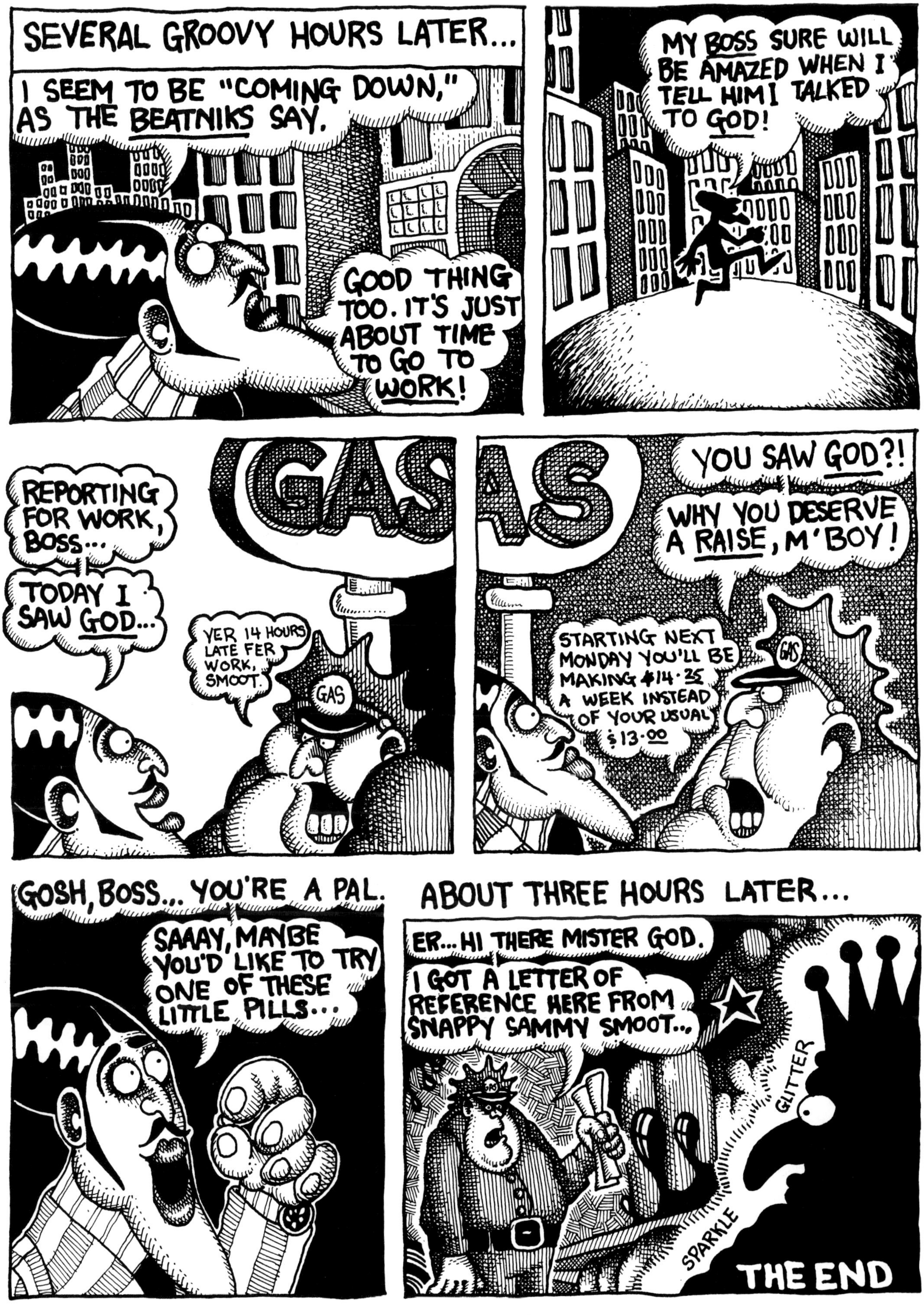

SEVERAL GROOVY HOURS LATER...
I SEEM TO BE "COMING DOWN," AS THE BEATNIKS SAY.
GOOD THING TOO. IT'S JUST ABOUT TIME TO GO TO WORK!
MY BOSS SURE WILL BE AMAZED WHEN I TELL HIM I TALKED TO GOD!
GAS
REPORTING FOR WORK, BOSS...
TODAY I SAW GOD...
YER 14 HOURS LATE FER WORK, SMOOT.
GAS
YOU SAW GOD?!
WHY YOU DESERVE A RAISE, M'BOY!
STARTING NEXT MONDAY YOU'LL BE MAKING $14.25 A WEEK INSTEAD OF YOUR USUAL $13.00
GAS
GOSH, BOSS... YOU'RE A PAL.
SAAAY, MAYBE YOU'D LIKE TO TRY ONE OF THESE LITTLE PILLS...
ABOUT THREE HOURS LATER...
ER...HI THERE MISTER GOD.
I GOT A LETTER OF REFERENCE HERE FROM SNAPPY SAMMY SMOOT...
GLITTER
SPARKLE
THE END

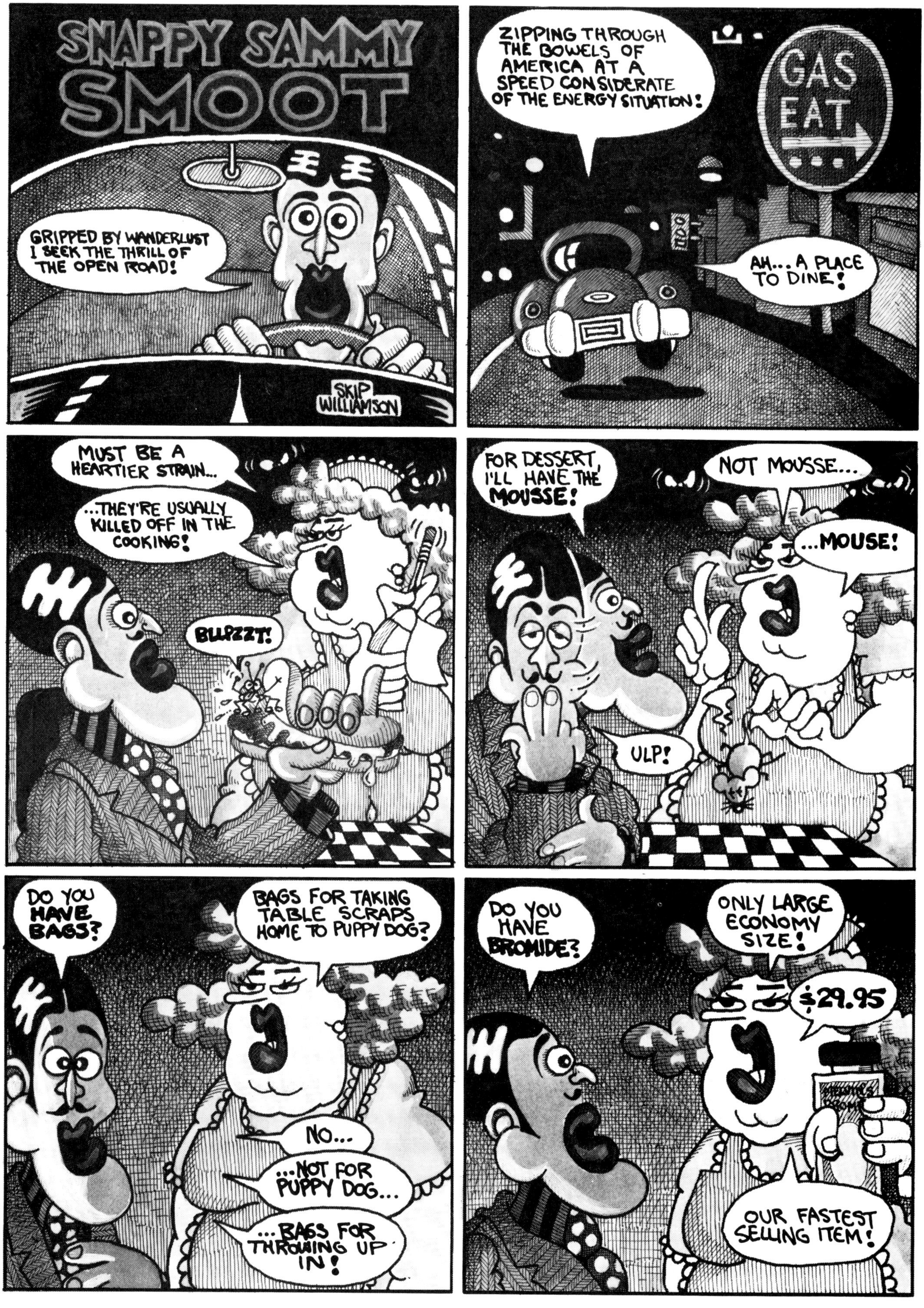
SNAPPY SAMMY SMOOT
GRIPPED BY WANDERLUST I SEEK THE THRILL OF THE OPEN ROAD!
SKIP WILLIAMSON
ZIPPING THROUGH THE BOWELS OF AMERICA AT A SPEED CONSIDERATE OF THE ENERGY SITUATION!
GAS EAT
AH... A PLACE TO DINE!
MUST BE A HEARTIER STRAIN...
...THEY'RE USUALLY KILLED OFF IN THE COOKING!
BLLPZZT!
FOR DESSERT, I'LL HAVE THE MOUSSE!
NOT MOUSSE...
...MOUSE!
ULP!
DO YOU HAVE BAGS?
BAGS FOR TAKING TABLE SCRAPS HOME TO PUPPY DOG?
NO...
...NOT FOR PUPPY DOG...
...BAGS FOR THROWING UP IN!
DO YOU HAVE BROMIDE?
ONLY LARGE ECONOMY SIZE!
$29.95
OUR FASTEST SELLING ITEM!

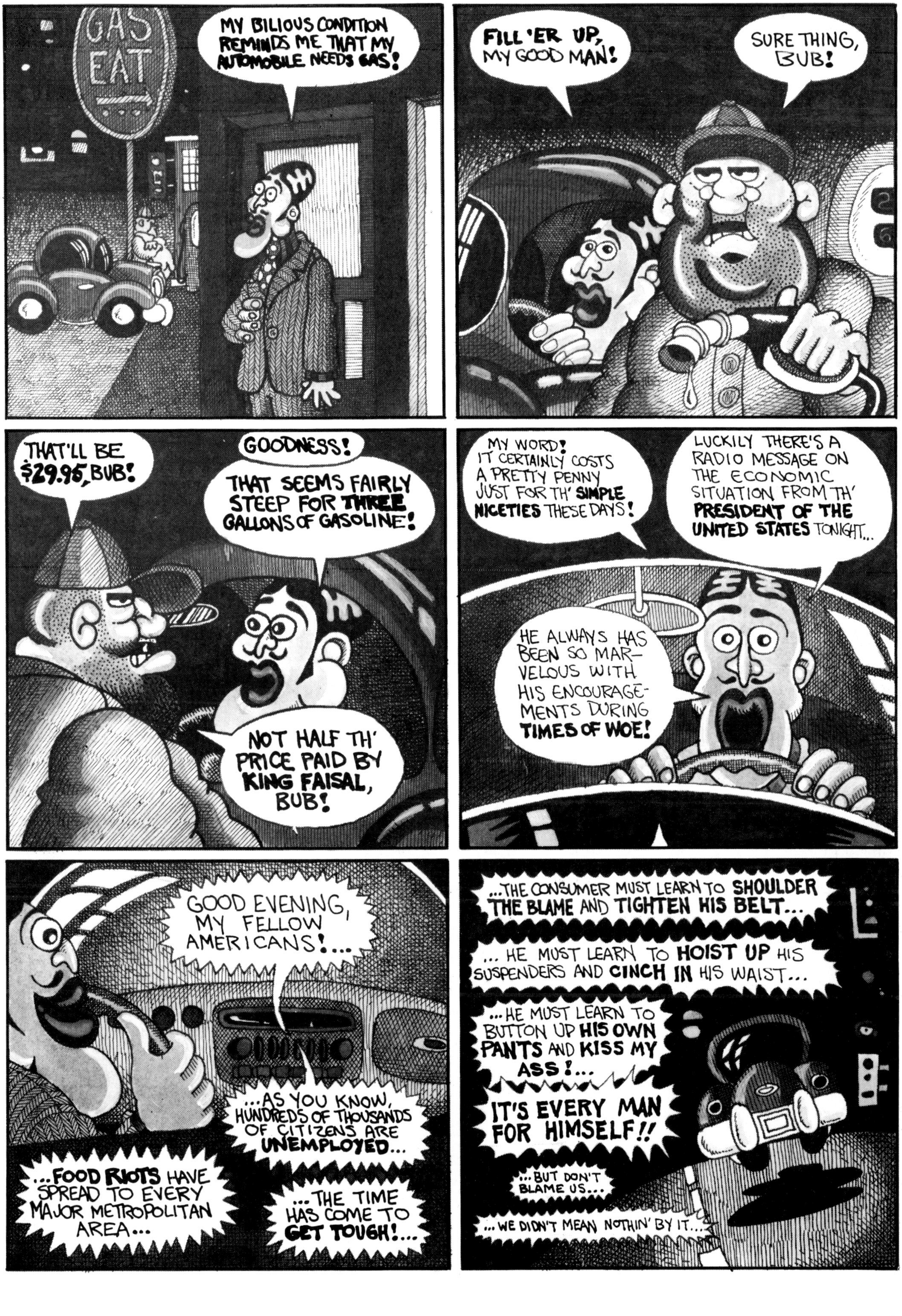
GAS
EAT
MY BILIOUS CONDITION REMINDS ME THAT MY AUTOMOBILE NEEDS GAS!
FILL 'ER UP, MY GOOD MAN!
SURE THING, BUB!
THAT'LL BE $29.95, BUB!
GOODNESS!
THAT SEEMS FAIRLY STEEP FOR THREE GALLONS OF GASOLINE!
NOT HALF TH' PRICE PAID BY KING FAISAL, BUB!
MY WORD! IT CERTAINLY COSTS A PRETTY PENNY JUST FOR TH' SIMPLE NICETIES THESE DAYS!
LUCKILY THERE'S A RADIO MESSAGE ON THE ECONOMIC SITUATION FROM TH' PRESIDENT OF THE UNITED STATES TONIGHT...
HE ALWAYS HAS BEEN SO MAR-VELOUS WITH HIS ENCOURAGE-MENTS DURING TIMES OF WOE!
GOOD EVENING, MY FELLOW AMERICANS!...
...AS YOU KNOW, HUNDREDS OF THOUSANDS OF CITIZENS ARE UNEMPLOYED...
...FOOD RIOTS HAVE SPREAD TO EVERY MAJOR METROPOLITAN AREA...
...THE TIME HAS COME TO GET TOUGH!...
...THE CONSUMER MUST LEARN TO SHOULDER THE BLAME AND TIGHTEN HIS BELT...
... HE MUST LEARN TO HOIST UP HIS SUSPENDERS AND CINCH IN HIS WAIST...
...HE MUST LEARN TO BUTTON UP HIS OWN PANTS AND KISS MY ASS!...
IT'S EVERY MAN FOR HIMSELF!!
...BUT DON'T BLAME US...
...WE DIDN'T MEAN NOTHIN' BY IT...

OF COURSE, YOUNG MAN! HERE IS A NICE CRISP DOLLAR BILL FOR YOU...

HARDLY COMPENSATION, I MIGHT ADD, FOR MORAL IDEALISM THE LIKES OF YOURS!

MAY TH' GOOD LORD BLESS YOU!

HEY... WE FINALLY GOT ENOUGH T' SCORE SOME BOONE'S FARM STRAWBERRY HILL.

FAR OUT

DIS IS BETTER 'N' TH' ECOLOGY RACKET

BUT THAT WAS NOT YET THE LAST RELIGIOUS ENCOUNTER OF SAM'S EVENING... LATER... AT HOME...

WONDER WHUT'S ON TH' TEEVEE?

CLIK

KUP'S SHOW

OUR FIRST GUEST TONIGHT IS RELIGIOUS ZEALOT, PAT BOONE...

BUT FIRST A WORD FROM MAXWELL COFFEE

THIS WONDERFUL, PAT!

TH' KIDS ARE INCREDIBLE THESE DAYS, KUP... THEY'RE TURNING OFF TO DRUGS AND TURNING ON TO CHRIST...

LATER... THE SAME EVENING...

GOLLY... THE YOUNG FOLKS THESE DAYS ARE POSITIVELY SACRED!

I HAVEN'T FELT THIS SPIRITUAL SINCE THE LAST DONOVAN CONCERT!

SMOOT'S PEACEFUL SLUMBER IS DISTURBED BY RESTLESS DREAMS...

SAM SMOOT! I HAVE A MESSAGE FOR YOU!

I'VE SEARCHED YOUR HEART AND FOUND IT TO BE GOOD... YOU HAVE BEEN CHOSEN FOR A VERY IMPORTANT TASK. A TASK THAT WILL REQUIRE SACRIFICE AND MORAL PURPOSE ON YOUR PART...

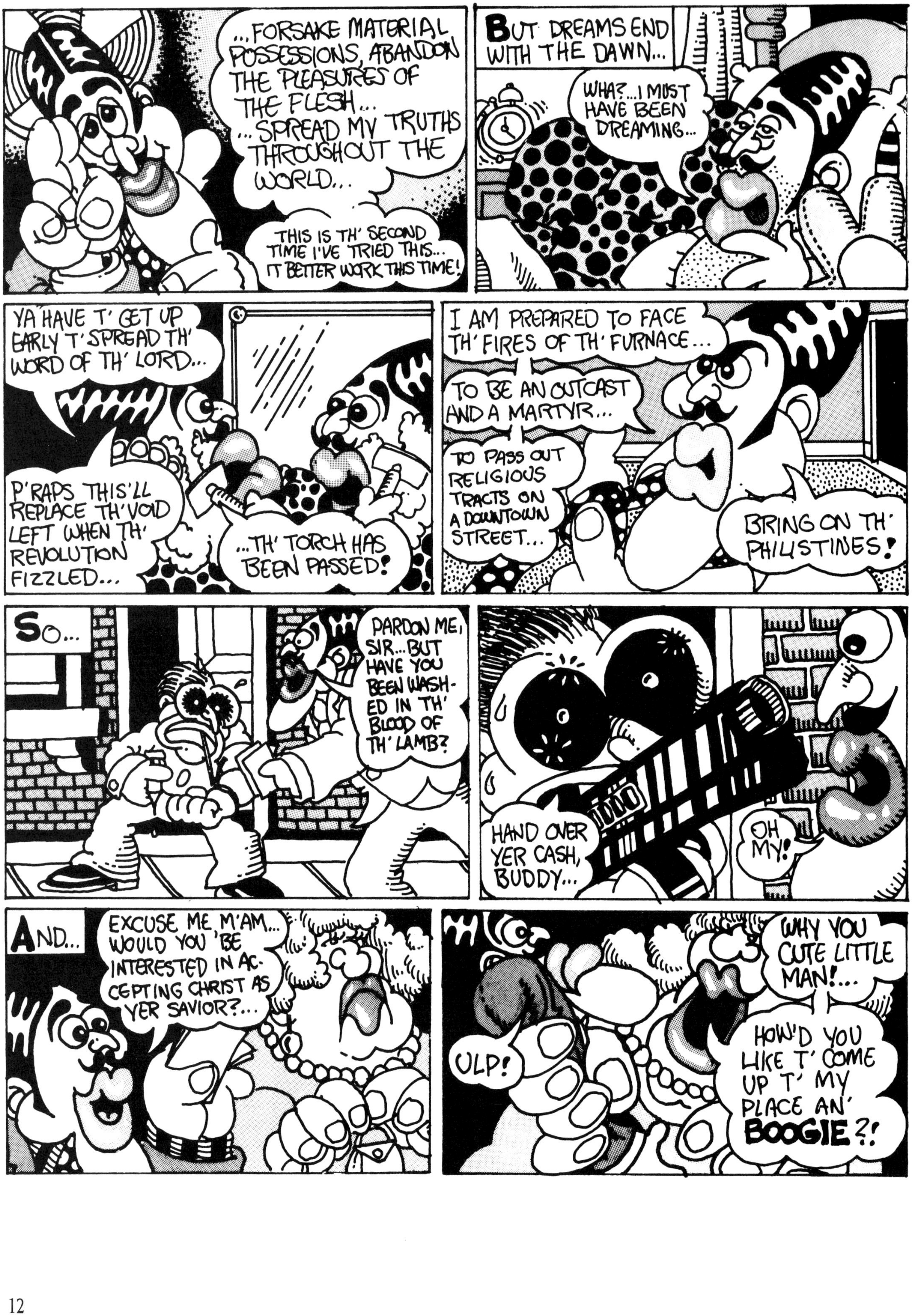
...FORSAKE MATERIAL POSSESSIONS, ABANDON THE PLEASURES OF THE FLESH... ...SPREAD MY TRUTHS THROUGHOUT THE WORLD...
THIS IS TH' SECOND TIME I'VE TRIED THIS... IT BETTER WORK THIS TIME!
BUT DREAMS END WITH THE DAWN...
WHA?...I MUST HAVE BEEN DREAMING...
YA HAVE T' GET UP EARLY T' SPREAD TH' WORD OF TH' LORD...
P'RAPS THIS'LL REPLACE TH' VOID LEFT WHEN TH' REVOLUTION FIZZLED...
...TH' TORCH HAS BEEN PASSED!
I AM PREPARED TO FACE TH' FIRES OF TH' FURNACE...
TO BE AN OUTCAST AND A MARTYR...
TO PASS OUT RELIGIOUS TRACTS ON A DOWNTOWN STREET...
BRING ON TH' PHILISTINES!
SO...
PARDON ME, SIR...BUT HAVE YOU BEEN WASHED IN TH' BLOOD OF TH' LAMB?
HAND OVER YER CASH, BUDDY...
OH MY!
AND...
EXCUSE ME, M'AM... WOULD YOU BE INTERESTED IN ACCEPTING CHRIST AS YER SAVIOR?...
ULP!
WHY YOU CUTE LITTLE MAN!...
HOW'D YOU LIKE T' COME UP T' MY PLACE AN' BOOGIE?!

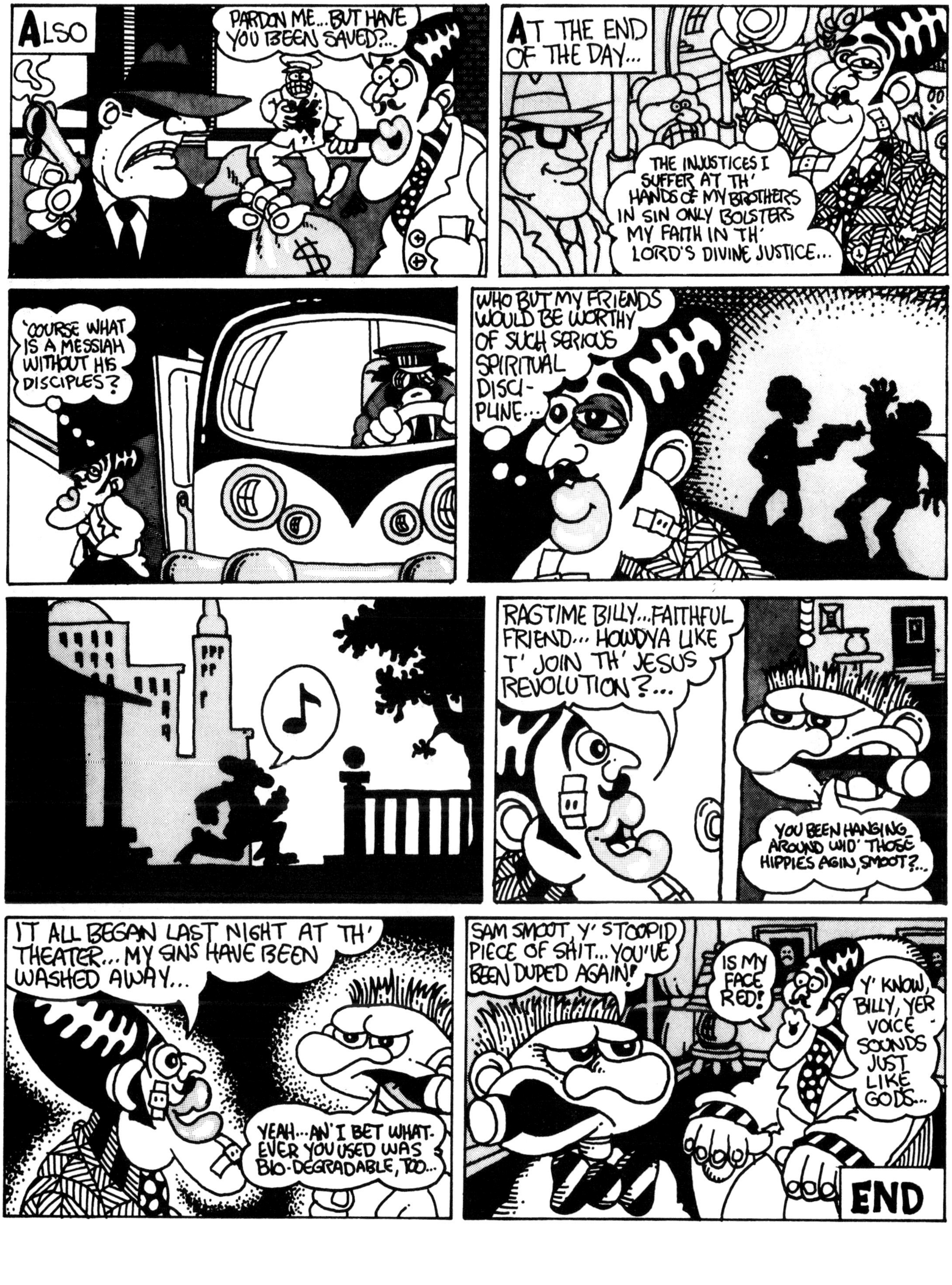
ALSO
PARDON ME... BUT HAVE YOU BEEN SAVED?...
AT THE END OF THE DAY...
THE INJUSTICES I SUFFER AT TH' HANDS OF MY BROTHERS IN SIN ONLY BOLSTERS MY FAITH IN TH' LORD'S DIVINE JUSTICE...
'COURSE WHAT IS A MESSIAH WITHOUT HIS DISCIPLES?
WHO BUT MY FRIENDS WOULD BE WORTHY OF SUCH SERIOUS SPIRITUAL DISCI-PLINE...
RAGTIME BILLY... FAITHFUL FRIEND... HOWDYA LIKE T' JOIN TH' JESUS REVOLUTION?...
YOU BEEN HANGING AROUND WID' THOSE HIPPIES AGIN, SMOOT?...
IT ALL BEGAN LAST NIGHT AT TH' THEATER... MY SINS HAVE BEEN WASHED AWAY...
YEAH... AN' I BET WHAT-EVER YOU USED WAS BIO-DEGRADABLE, TOO...
SAM SMOOT, Y' STOOPID PIECE OF SHIT... YOU'VE BEEN DUPED AGAIN!
IS MY FACE RED!
Y' KNOW, BILLY, YER VOICE SOUNDS JUST LIKE GODS...
END

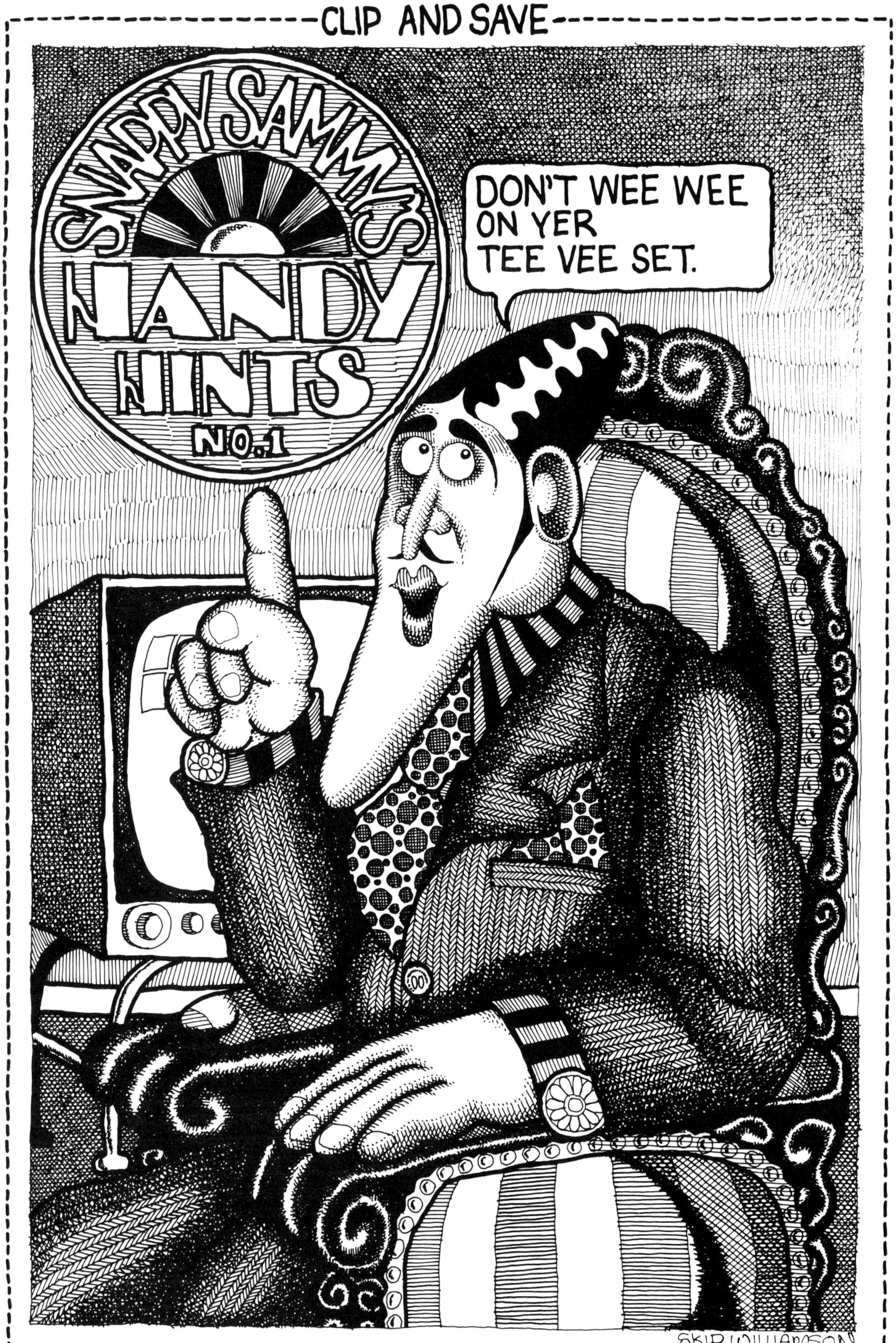
CLIP AND SAVE
SNAPPY SAMMY'S HANDY HINTS NO. 1
DON'T WEE WEE ON YER TEE VEE SET.
SKIP WILLIAMSON

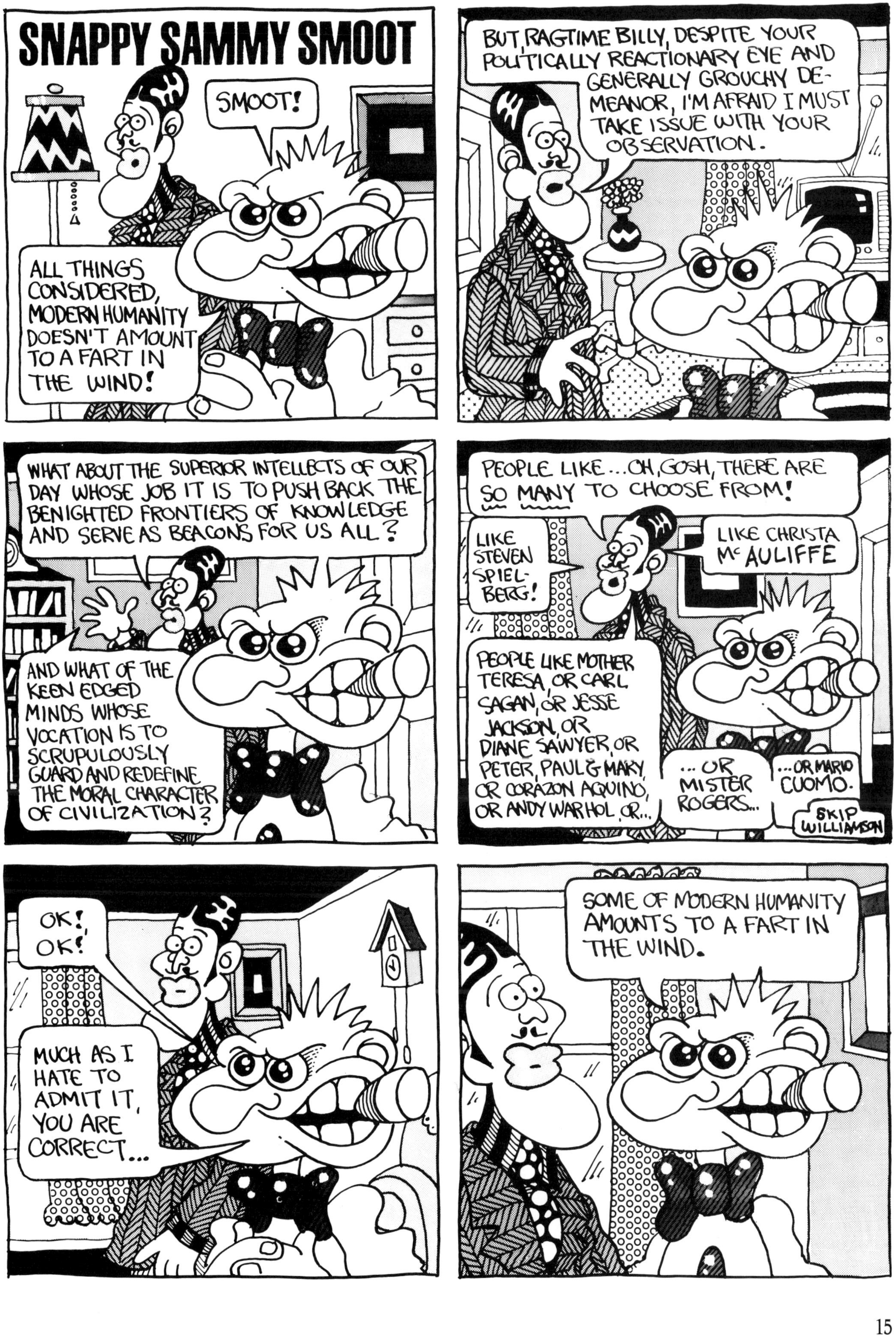
SNAPPY SAMMY SMOOT
SMOOT!
ALL THINGS CONSIDERED, MODERN HUMANITY DOESN'T AMOUNT TO A FART IN THE WIND!
BUT, RAGTIME BILLY, DESPITE YOUR POLITICALLY REACTIONARY EYE AND GENERALLY GROUCHY DE-MEANOR, I'M AFRAID I MUST TAKE ISSUE WITH YOUR OBSERVATION.
WHAT ABOUT THE SUPERIOR INTELLECTS OF OUR DAY WHOSE JOB IT IS TO PUSH BACK THE BENIGHTED FRONTIERS OF KNOWLEDGE AND SERVE AS BEACONS FOR US ALL?
AND WHAT OF THE KEEN EDGED MINDS WHOSE VOCATION IS TO SCRUPULOUSLY GUARD AND REDEFINE THE MORAL CHARACTER OF CIVILIZATION?
PEOPLE LIKE...OH, GOSH, THERE ARE SO MANY TO CHOOSE FROM!
LIKE STEVEN SPIEL-BERG!
LIKE CHRISTA McAULIFFE
PEOPLE LIKE MOTHER TERESA, OR CARL SAGAN, OR JESSE JACKSON, OR DIANE SAWYER, OR PETER, PAUL & MARY, OR CORAZON AQUINO, OR ANDY WARHOL, OR...
...OR MISTER ROGERS...
...OR MARIO CUOMO.
SKIP WILLIAMSON
OK! OK!
MUCH AS I HATE TO ADMIT IT, YOU ARE CORRECT...
SOME OF MODERN HUMANITY AMOUNTS TO A FART IN THE WIND.

AW HECK!

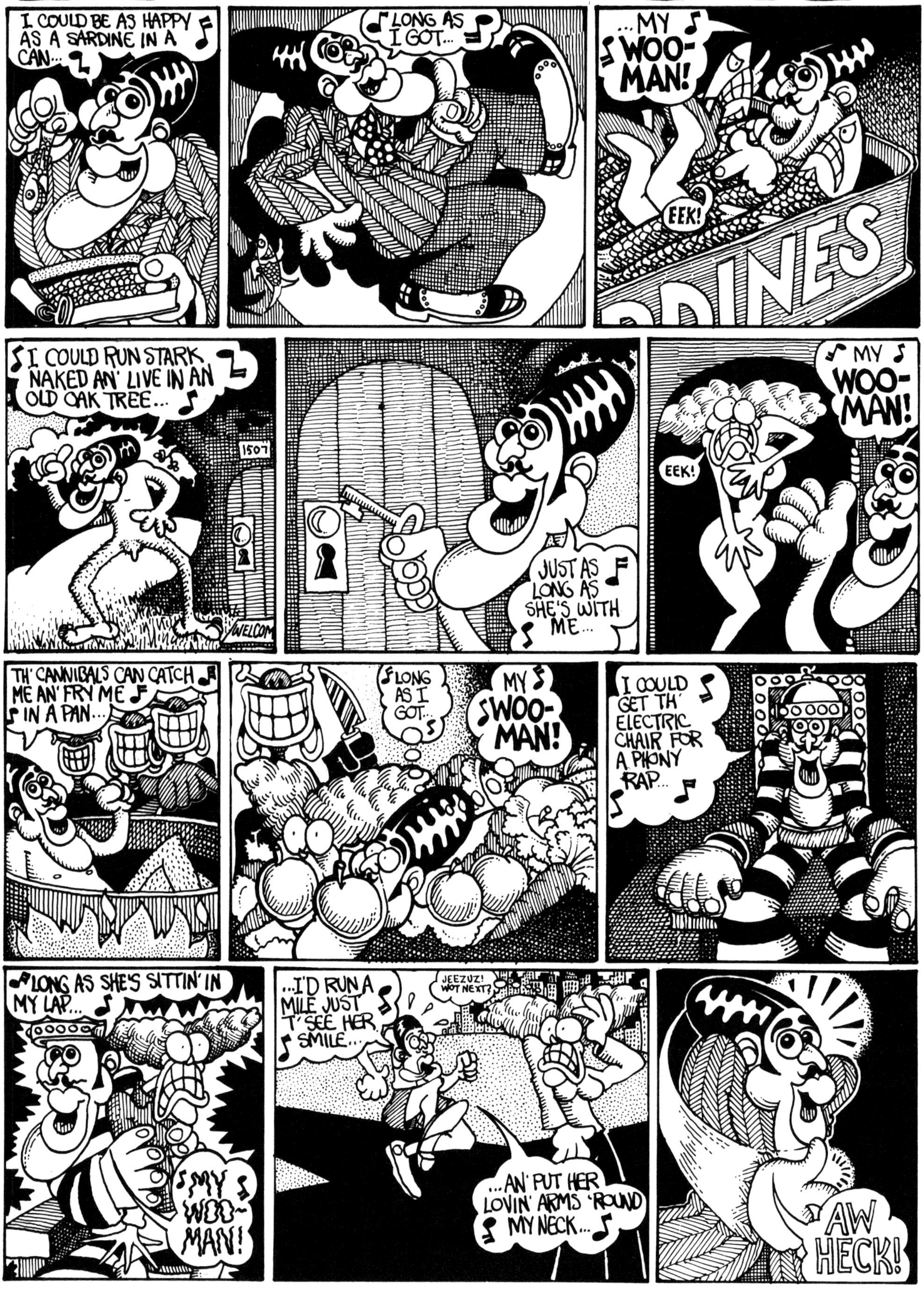

I COULD BE AS HAPPY AS A SARDINE IN A CAN...
LONG AS I GOT...
...MY WOO-MAN!
EEK!
I COULD RUN STARK NAKED AN' LIVE IN AN OLD OAK TREE...
1507
WELCOM
JUST AS LONG AS SHE'S WITH ME...
MY WOO-MAN!
EEK!
TH' CANNIBALS CAN CATCH ME AN' FRY ME IN A PAN...
LONG AS I GOT...
MY WOO-MAN!
I COULD GET TH' ELECTRIC CHAIR FOR A PHONY RAP...
LONG AS SHE'S SITTIN' IN MY LAP...
MY WOO-MAN!
...I'D RUN A MILE JUST T' SEE HER SMILE...
JEEZUZ! WOT NEXT?
...AN' PUT HER LOVIN' ARMS 'ROUND MY NECK...
AW HECK!

"AW HECK" LYRICS © COPYRIGHT 1971 BY JOHN PRINE

SNAPPY SAMMY SMOOT

OL' SAM HAS A REVELATION

LADIES & GENTLEMEN, THE PRESIDENT OF THE UNITED STATES!

WHY, THAT MAN IS **GENUINELY CRAZY!**

LOVE IS HATE

WAR IS PEACE

CHICKENS ARE FROGS

NOT THAT THAT'S **UNUSUAL** IN PRESIDENTS...

...IT'S KIND OF **ENDEARING** REALLY... LIKE **LBJ**...

SPECIAL INTERESTS BEING SERVED...ESPIONAGE AND SABOTAGE ON TH' **HIGHEST NATIONAL LEVEL**...ALL CLOAKED BEHIND TH' THIN FABRIC OF **POLITICAL EXPEDIENCE!**

I ACTUALLY DETECT **A BIAS** IN TH' MEDIA...

TIME

MAN OF THE YEAR

HISTORY BOOKS ARE HALF TRUTHS AND GLORIFICATION OF THE CORRUPTION OF POWER!

TH' REALITY OF OUR NATIONAL SPIRIT IS AND HAS BEEN NOTHING MORE THAN RACISM, SEXISM, EXPLOITATION AND GENOCIDE!

RELIGIOUS PROPHETS FROM TH' ILLUMINATE TO BILLY GRAHAM PREACH IMPENDING APOCALYPSE!

SNAKES ARE DUCKS!

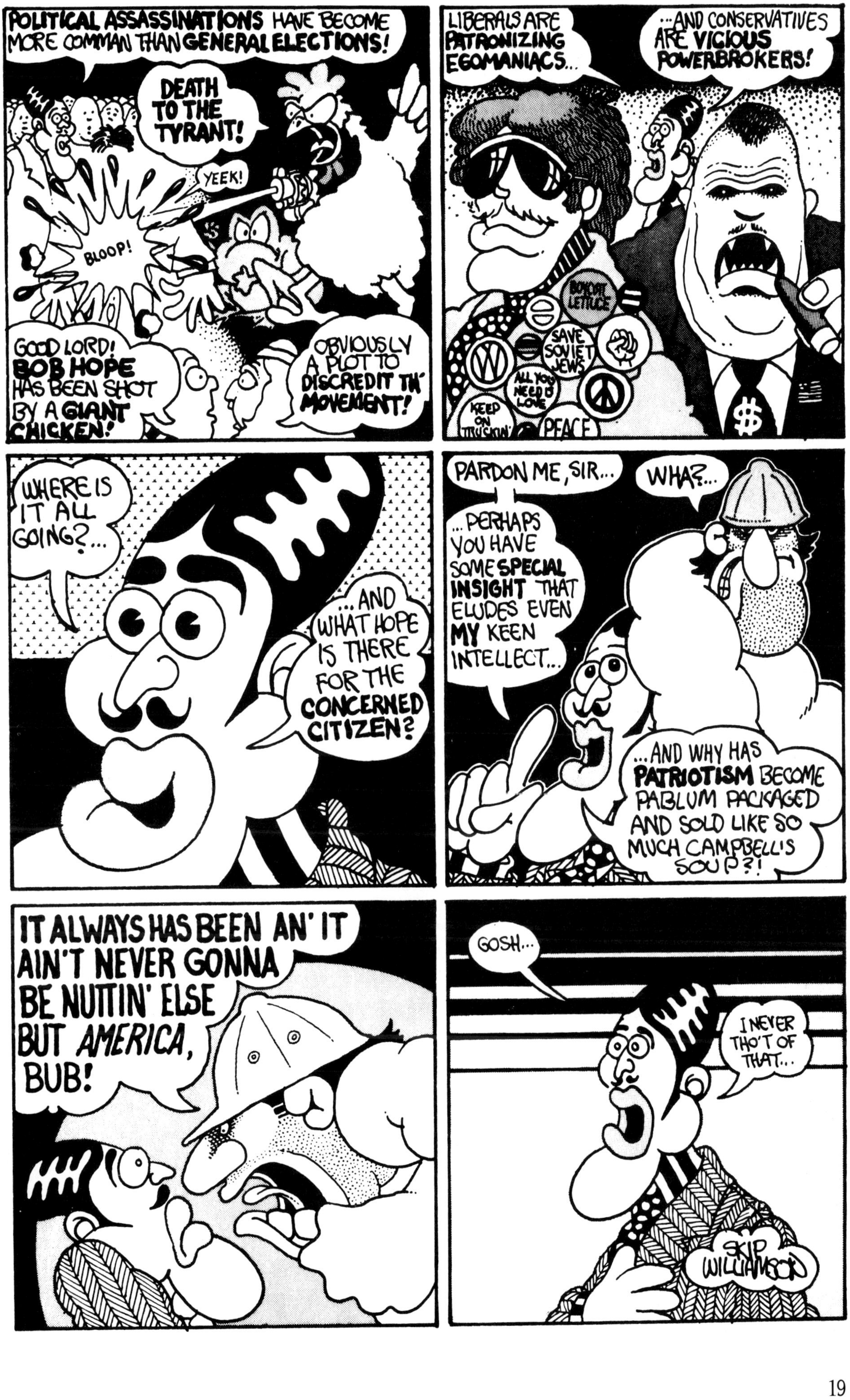
POLITICAL ASSASSINATIONS HAVE BECOME MORE COMMAN THAN GENERAL ELECTIONS!
DEATH TO THE TYRANT!
YEEK!
BLOOP!
GOOD LORD! BOB HOPE HAS BEEN SHOT BY A GIANT CHICKEN!
OBVIOUSLY A PLOT TO DISCREDIT TH' MOVEMENT!
LIBERALS ARE PATRONIZING EGOMANIACS...
...AND CONSERVATIVES ARE VICIOUS POWERBROKERS!
BOYCOTT LETTUCE
SAVE SOVIET JEWS
ALL YOU NEED IS LOVE
KEEP ON TRUCKIN'
PEACE
$
WHERE IS IT ALL GOING?...
...AND WHAT HOPE IS THERE FOR THE CONCERNED CITIZEN?
PARDON ME, SIR...
WHA?...
...PERHAPS YOU HAVE SOME SPECIAL INSIGHT THAT ELUDES EVEN MY KEEN INTELLECT...
...AND WHY HAS PATRIOTISM BECOME PABLUM PACKAGED AND SOLD LIKE SO MUCH CAMPBELL'S SOUP?!
IT ALWAYS HAS BEEN AN' IT AIN'T NEVER GONNA BE NUTTIN' ELSE BUT AMERICA, BUB!
GOSH...
I NEVER THO'T OF THAT...
SKIP WILLIAMSON

SNAPPY SAMMY SMOOT

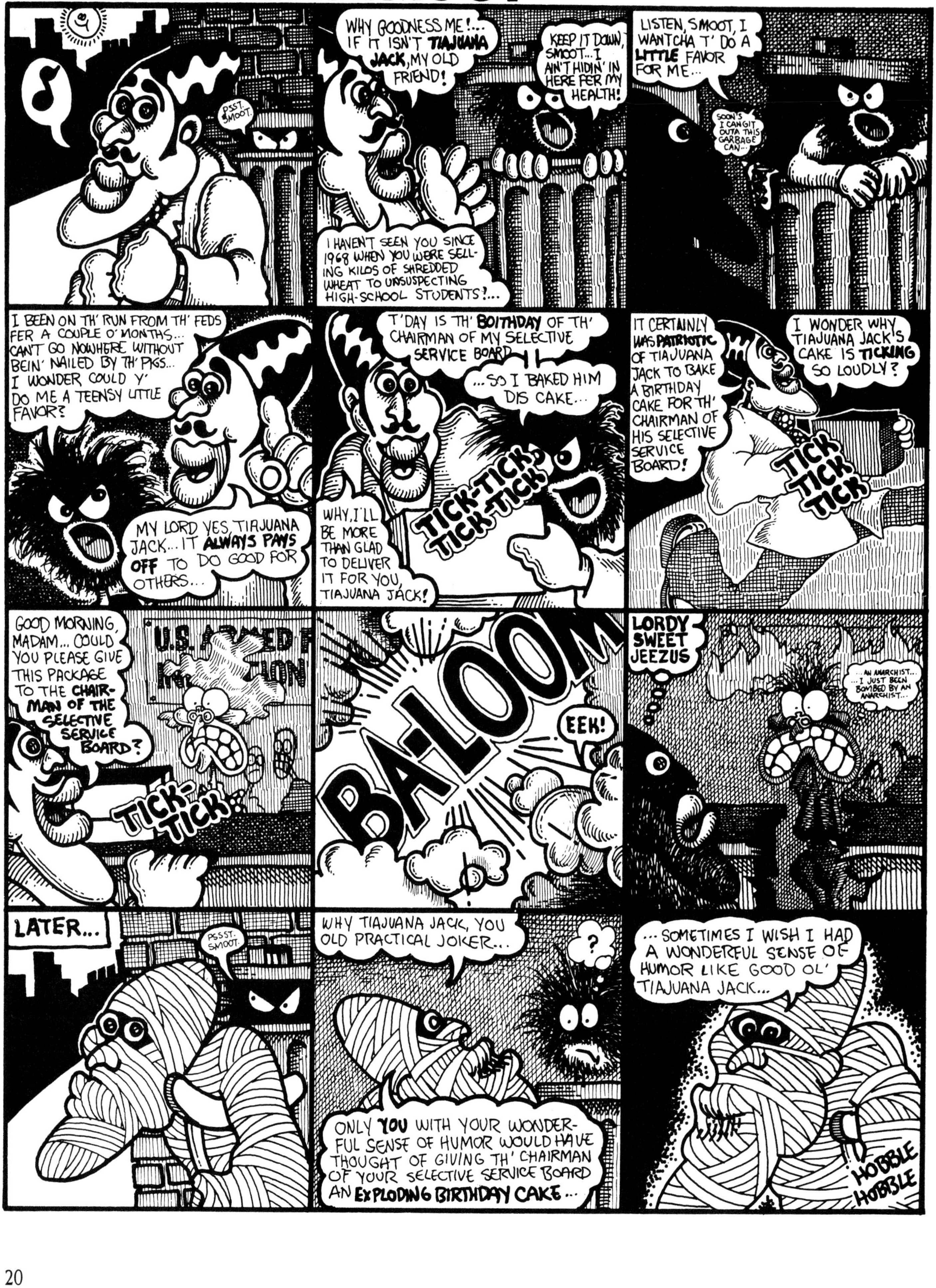

PSST. SMOOT.
WHY GOODNESS ME!... IF IT ISN'T TIAJUANA JACK, MY OLD FRIEND!
KEEP IT DOWN, SMOOT... I AIN'T HIDIN' IN HERE FER MY HEALTH!
I HAVEN'T SEEN YOU SINCE 1968 WHEN YOU WERE SELLING KILOS OF SHREDDED WHEAT TO UNSUSPECTING HIGH-SCHOOL STUDENTS!...
LISTEN, SMOOT, I WANTCHA T' DO A LITTLE FAVOR FOR ME...
SOON'S I CAN GIT OUTA THIS GARBAGE CAN...
I BEEN ON TH' RUN FROM TH' FEDS FER A COUPLE O' MONTHS... CAN'T GO NOWHERE WITHOUT BEIN' NAILED BY TH' PIGS... I WONDER COULD Y' DO ME A TEENSY LITTLE FAVOR?
MY LORD YES TIAJUANA JACK... IT ALWAYS PAYS OFF TO DO GOOD FOR OTHERS...
T'DAY IS TH' BOITHDAY OF TH' CHAIRMAN OF MY SELECTIVE SERVICE BOARD...
...SO I BAKED HIM DIS CAKE...
TICK-TICK TICK-TICK
WHY, I'LL BE MORE THAN GLAD TO DELIVER IT FOR YOU, TIAJUANA JACK!
IT CERTAINLY WAS PATRIOTIC OF TIAJUANA JACK TO BAKE A BIRTHDAY CAKE FOR TH' CHAIRMAN OF HIS SELECTIVE SERVICE BOARD!
I WONDER WHY TIAJUANA JACK'S CAKE IS TICKING SO LOUDLY?
TICK TICK TICK
GOOD MORNING, MADAM... COULD YOU PLEASE GIVE THIS PACKAGE TO THE CHAIRMAN OF THE SELECTIVE SERVICE BOARD?
TICK-TICK
BA-LOOM
EEK!
LORDY SWEET JEEZUS
...AN ANARCHIST... ...I JUST BEEN BOMBED BY AN ANARCHIST...
LATER...
PSSST. SMOOT.
WHY TIAJUANA JACK, YOU OLD PRACTICAL JOKER...
?
ONLY YOU WITH YOUR WONDERFUL SENSE OF HUMOR WOULD HAVE THOUGHT OF GIVING TH' CHAIRMAN OF YOUR SELECTIVE SERVICE BOARD AN EXPLODING BIRTHDAY CAKE...
...SOMETIMES I WISH I HAD A WONDERFUL SENSE OF HUMOR LIKE GOOD OL' TIAJUANA JACK...
HOBBLE HOBBLE

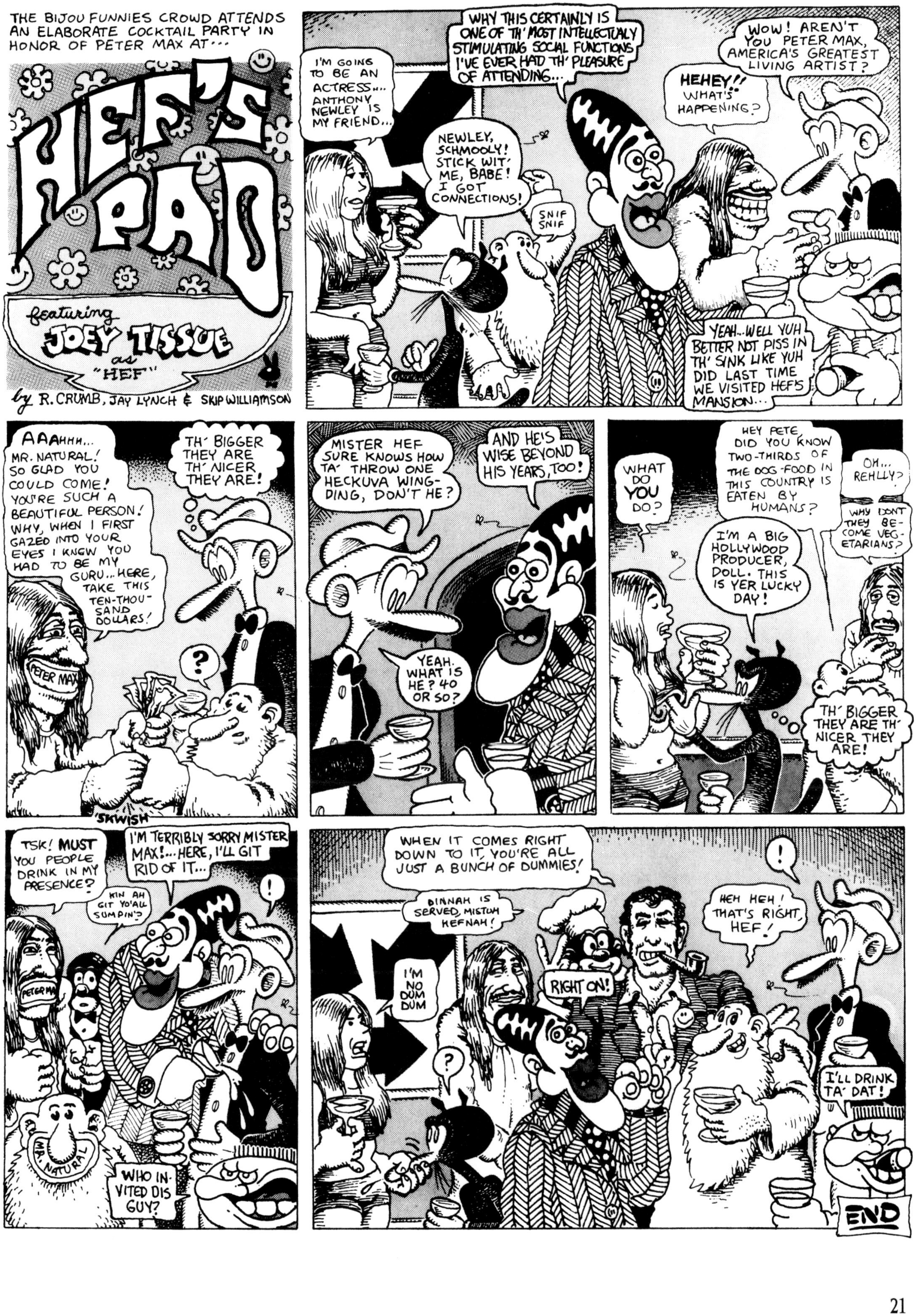

THE BIJOU FUNNIES CROWD ATTENDS AN ELABORATE COCKTAIL PARTY IN HONOR OF PETER MAX AT...
HEF'S PAD
featuring JOEY TISSUE as "HEF"
by R. CRUMB, JAY LYNCH & SKIP WILLIAMSON
I'M GOING TO BE AN ACTRESS... ANTHONY NEWLEY IS MY FRIEND...
WHY THIS CERTAINLY IS ONE OF TH' MOST INTELLECTUALY STIMULATING SOCIAL FUNCTIONS I'VE EVER HAD TH' PLEASURE OF ATTENDING...
NEWLEY, SCHMOOLY! STICK WIT' ME, BABE! I GOT CONNECTIONS!
SNIF SNIF
HEHEY!! WHAT'S HAPPENING?
WOW! AREN'T YOU PETER MAX, AMERICA'S GREATEST LIVING ARTIST?
YEAH... WELL YUH BETTER NOT PISS IN TH' SINK LIKE YUH DID LAST TIME WE VISITED HEF'S MANSION...
AAAHHH... MR. NATURAL! SO GLAD YOU COULD COME! YOU'RE SUCH A BEAUTIFUL PERSON! WHY, WHEN I FIRST GAZED INTO YOUR EYES I KNEW YOU HAD TO BE MY GURU... HERE, TAKE THIS TEN-THOUSAND DOLLARS!
TH' BIGGER THEY ARE TH' NICER THEY ARE!
PETER MAX
?
SKWISH
MISTER HEF SURE KNOWS HOW TA' THROW ONE HECKUVA WING-DING, DON'T HE?
AND HE'S WISE BEYOND HIS YEARS, TOO!
YEAH. WHAT IS HE? 40 OR SO?
WHAT DO YOU DO?
HEY PETE, DID YOU KNOW TWO-THIRDS OF THE DOG-FOOD IN THIS COUNTRY IS EATEN BY HUMANS?
OH... REHLLY?
WHY DON'T THEY BE-COME VEG-ETARIANS?
I'M A BIG HOLLYWOOD PRODUCER, DOLL. THIS IS YER LUCKY DAY!
TH' BIGGER THEY ARE TH' NICER THEY ARE!
TSK! MUST YOU PEOPLE DRINK IN MY PRESENCE?
I'M TERRIBLY SORRY MISTER MAX!... HERE, I'LL GIT RID OF IT...
KIN AH GIT YO'ALL SUMPIN'?
!
PETER MAX
MR. NATURAL
WHO IN-VITED DIS GUY?
WHEN IT COMES RIGHT DOWN TO IT, YOU'RE ALL JUST A BUNCH OF DUMMIES!
!
DINNAH IS SERVED, MISTUH HEFNAH!
HEH HEH! THAT'S RIGHT, HEF!
I'M NO DUM DUM
RIGHT ON!
?
I'LL DRINK TA' DAT!
END

SNAPPY SAMMY SMOOT *in* SEX & DEATH

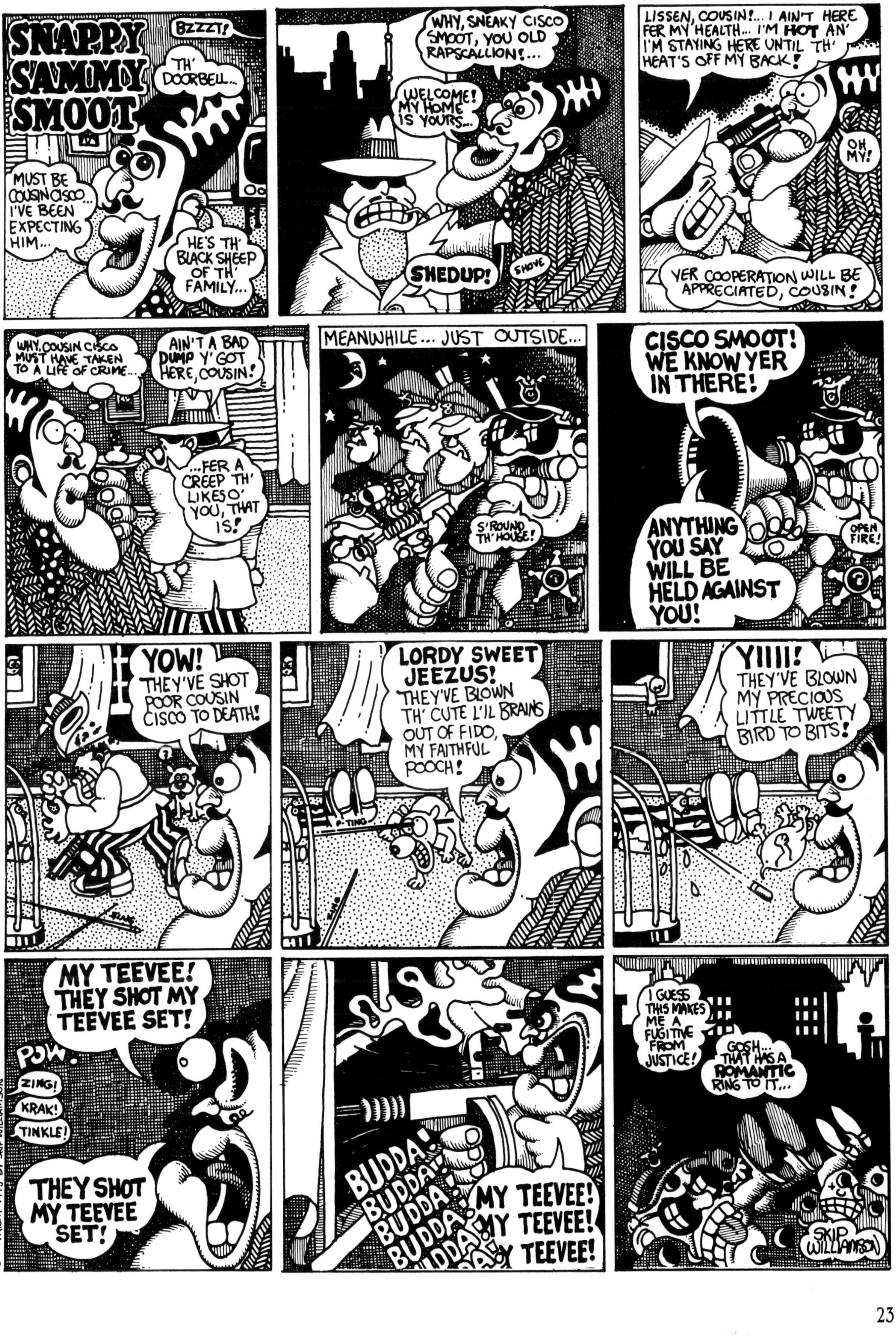
SNAPPY SAMMY SMOOT
BZZZT!
TH' DOORBELL...
MUST BE COUSIN CISCO... I'VE BEEN EXPECTING HIM...
HE'S TH' BLACK SHEEP OF TH' FAMILY...
WHY, SNEAKY CISCO SMOOT, YOU OLD RAPSCALLION!...
WELCOME! MY HOME IS YOURS...
SHEDUP!
SHOVE
LISSEN, COUSIN!... I AIN'T HERE FER MY HEALTH... I'M HOT AN' I'M STAYING HERE UNTIL TH' HEAT'S OFF MY BACK!
OH MY!
YER COOPERATION WILL BE APPRECIATED, COUSIN!
WHY, COUSIN CISCO MUST HAVE TAKEN TO A LIFE OF CRIME...
AIN'T A BAD DUMP Y'GOT HERE, COUSIN!
...FER A CREEP TH' LIKES O' YOU, THAT IS!
MEANWHILE... JUST OUTSIDE...
S'ROUND TH' HOUSE!
CISCO SMOOT! WE KNOW YER IN THERE!
ANYTHING YOU SAY WILL BE HELD AGAINST YOU!
OPEN FIRE!
YOW! THEY'VE SHOT POOR COUSIN CISCO TO DEATH!
LORDY SWEET JEEZUS! THEY'VE BLOWN TH' CUTE L'IL BRAINS OUT OF FIDO, MY FAITHFUL POOCH!
P-TING
YIIII! THEY'VE BLOWN MY PRECIOUS LITTLE TWEETY BIRD TO BITS!
MY TEEVEE! THEY SHOT MY TEEVEE SET!
POW
ZING!
KRAK!
TINKLE!
THEY SHOT MY TEEVEE SET!
BUDDA! BUDDA! BUDDA! BUDDA!
MY TEEVEE! MY TEEVEE! Y TEEVEE!
I GUESS THIS MAKES ME A FUGITIVE FROM JUSTICE!
GOSH... THAT HAS A ROMANTIC RING TO IT...
SKIP WILLIAMSON

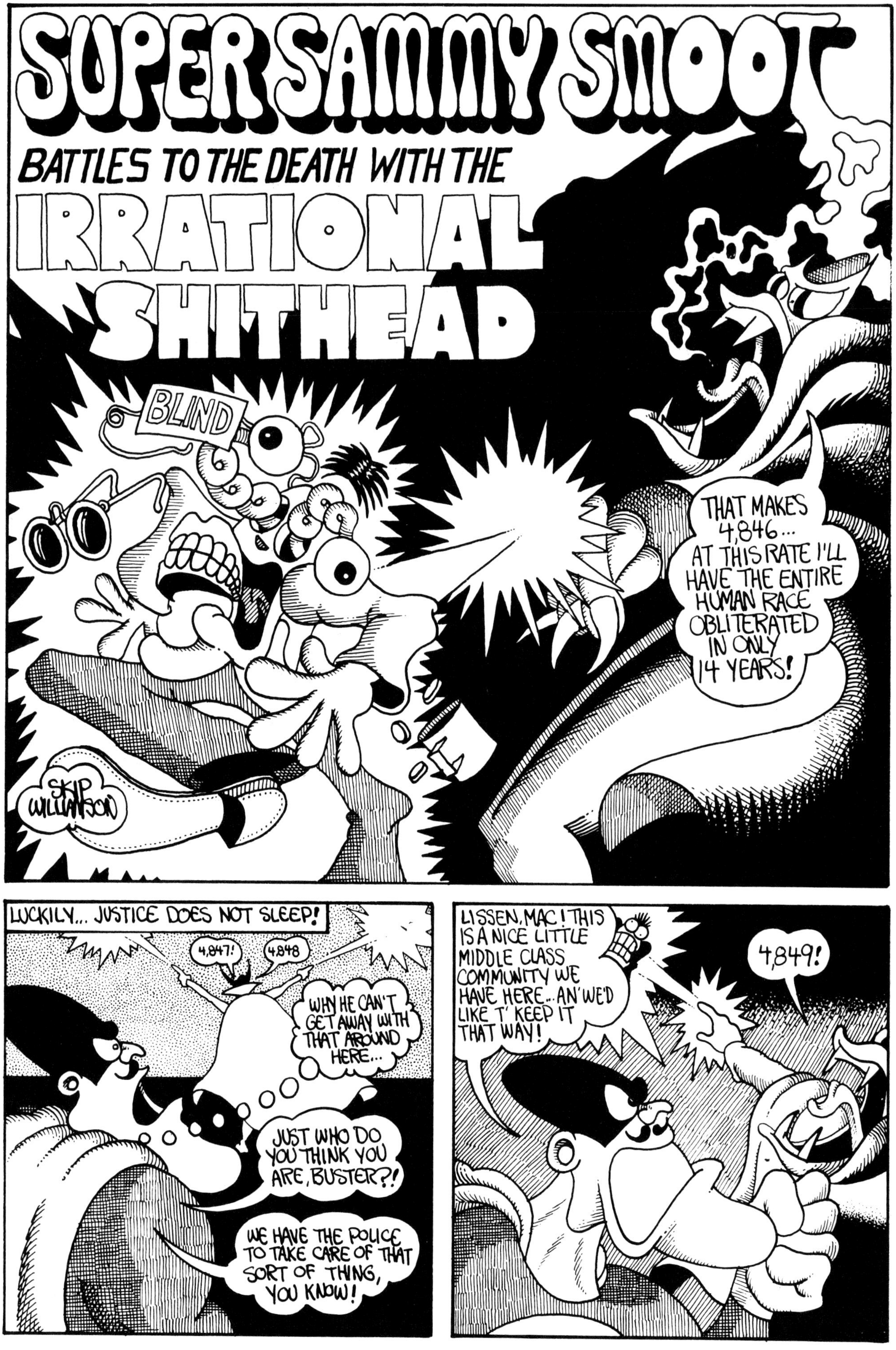
SUPER SAMMY SMOOT
BATTLES TO THE DEATH WITH THE
IRRATIONAL SHITHEAD
BLIND
SKIP WILLIAMSON
THAT MAKES 4,846... AT THIS RATE I'LL HAVE THE ENTIRE HUMAN RACE OBLITERATED IN ONLY 14 YEARS!
LUCKILY... JUSTICE DOES NOT SLEEP!
4,847!
4,848
WHY HE CAN'T GET AWAY WITH THAT AROUND HERE...
JUST WHO DO YOU THINK YOU ARE, BUSTER?!
WE HAVE THE POLICE TO TAKE CARE OF THAT SORT OF THING, YOU KNOW!
LISSEN, MAC! THIS IS A NICE LITTLE MIDDLE CLASS COMMUNITY WE HAVE HERE.. AN' WE'D LIKE T' KEEP IT THAT WAY!
4,849!

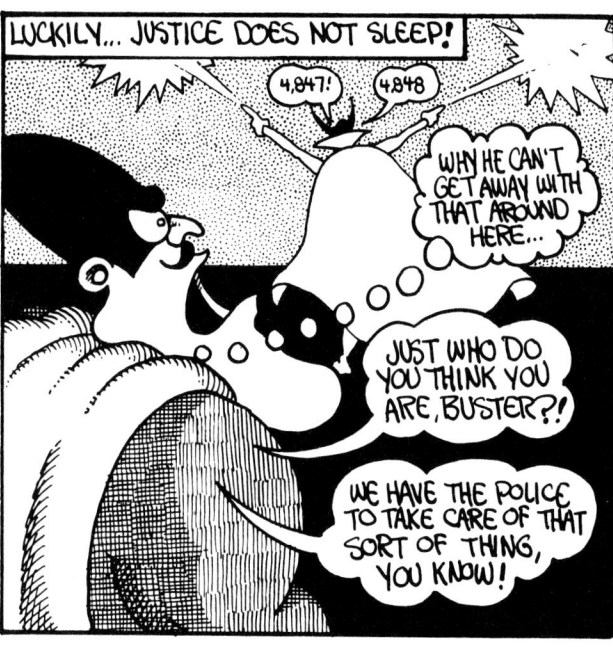

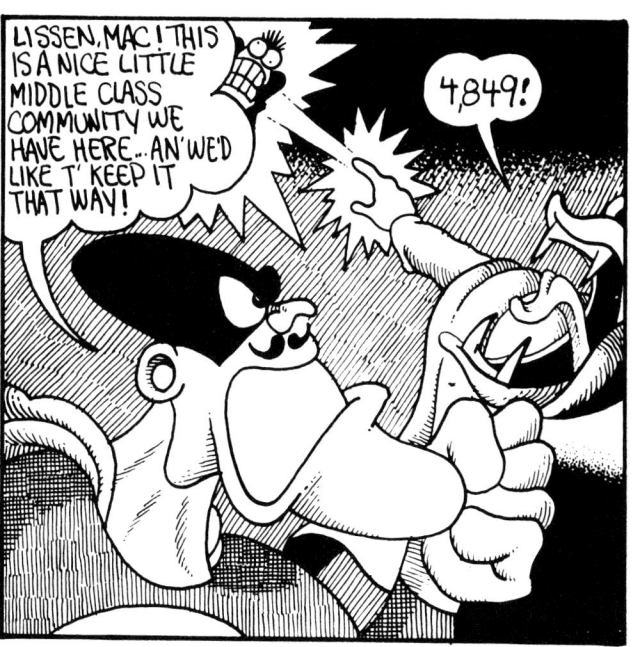

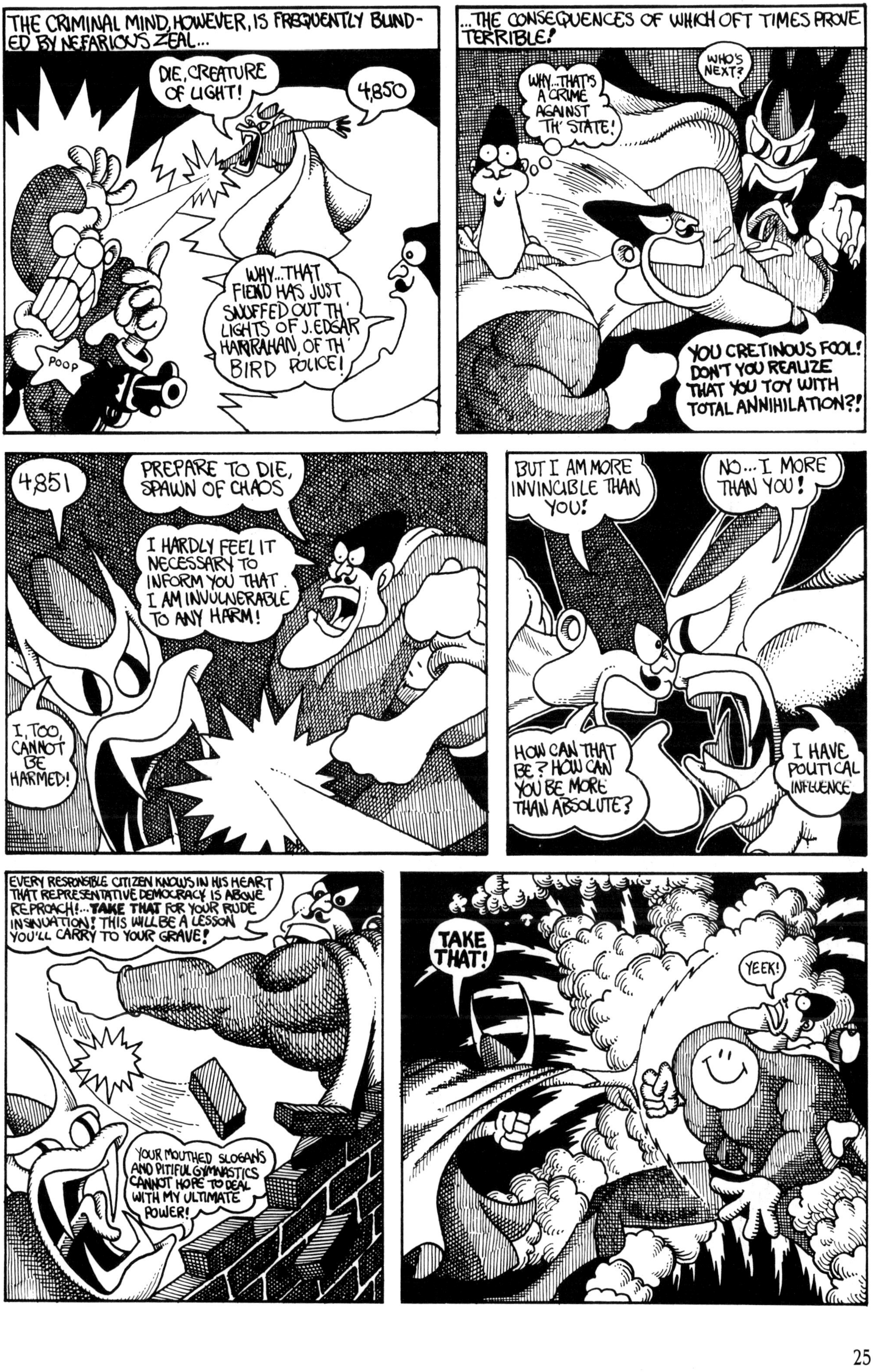
THE CRIMINAL MIND, HOWEVER, IS FREQUENTLY BLINDED BY NEFARIOUS ZEAL...
DIE, CREATURE OF LIGHT!
4,850
POOP
WHY...THAT FIEND HAS JUST SNUFFED OUT TH' LIGHTS OF J. EDGAR HARRAHAN, OF TH' BIRD POLICE!
...THE CONSEQUENCES OF WHICH OFT TIMES PROVE TERRIBLE!
WHO'S NEXT?
WHY...THAT'S A CRIME AGAINST TH' STATE!
YOU CRETINOUS FOOL! DON'T YOU REALIZE THAT YOU TOY WITH TOTAL ANNIHILATION?!
4,851
PREPARE TO DIE, SPAWN OF CHAOS
I HARDLY FEEL IT NECESSARY TO INFORM YOU THAT I AM INVULNERABLE TO ANY HARM!
I, TOO, CANNOT BE HARMED!
BUT I AM MORE INVINCIBLE THAN YOU!
NO... I MORE THAN YOU!
HOW CAN THAT BE? HOW CAN YOU BE MORE THAN ABSOLUTE?
I HAVE POLITICAL INFLUENCE
EVERY RESPONSIBLE CITIZEN KNOWS IN HIS HEART THAT REPRESENTATIVE DEMOCRACY IS ABOVE REPROACH!... TAKE THAT FOR YOUR RUDE INSINUATION! THIS WILL BE A LESSON YOU'LL CARRY TO YOUR GRAVE!
YOUR MOUTHED SLOGANS AND PITIFUL GYMNASTICS CANNOT HOPE TO DEAL WITH MY ULTIMATE POWER!
TAKE THAT!
YEEK!

THE FABRIC OF ORDER WITH HONOR CANNOT BE RENDED BY A SECOND RATE FIREWORKS DISPLAY!
KISS YOUR ASS GOODBYE, ANARCHIST SWINE!
HOWEVER, NATURE'S WIRING IS NOT PREPARED TO HANDLE SUCH AN ENERGY OVERLOAD...
FOOM!
...THE RESULT IS AN UNFORTUNATE INTERGALACTIC SHORT CIRUIT (WHICH SAYS SOMETHING ABOUT EXCESSES OF POWER).
HEY!...WAITAMINUTE!
WE'VE DESTROYED TH' ENTIRE UNIVERSE!
EVERYTHING WAS ATOMIZED... EXCEPT FOR US...
WE'RE INVULNERABLE!
IT'S ALL DARK!...
...AND SCARY!
WHY...IT'S JUST TH' SAME AS BEING DEAD!
NOW YOU'VE DONE IT, YOU FOOL!
YOU BLEEDING HEARTS MAKE ME SICK!
CLANG!
BONK!
BIFF!
ETC.

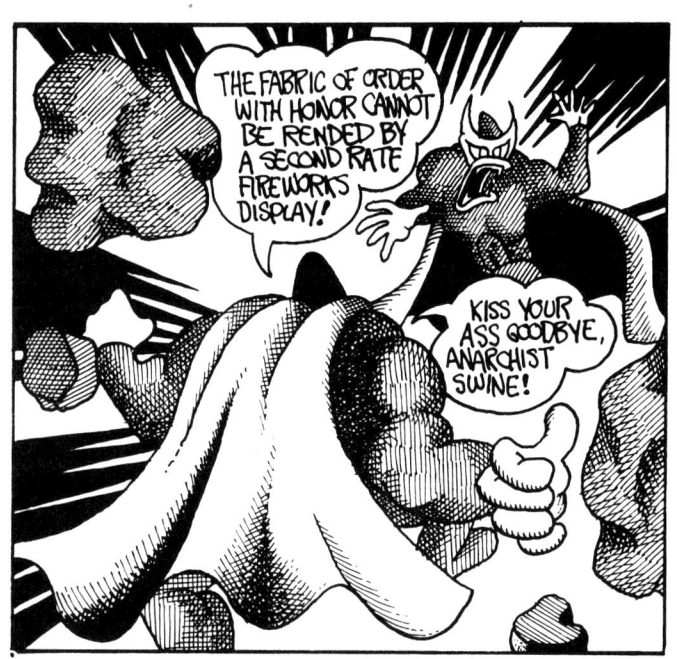

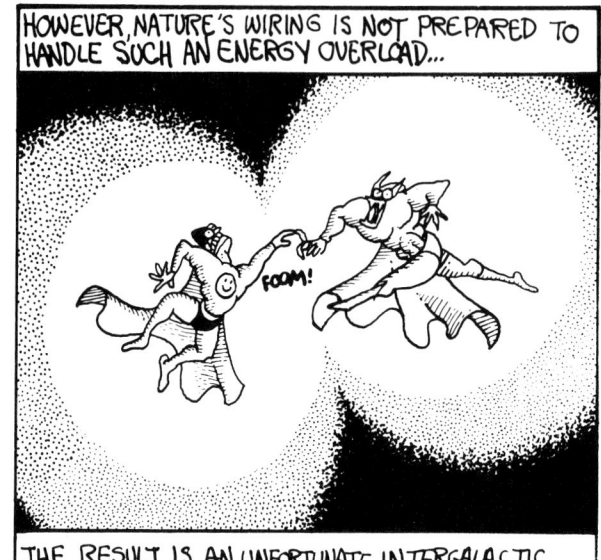

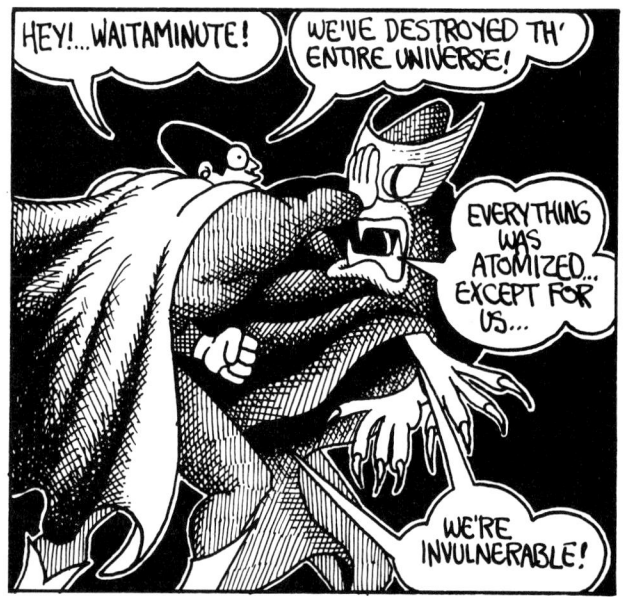

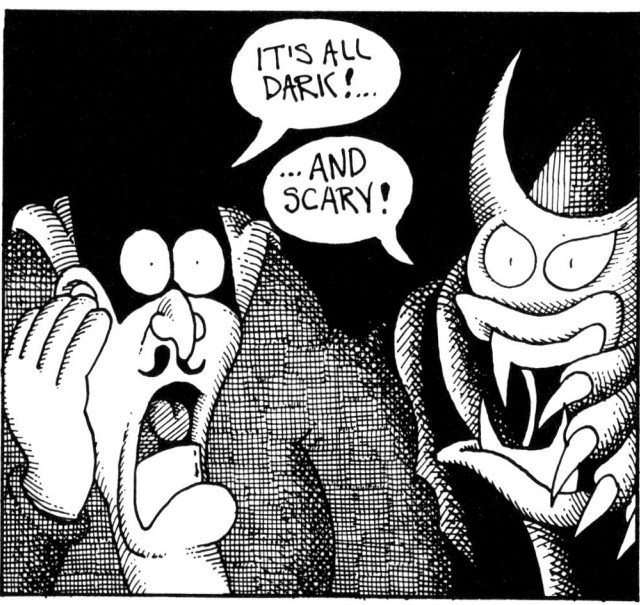

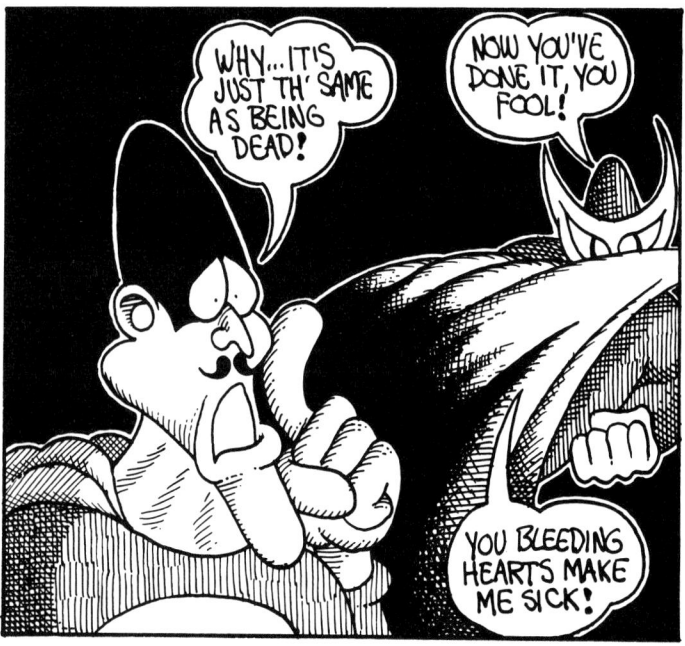

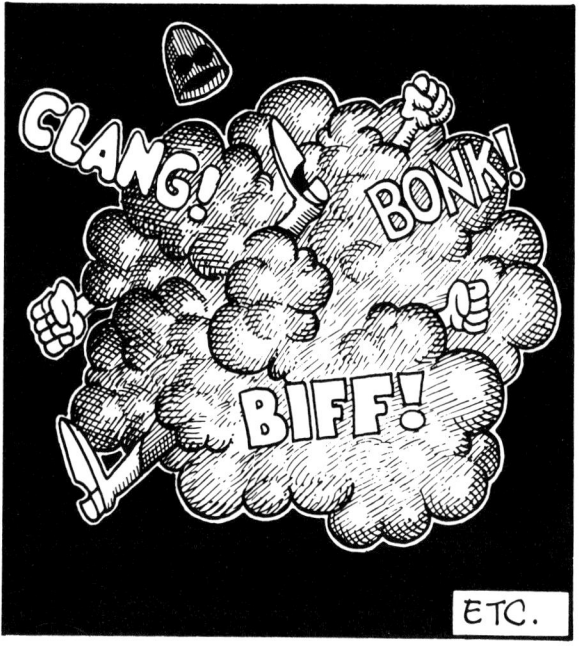

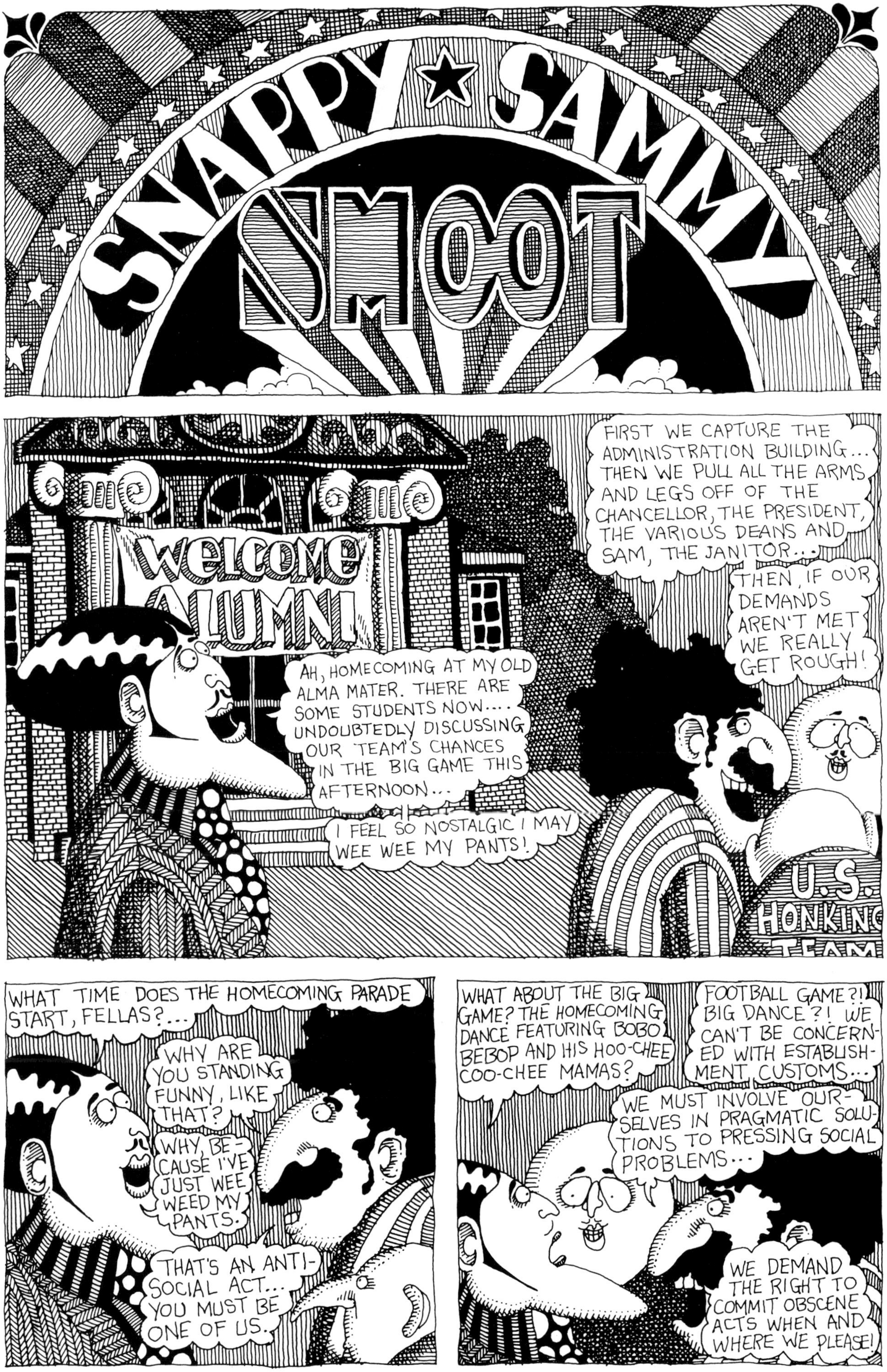

SNAPPY SAMMY SMOOT
WELCOME ALUMNI
AH, HOMECOMING AT MY OLD ALMA MATER. THERE ARE SOME STUDENTS NOW.... UNDOUBTEDLY DISCUSSING OUR TEAM'S CHANCES IN THE BIG GAME THIS AFTERNOON...
I FEEL SO NOSTALGIC I MAY WEE WEE MY PANTS!
FIRST WE CAPTURE THE ADMINISTRATION BUILDING... THEN WE PULL ALL THE ARMS AND LEGS OFF OF THE CHANCELLOR, THE PRESIDENT, THE VARIOUS DEANS AND SAM, THE JANITOR...
THEN, IF OUR DEMANDS AREN'T MET WE REALLY GET ROUGH!
U.S. HONKING TEAM
WHAT TIME DOES THE HOMECOMING PARADE START, FELLAS?...
WHY ARE YOU STANDING FUNNY, LIKE THAT?
WHY, BECAUSE I'VE JUST WEE WEED MY PANTS.
THAT'S AN ANTI-SOCIAL ACT... YOU MUST BE ONE OF US.
WHAT ABOUT THE BIG GAME? THE HOMECOMING DANCE FEATURING BOBO BEBOP AND HIS HOO-CHEE COO-CHEE MAMAS?
FOOTBALL GAME?! BIG DANCE?! WE CAN'T BE CONCERNED WITH ESTABLISHMENT CUSTOMS...
WE MUST INVOLVE OURSELVES IN PRAGMATIC SOLUTIONS TO PRESSING SOCIAL PROBLEMS...
WE DEMAND THE RIGHT TO COMMIT OBSCENE ACTS WHEN AND WHERE WE PLEASE!

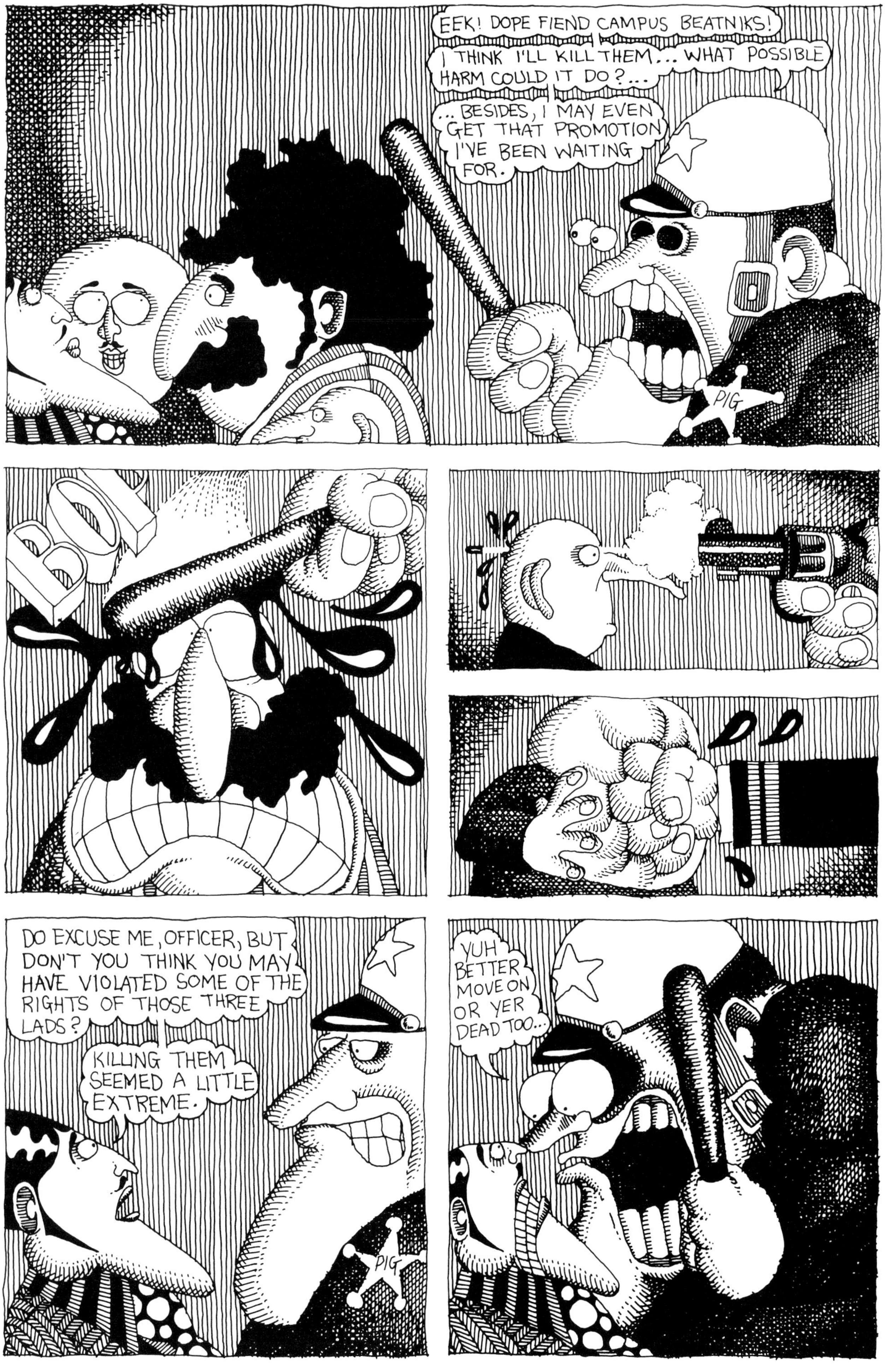
EEK! DOPE FIEND CAMPUS BEATNIKS!
I THINK I'LL KILL THEM... WHAT POSSIBLE HARM COULD IT DO?...
...BESIDES, I MAY EVEN GET THAT PROMOTION I'VE BEEN WAITING FOR.
PIG
BOP
DO EXCUSE ME, OFFICER, BUT DON'T YOU THINK YOU MAY HAVE VIOLATED SOME OF THE RIGHTS OF THOSE THREE LADS?
KILLING THEM SEEMED A LITTLE EXTREME.
PIG
YUH BETTER MOVE ON OR YER DEAD TOO...

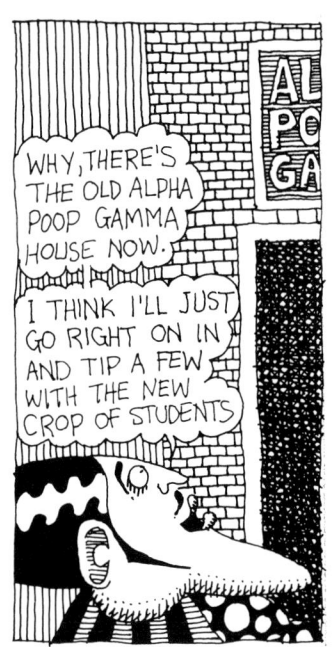

SKIP WILLIAMSON

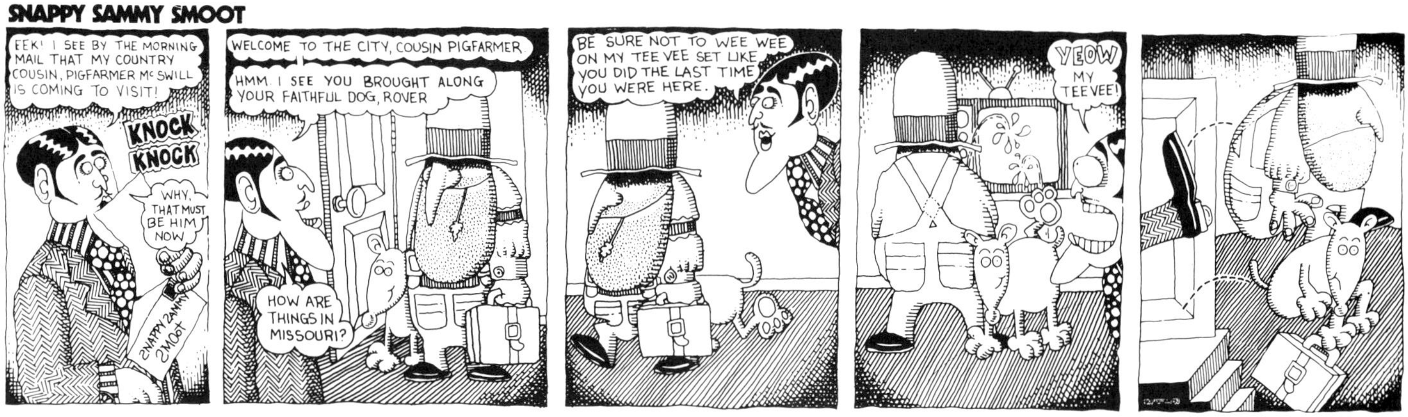
SNAPPY SAMMY SMOOT
EEK! I SEE BY THE MORNING MAIL THAT MY COUNTRY COUSIN, PIGFARMER McSWILL IS COMING TO VISIT!
KNOCK KNOCK
WHY, THAT MUST BE HIM NOW.
SNAPPY SAMMY SMOOT
WELCOME TO THE CITY, COUSIN PIGFARMER
HMM. I SEE YOU BROUGHT ALONG YOUR FAITHFUL DOG, ROVER
HOW ARE THINGS IN MISSOURI?
BE SURE NOT TO WEE WEE ON MY TEE VEE SET LIKE YOU DID THE LAST TIME YOU WERE HERE.
YEOW MY TEE VEE!

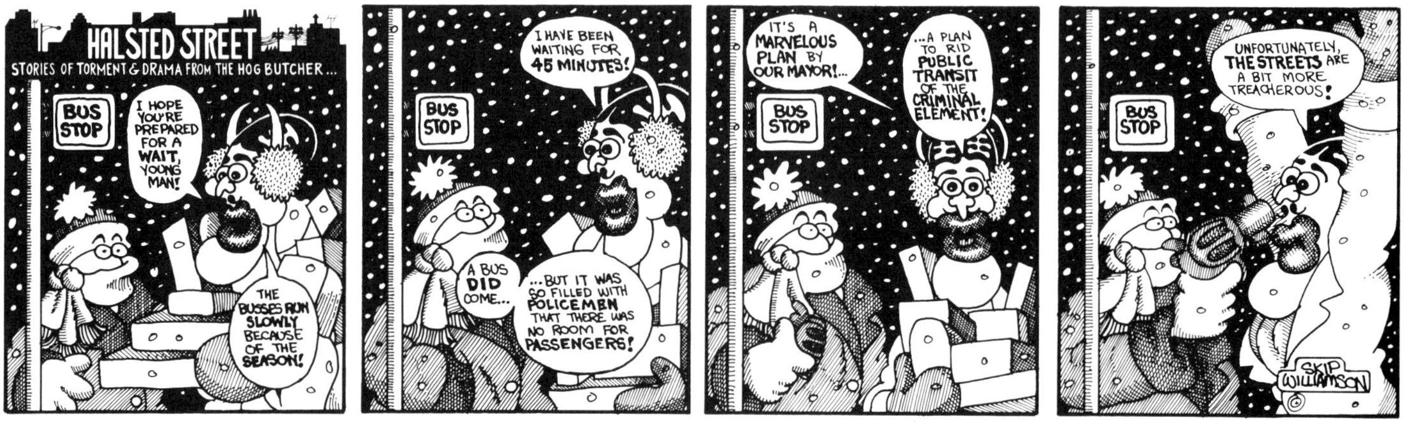
HALSTED STREET
STORIES OF TORMENT & DRAMA FROM THE HOG BUTCHER...
BUS STOP
I HOPE YOU'RE PREPARED FOR A WAIT, YOUNG MAN!
THE BUSSES RUN SLOWLY BECAUSE OF THE SEASON!
I HAVE BEEN WAITING FOR 45 MINUTES!
A BUS DID COME...
...BUT IT WAS SO FILLED WITH POLICEMEN THAT THERE WAS NO ROOM FOR PASSENGERS!
IT'S A MARVELOUS PLAN BY OUR MAYOR!...
...A PLAN TO RID PUBLIC TRANSIT OF THE CRIMINAL ELEMENT!
UNFORTUNATELY, THE STREETS ARE A BIT MORE TREACHEROUS!
SKIP WILLIAMSON ©

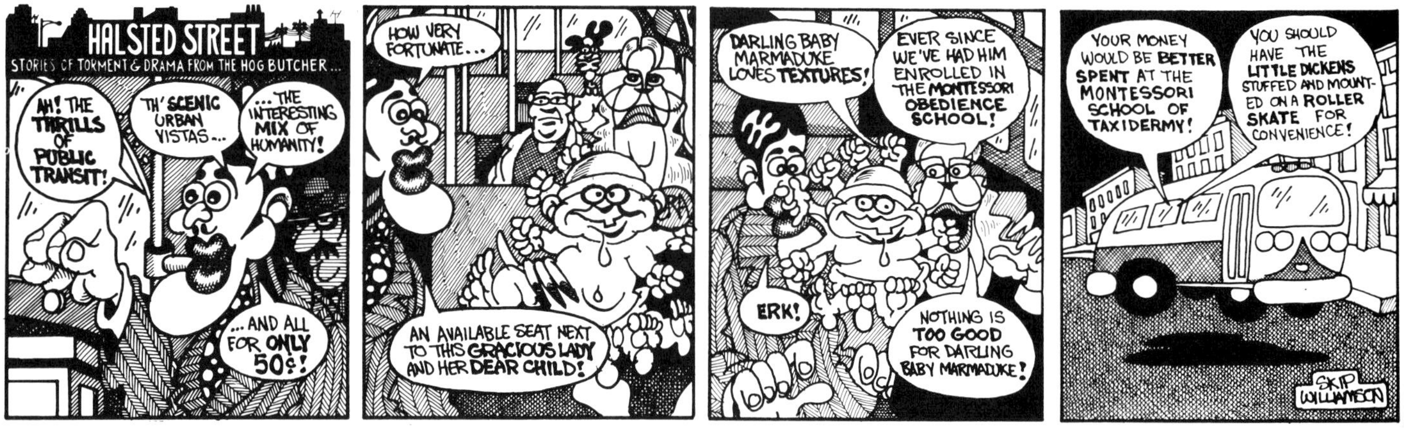
HALSTED STREET
STORIES OF TORMENT & DRAMA FROM THE HOG BUTCHER...
AH! THE THRILLS OF PUBLIC TRANSIT!
TH' SCENIC URBAN VISTAS...
...THE INTERESTING MIX OF HUMANITY!
...AND ALL FOR ONLY 50¢!
HOW VERY FORTUNATE...
AN AVAILABLE SEAT NEXT TO THIS GRACIOUS LADY AND HER DEAR CHILD!
DARLING BABY MARMADUKE LOVES TEXTURES!
EVER SINCE WE'VE HAD HIM ENROLLED IN THE MONTESSORI OBEDIENCE SCHOOL!
ERK!
NOTHING IS TOO GOOD FOR DARLING BABY MARMADUKE!
YOUR MONEY WOULD BE BETTER SPENT AT THE MONTESSORI SCHOOL OF TAXIDERMY!
YOU SHOULD HAVE THE LITTLE DICKENS STUFFED AND MOUNTED ON A ROLLER SKATE FOR CONVENIENCE!
SKIP WILLIAMSON

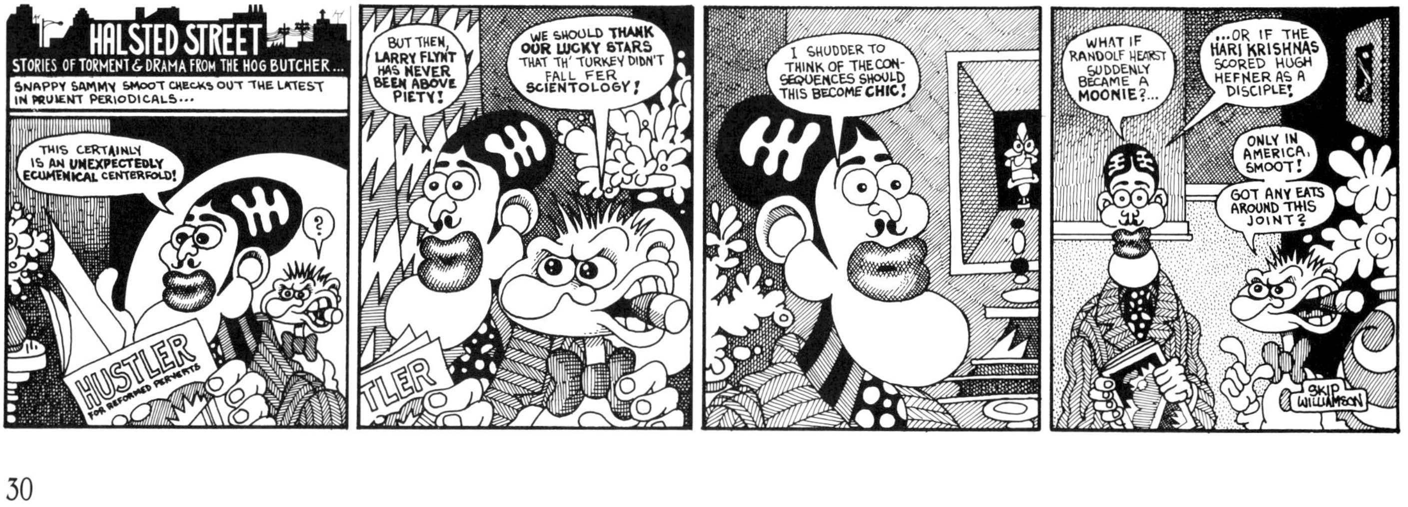
HALSTED STREET
STORIES OF TORMENT & DRAMA FROM THE HOG BUTCHER...
SNAPPY SAMMY SMOOT CHECKS OUT THE LATEST IN PRURIENT PERIODICALS...
THIS CERTAINLY IS AN UNEXPECTEDLY ECUMENICAL CENTERFOLD!
?
HUSTLER
FOR REFORMED PERVERTS
BUT THEN, LARRY FLYNT HAS NEVER BEEN ABOVE PIETY!
WE SHOULD THANK OUR LUCKY STARS THAT TH' TURKEY DIDN'T FALL FER SCIENTOLOGY!
TLER
I SHUDDER TO THINK OF THE CONSEQUENCES SHOULD THIS BECOME CHIC!
WHAT IF RANDOLF HEARST SUDDENLY BECAME A MOONIE?...
...OR IF THE HARI KRISHNAS SCORED HUGH HEFNER AS A DISCIPLE!
ONLY IN AMERICA, SMOOT!
GOT ANY EATS AROUND THIS JOINT?
SKIP WILLIAMSON

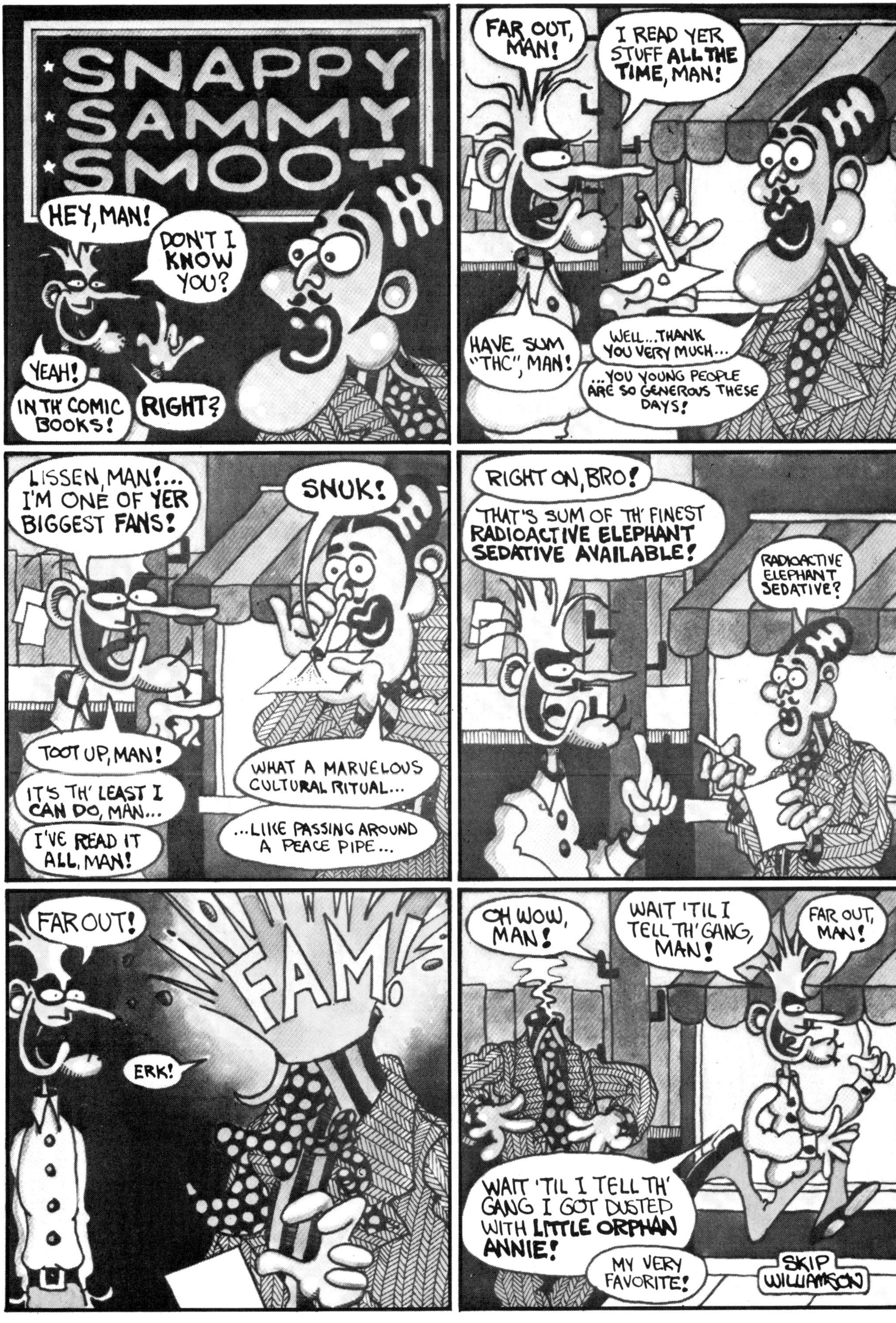
SNAPPY SAMMY SMOOT
HEY, MAN!
DON'T I KNOW YOU?
YEAH!
IN TH' COMIC BOOKS!
RIGHT?
FAR OUT, MAN!
I READ YER STUFF ALL THE TIME, MAN!
HAVE SUM "THC", MAN!
WELL...THANK YOU VERY MUCH...
...YOU YOUNG PEOPLE ARE SO GENEROUS THESE DAYS!
LISSEN, MAN!... I'M ONE OF YER BIGGEST FANS!
SNUK!
TOOT UP, MAN!
IT'S TH' LEAST I CAN DO, MAN...
I'VE READ IT ALL, MAN!
WHAT A MARVELOUS CULTURAL RITUAL...
...LIKE PASSING AROUND A PEACE PIPE...
RIGHT ON, BRO!
THAT'S SUM OF TH' FINEST RADIOACTIVE ELEPHANT SEDATIVE AVAILABLE!
RADIOACTIVE ELEPHANT SEDATIVE?
FAR OUT!
FAM!
ERK!
OH WOW, MAN!
WAIT 'TIL I TELL TH' GANG, MAN!
FAR OUT, MAN!
WAIT 'TIL I TELL TH' GANG I GOT DUSTED WITH LITTLE ORPHAN ANNIE!
MY VERY FAVORITE!
SKIP WILLIAMSON

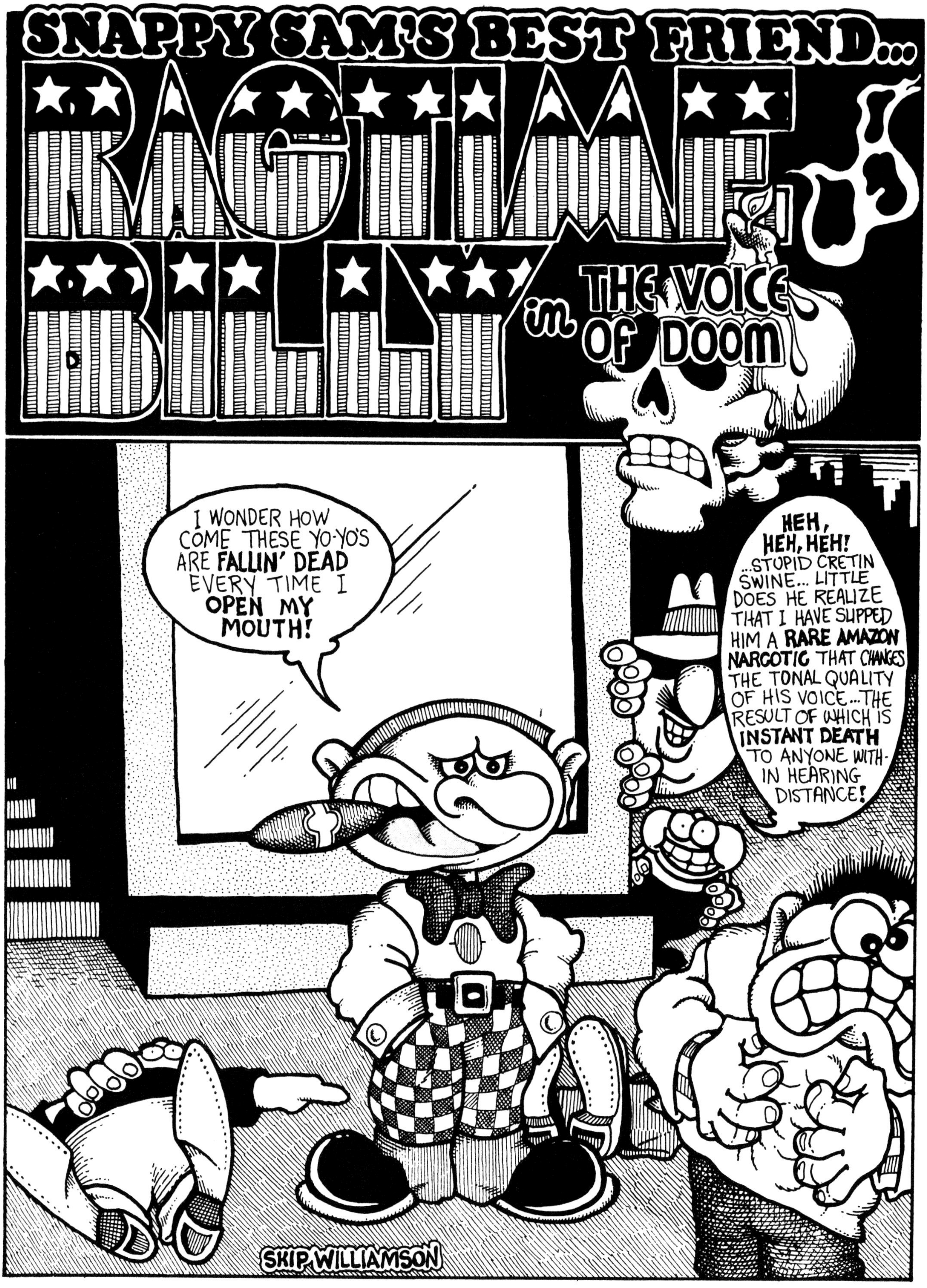
SNAPPY SAM'S BEST FRIEND...
RAGTIME BILLY in THE VOICE OF DOOM
I WONDER HOW COME THESE YO-YO'S ARE FALLIN' DEAD EVERY TIME I OPEN MY MOUTH!
HEH, HEH, HEH! ...STUPID CRETIN SWINE... LITTLE DOES HE REALIZE THAT I HAVE SLIPPED HIM A RARE AMAZON NARCOTIC THAT CHANGES THE TONAL QUALITY OF HIS VOICE...THE RESULT OF WHICH IS INSTANT DEATH TO ANYONE WITHIN HEARING DISTANCE!
SKIP WILLIAMSON

CRIMINAL GENIUS, FLUBBER McGEE, ONE-TIME HARVARD BUSINESS ADMINISTRATION MAJOR EXPELLED FOR PERFORMING UNNATURAL ACTS WITH THE SCHOOL'S RADICAL FRINGE... NOW DEDICATED TO POWER/LUST AND STOLEN MILLIONS HE HEADS INTO THE AMAZON, SEEKING REFUGE...

THERE, IN ISOLATION FROM MODERN CIVILIZATION FOR FIVE YEARS, McGEE LEARNS THE BLACK ARTS UNDER THE MYSTIC GUIDANCE OF **MONTEZUMA CHARLIE**, AGELESS MASTER OF COSMIC CONSCIOUSNESS...

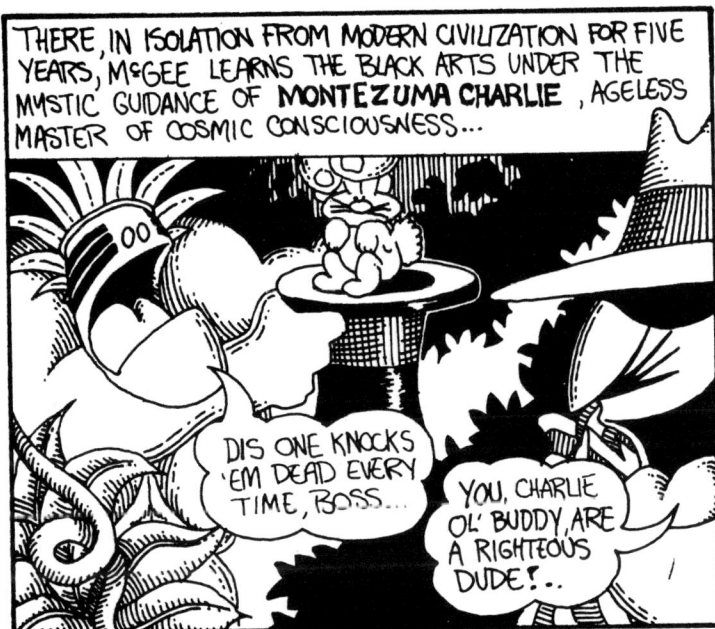

DIS ONE KNOCKS 'EM DEAD EVERY TIME, BOSS...

YOU, CHARLIE OL' BUDDY, ARE A RIGHTEOUS DUDE!...

MEANWHILE... CIVILIZATION RAGES ON... AND ACROSS AMERICA MILLIONS OF TEEVEE SETS ARE TUNED TO THE SAME CHANNEL... IT'S TIME FOR THE INCREDIBLY POPULAR...

RAGTIME BILLY show

WELCOME MR. + MRS. PATRIOTIC AMERICAN... ON T'NIGHT'S BROADCAST I'D LIKE T' TALK WITH YA ABOUT ANOTHER **DIRE THREAT** T' AMERICAN SECURITY...

...'COURSE I'M TALKIN' ABOUT...

HOMER-SEXUAL QUEERS!

WHO DO THEM FAGGOTY JOIKS T'INK THEY ARE, ANYWAY...

...TOYING AS THEY DO WID TH' VERY MORAL FIBRE OF **PLAIN FOLKS** LIKE ME AN' YOU!...

80,000,000 AMERICANS RESPOND UNANIMOUSLY AND THE INFLUENCE OF THE SHOW IS FELT THROUGHOUT THE LAND...

GROAN... I'M A YOUTHFUL ANARCHIST... BROUGHT TO JUSTICE BECAUSE OF INFORMATION BROUGHT TO LIGHT ON TH' RAGTIME BILLY SHOW!

GROAN... EVER SINCE RAGTIME BILLY TOOK A PUBLIC POSITION A-GAINST DRUGS I CAN'T SELL HEROIN AND MARIUANA TO GRADE-SCHOOLERS ON TH' PLAYGROUND!

GROAN... I'M A SEX-PLOITATION FILM-MAKER- ONLY NOBODY COMES TO SEE MY MOVIES NOW THAT RAGTIME BILLY HAS GIVEN HIS ENDORSEMENT TO ANTI-SMUT CRUSADERS!

GROAN GROAN GROAN

MEANWHILE...

HMMM... THIS RAGTIME BILLY CHARACTER GIVES ME AN IDEA

HEY CHARLIE... BE A GOOD INDIAN AN' GO BOOK ME PASSAGE ON TH' FIRST BOAT BACK T' TH' STATES...

NEW YORK TIMES MAGAZINE
RAGTIME BILLY, T.V. PHENOMENON

McGEE PACKS HIS BAGS

WITH THIS SINISTER AMAZONIAN DRUG AND THIS RAGTIME BILLY'S ENORMOUS POPULARITY I CAN AT LAST REALIZE MY CHILDHOOD FANTASY OF WORLD DOMINATION!

ONE DOSE OF THIS ANCIENT NARCOTIC WILL SO ALTER THE VICTIM'S VOICE SO THAT ANYONE WITHIN ITS RANGE WILL INSTANTLY DIE!

THE STICKY THREADS OF MY NEFARIOUS PLOT ARE WEAVING THEMSELVES INTO A WEB OF INTERNATIONAL INTRIGUE...

BACK IN THE STATES...

THE DAILY
RAGTIME BILLY RAIDS GAY BAR

WE'LL RID CITY OF EFFETE VERMIN, CRUSADER VOWS

YA SHOULD'A SEEN THE JEERS RAGTIME BILLY IN A PRESS CON- SHORTLY

WORLD UNREST

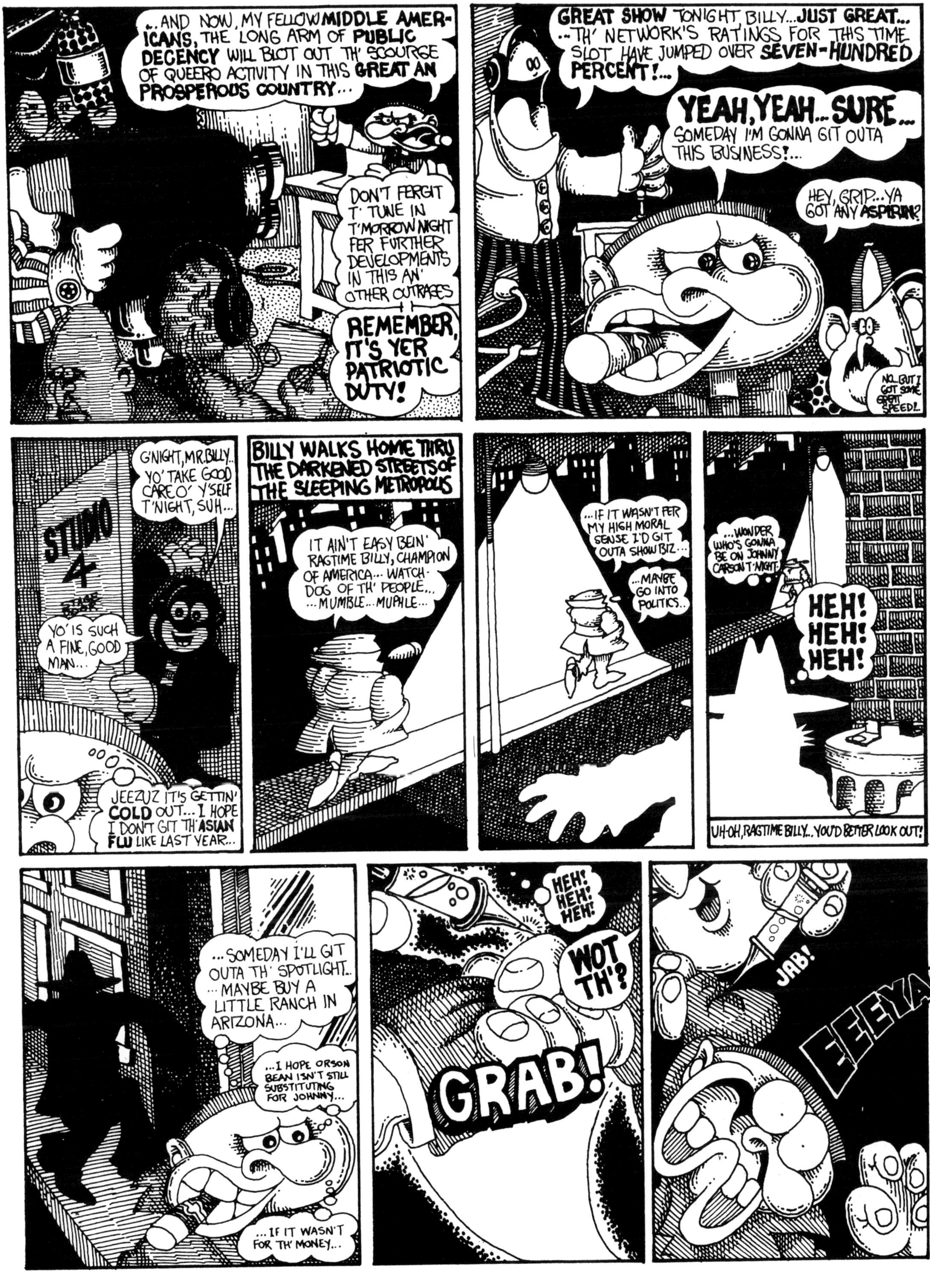
...AND NOW, MY FELLOW MIDDLE AMERICANS, THE LONG ARM OF PUBLIC DECENCY WILL BLOT OUT TH' SCOURGE OF QUEERO ACTIVITY IN THIS GREAT AN PROSPEROUS COUNTRY...
DON'T FERGIT T' TUNE IN T'MORROW NIGHT FER FURTHER DEVELOPMENTS IN THIS AN' OTHER OUTRAGES
REMEMBER, IT'S YER PATRIOTIC DUTY!
GREAT SHOW TONIGHT, BILLY... JUST GREAT... ...TH' NETWORK'S RATINGS FOR THIS TIME SLOT HAVE JUMPED OVER SEVEN-HUNDRED PERCENT!...
YEAH, YEAH... SURE... SOMEDAY I'M GONNA GIT OUTA THIS BUSINESS!...
HEY, GRIP... YA GOT ANY ASPIRIN?
NO, BUT I GOT SOME GREAT SPEED!
G'NIGHT, MR. BILLY... YO' TAKE GOOD CARE O' Y'SELF T'NIGHT, SUH...
STUDIO 4
YO' IS SUCH A FINE, GOOD MAN...
JEEZUZ IT'S GETTIN' COLD OUT... I HOPE I DON'T GIT TH' ASIAN FLU LIKE LAST YEAR...
BILLY WALKS HOME THRU THE DARKENED STREETS OF THE SLEEPING METROPOLIS
IT AIN'T EASY BEIN' RAGTIME BILLY, CHAMPION OF AMERICA... WATCH-DOG OF TH' PEOPLE... ...MUMBLE... MUMBLE...
...IF IT WASN'T FER MY HIGH MORAL SENSE I'D GIT OUTA SHOW BIZ...
...MAYBE GO INTO POLITICS...
...WONDER WHO'S GONNA BE ON JOHNNY CARSON T'NIGHT...
HEH! HEH! HEH!
UH-OH, RAGTIME BILLY... YOU'D BETTER LOOK OUT!
...SOMEDAY I'LL GIT OUTA TH' SPOTLIGHT... ...MAYBE BUY A LITTLE RANCH IN ARIZONA...
...I HOPE ORSON BEAN ISN'T STILL SUBSTITUTING FOR JOHNNY...
...IF IT WASN'T FOR TH' MONEY...
HEH! HEH! HEH!
WOT TH'?
GRAB!
JAB!
EEEYAH

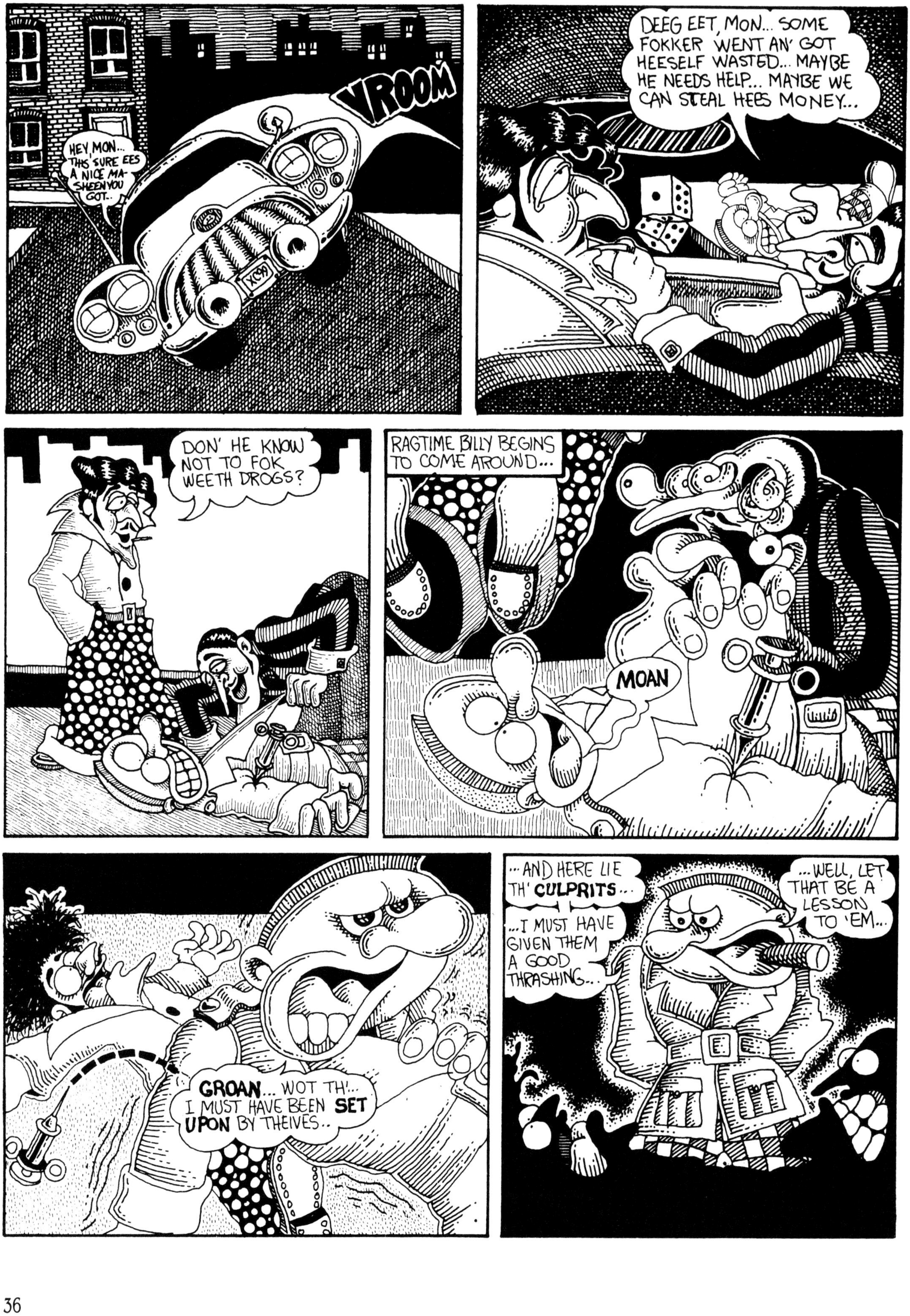
VROOM
HEY MON... THIS SURE EES A NICE MA-SHEEN YOU GOT..
DEEG EET, MON... SOME FOKKER WENT AN' GOT HEESELF WASTED... MAYBE HE NEEDS HELP... MAYBE WE CAN STEAL HEES MONEY...
DON' HE KNOW NOT TO FOK WEETH DROGS?
RAGTIME BILLY BEGINS TO COME AROUND...
MOAN
GROAN... WOT TH'... I MUST HAVE BEEN SET UPON BY THEIVES..
...AND HERE LIE TH' CULPRITS...
...I MUST HAVE GIVEN THEM A GOOD THRASHING...
...WELL, LET THAT BE A LESSON TO 'EM...

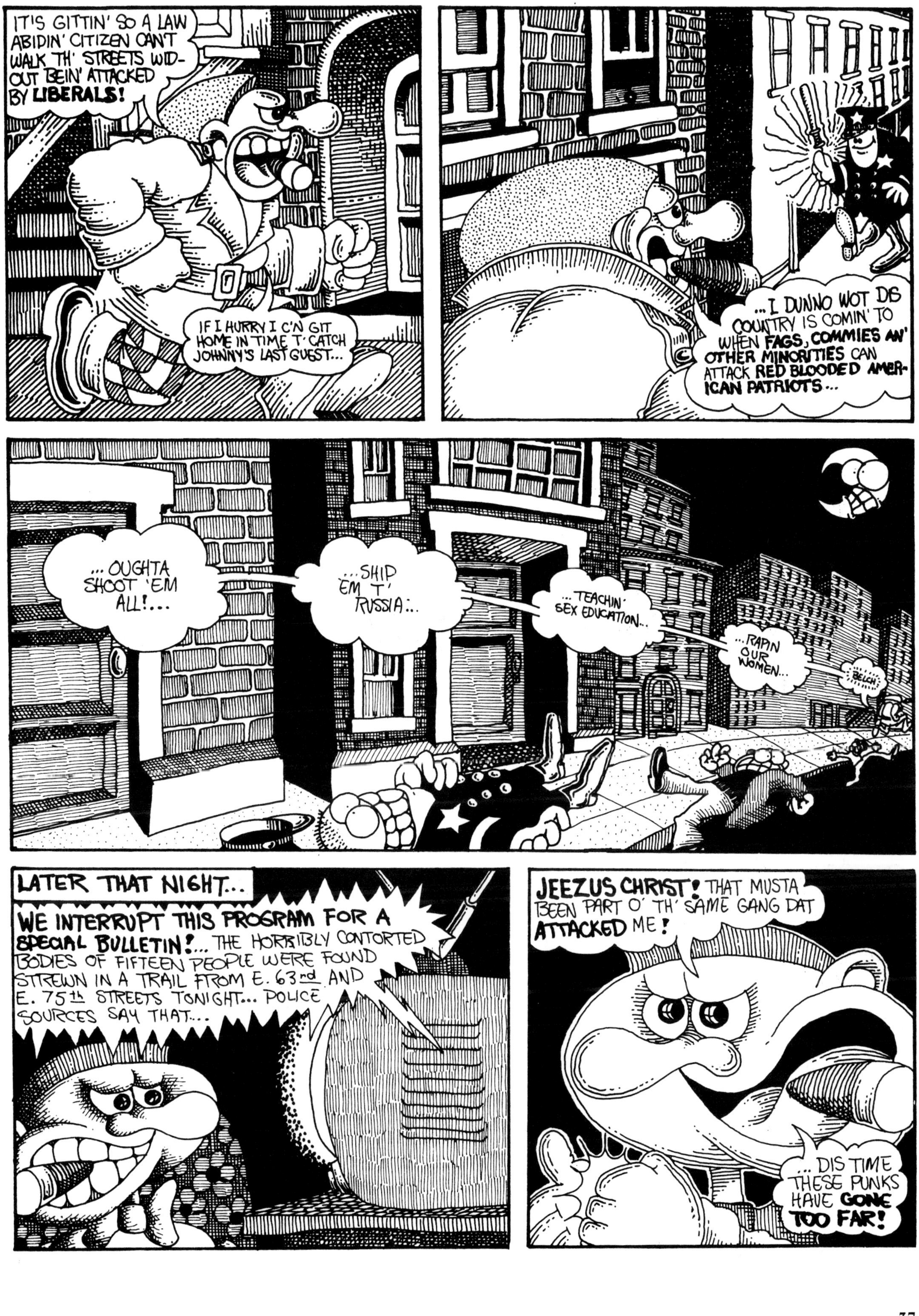
IT'S GITTIN' SO A LAW ABIDIN' CITIZEN CAN'T WALK TH' STREETS WID-OUT BEIN' ATTACKED BY LIBERALS!
IF I HURRY I C'N GIT HOME IN TIME T' CATCH JOHNNY'S LAST GUEST...
...I DUNNO WOT DIS COUNTRY IS COMIN' TO WHEN FAGS, COMMIES AN' OTHER MINORITIES CAN ATTACK RED BLOODED AMER-ICAN PATRIOTS...
...OUGHTA SHOOT 'EM ALL!...
...SHIP 'EM T' RUSSIA...
...TEACHIN' SEX EDUCATION...
...RAPIN OUR WOMEN...
BELCH
LATER THAT NIGHT...
WE INTERRUPT THIS PROGRAM FOR A SPECIAL BULLETIN!... THE HORRIBLY CONTORTED BODIES OF FIFTEEN PEOPLE WERE FOUND STREWN IN A TRAIL FROM E. 63rd AND E. 75th STREETS TONIGHT... POLICE SOURCES SAY THAT...
JEEZUS CHRIST! THAT MUSTA BEEN PART O' TH' SAME GANG DAT ATTACKED ME!
...DIS TIME THESE PUNKS HAVE GONE TOO FAR!

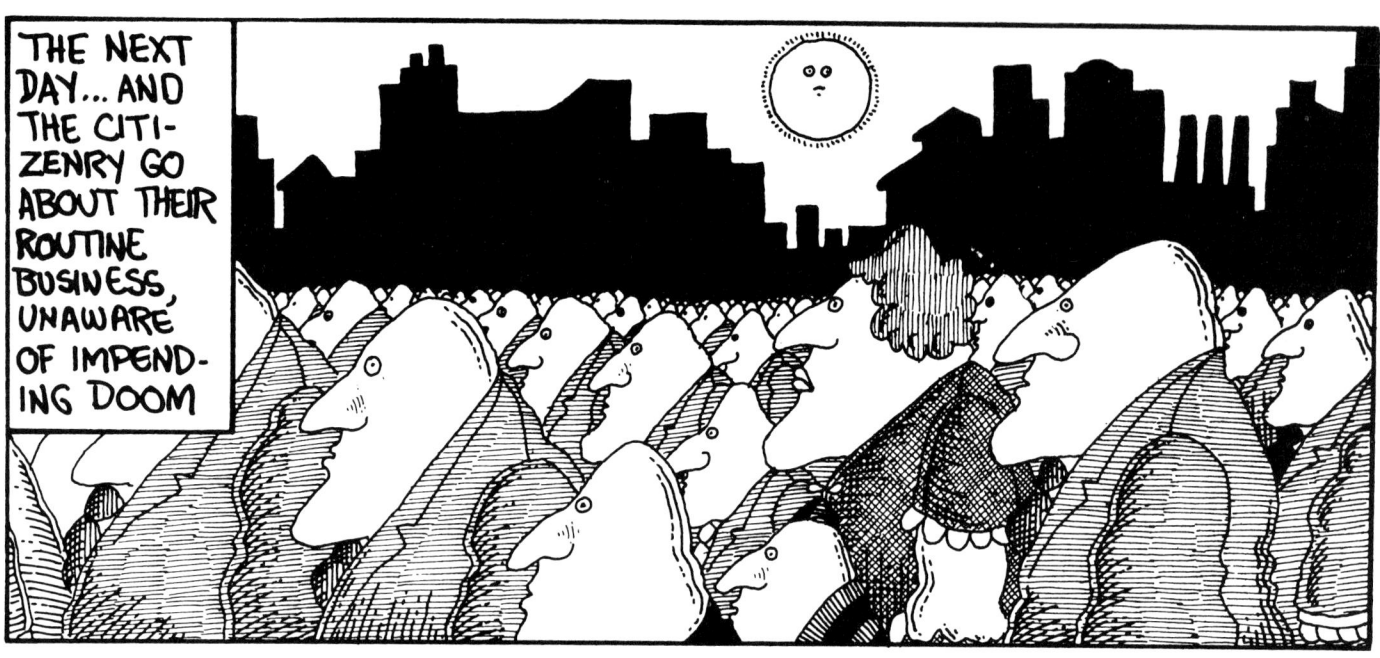

THE NEXT DAY... AND THE CITIZENRY GO ABOUT THEIR ROUTINE BUSINESS, UNAWARE OF IMPENDING DOOM

THAT EVENING...

MY GAWD! I ONLY GOT 15 MINUTES UNTIL AIR TIME!...

I C'N JUST MAKE IT IF I HURRY...

STUDIO A

ZIP

JUST IN TIME, RAGTIME BILLY...

ONLY 10 SECONDS TO AIR TIME...

10...
9...
8...
7...
6...
5...
4...
3...
2...

GOOD EVENING, MR. AND MRS. PATRIOTIC AMERICAN...

YER ON!

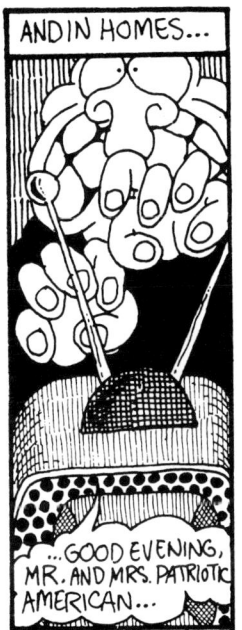

AND IN HOMES...

...GOOD EVENING, MR. AND MRS. PATRIOTIC AMERICAN...

...IN BARS...

...GOOD EVENING MR. AND MRS. PATRIOTIC AMERICANS...

...AND MOTELS ACROSS THE COUNTRY...

...GOOD EVENING, MR. AND MRS. AMERICAN PATRIOT...

BACK AT THE STUDIO... A FAMILIAR VOICE FROM BEHIND CAMERA "A" FILLS RAGTIME BILLY IN...

AN' THAT'S TH' WHOLE STORY, RAGTIME BILLY... ...BY JUST OPENING YOU MOUTH YOU'VE WIPED OUT 95% OF TH' COUNTRY'S POP-ULATION...

...LUCKILY I'VE INOCU-LATED MYSELF AGAINST TH' DRUG... YER VOICE HAS NO EFFECT ON ME...

...YOU AN' I CAN RULE TH' COUNTRY...

...WHO CARES ABOUT ALL THEM DEAD CREEPS, ANYWAY?

HMMM... MAYBE YER RIGHT...

...MOST EVERYBODY 'CEPT ME IS AN ASSHOLE...

YA KNOW, FLIBBER, YOU AIN'T HALF BAD FER AN ARCH-CRIMINAL...

...JUST THINK, RAG-TIME BILLY, YOU 'N' ME WALKIN' DOWN TH' ROAD OF LIFE T'GETHER...

...LONG AS YOU C'N KEEP YER HANDS OFF MY OL' WAZOO... YOU AN' ME 'LL GIT ALONG JUST FINE..

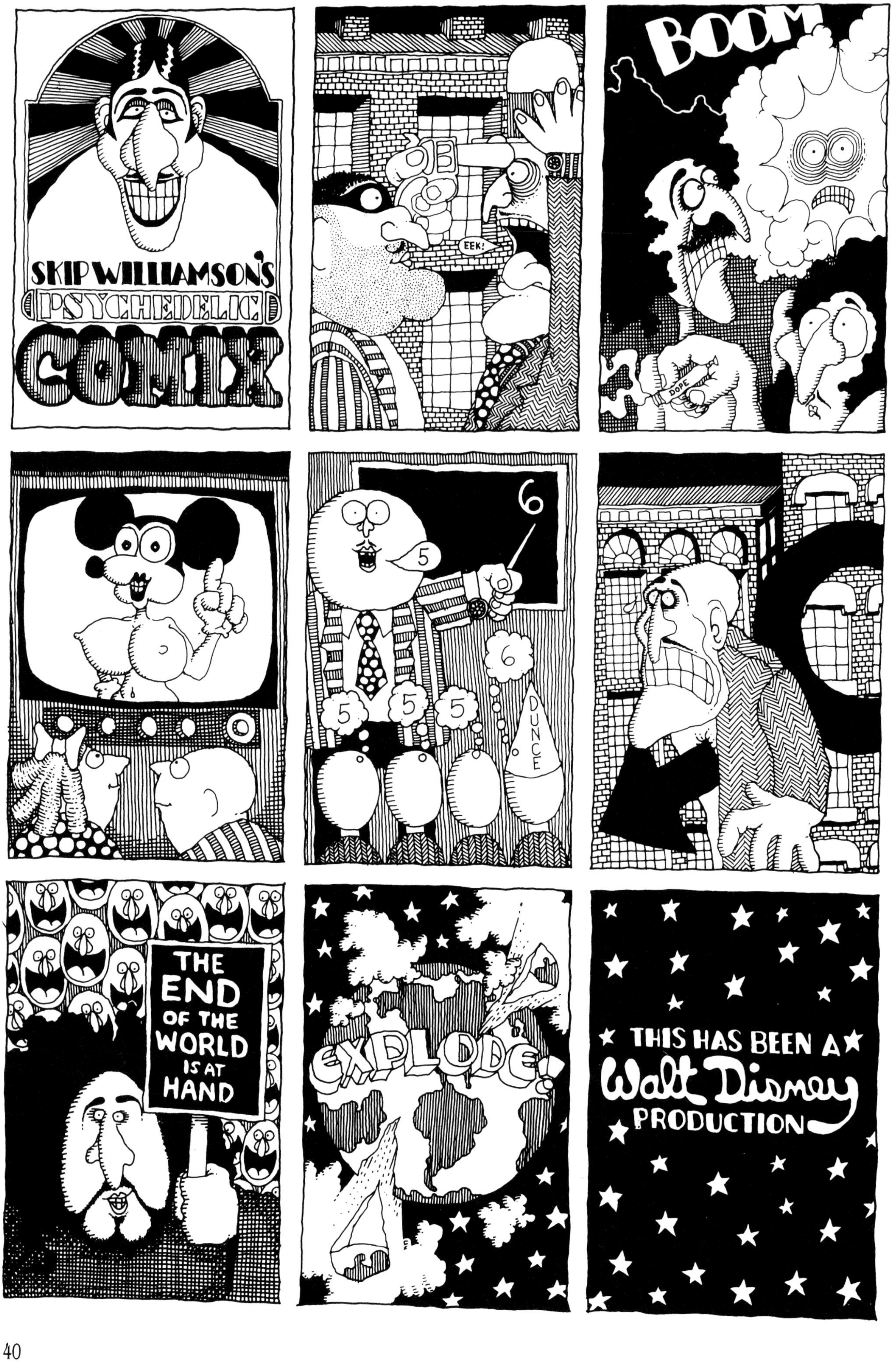
SKIP WILLIAMSON'S
PSYCHEDELIC
COMIX
EEK!
BOOM
DOPE
6
5
5
5
5
6
DUNCE
THE END OF THE WORLD IS AT HAND
EXPLODE!
THIS HAS BEEN A
Walt Disney
PRODUCTION

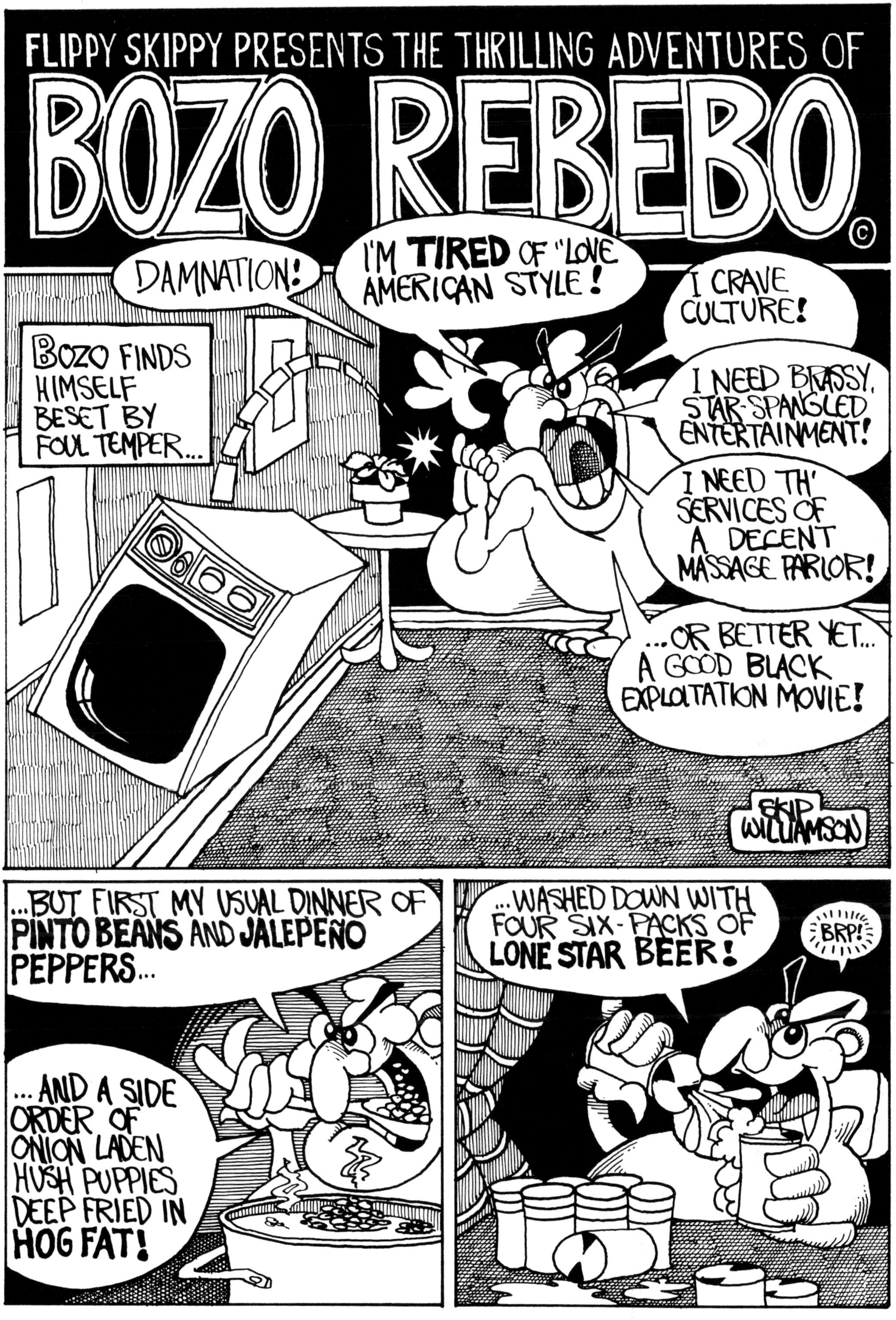

FLIPPY SKIPPY PRESENTS THE THRILLING ADVENTURES OF
BOZO REBEBO ©
DAMNATION!
I'M TIRED OF "LOVE AMERICAN STYLE!
I CRAVE CULTURE!
BOZO FINDS HIMSELF BESET BY FOUL TEMPER...
I NEED BRASSY, STAR-SPANGLED ENTERTAINMENT!
I NEED TH' SERVICES OF A DECENT MASSAGE PARLOR!
...OR BETTER YET... A GOOD BLACK EXPLOITATION MOVIE!
SKIP WILLIAMSON
...BUT FIRST MY USUAL DINNER OF PINTO BEANS AND JALEPEÑO PEPPERS...
...AND A SIDE ORDER OF ONION LADEN HUSH PUPPIES DEEP FRIED IN HOG FAT!
...WASHED DOWN WITH FOUR SIX-PACKS OF LONE STAR BEER!
BRP!

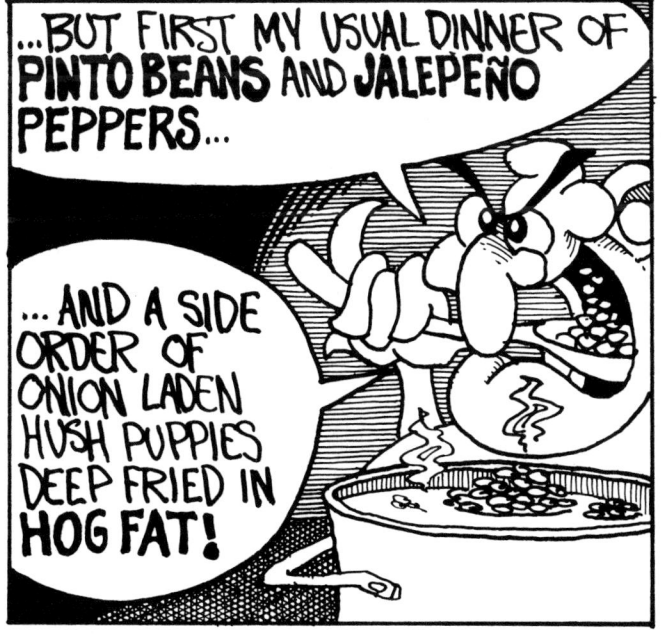

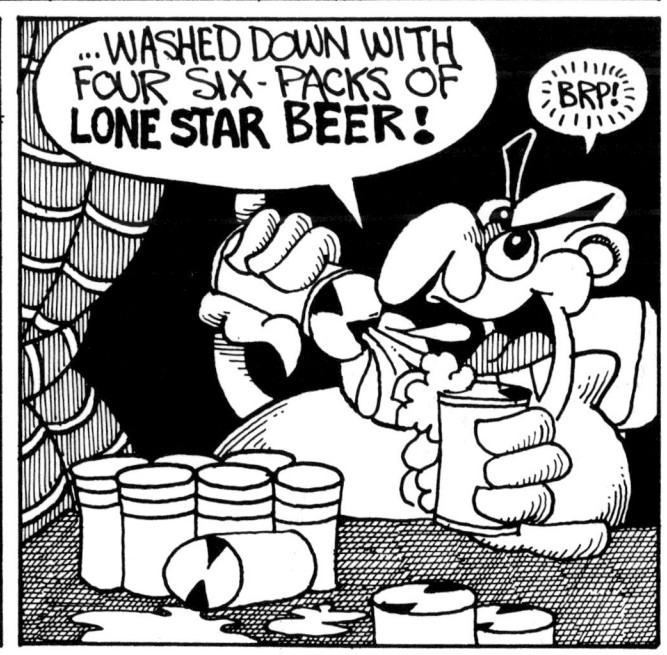

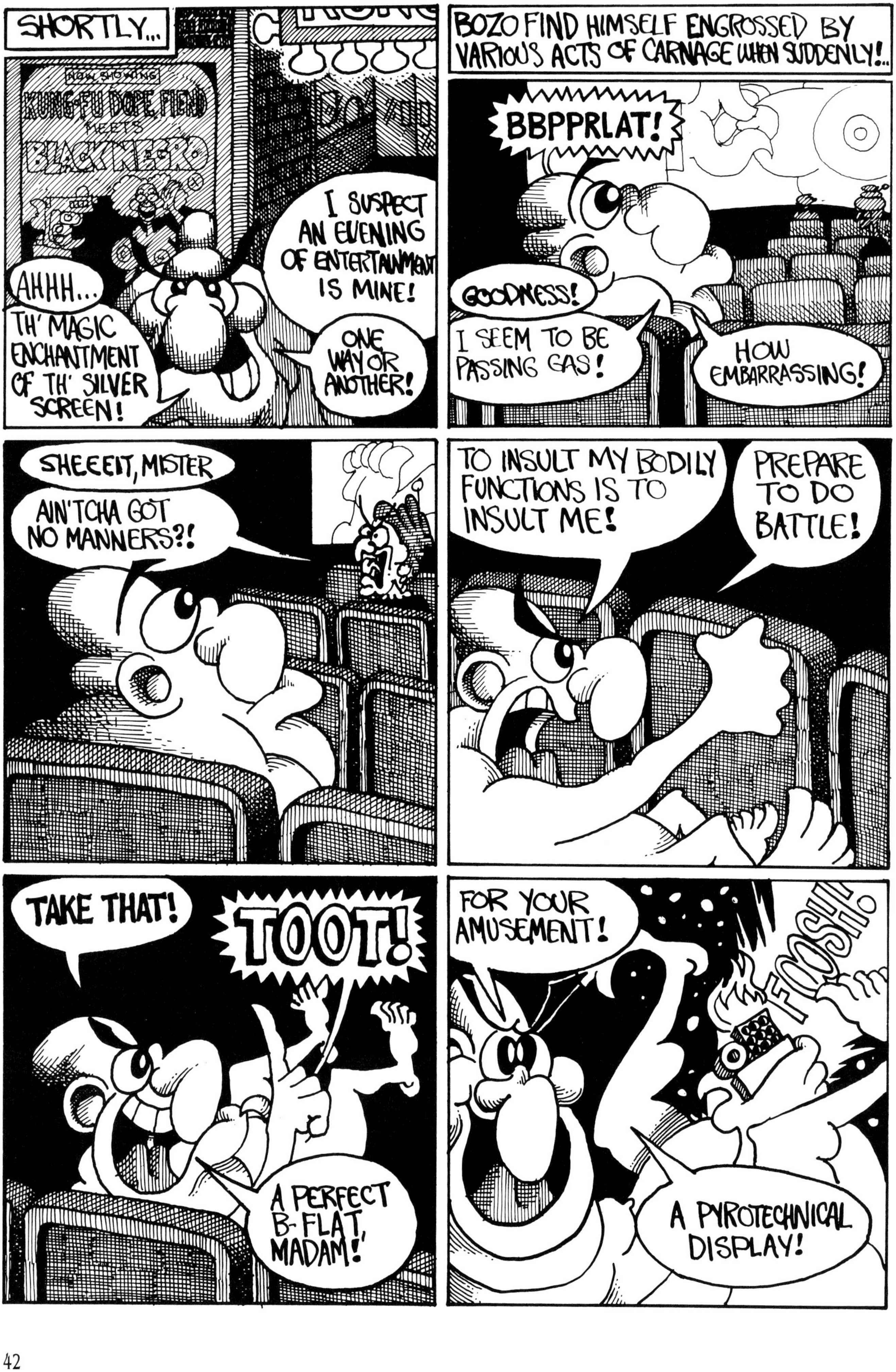
SHORTLY...
NOW SHOWING
KUNG-FU DOPE FIEND MEETS BLACK NEGRO
AHHH...
TH' MAGIC ENCHANTMENT OF TH' SILVER SCREEN!
I SUSPECT AN EVENING OF ENTERTAINMENT IS MINE!
ONE WAY OR ANOTHER!
BOZO FIND HIMSELF ENGROSSED BY VARIOUS ACTS OF CARNAGE WHEN SUDDENLY!..
BBPPRLAT!
GOODNESS!
I SEEM TO BE PASSING GAS!
HOW EMBARRASSING!
SHEEEIT, MISTER
AIN'TCHA GOT NO MANNERS?!
TO INSULT MY BODILY FUNCTIONS IS TO INSULT ME!
PREPARE TO DO BATTLE!
TAKE THAT!
TOOT!
A PERFECT B-FLAT, MADAM!
FOR YOUR AMUSEMENT!
FOOSH!
A PYROTECHNICAL DISPLAY!

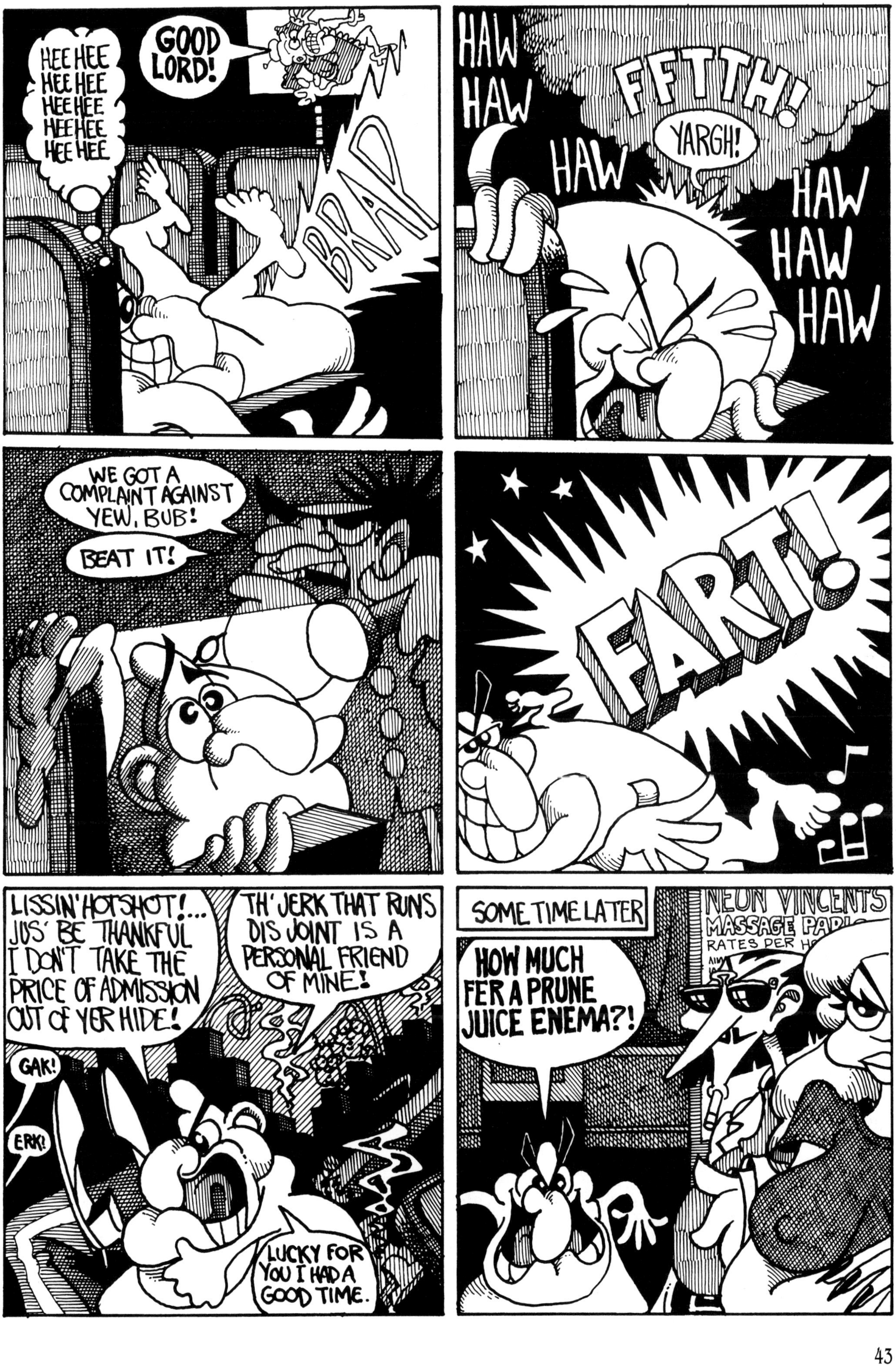
HEE HEE
HEE HEE
HEE HEE
HEE HEE
HEE HEE
GOOD LORD!
BRAP
HAW
HAW
FFTTH!
YARGH!
HAW
HAW
HAW
HAW
WE GOT A COMPLAINT AGAINST YEW, BUB!
BEAT IT!
FART!
LISSIN' HOTSHOT!... JUS' BE THANKFUL I DON'T TAKE THE PRICE OF ADMISSION OUT OF YER HIDE!
TH' JERK THAT RUNS DIS JOINT IS A PERSONAL FRIEND OF MINE!
GAK!
ERK!
LUCKY FOR YOU I HAD A GOOD TIME.
SOME TIME LATER
NEON VINCENTS
MASSAGE PARL
RATES PER H
HOW MUCH FER A PRUNE JUICE ENEMA?!

FILM FUN

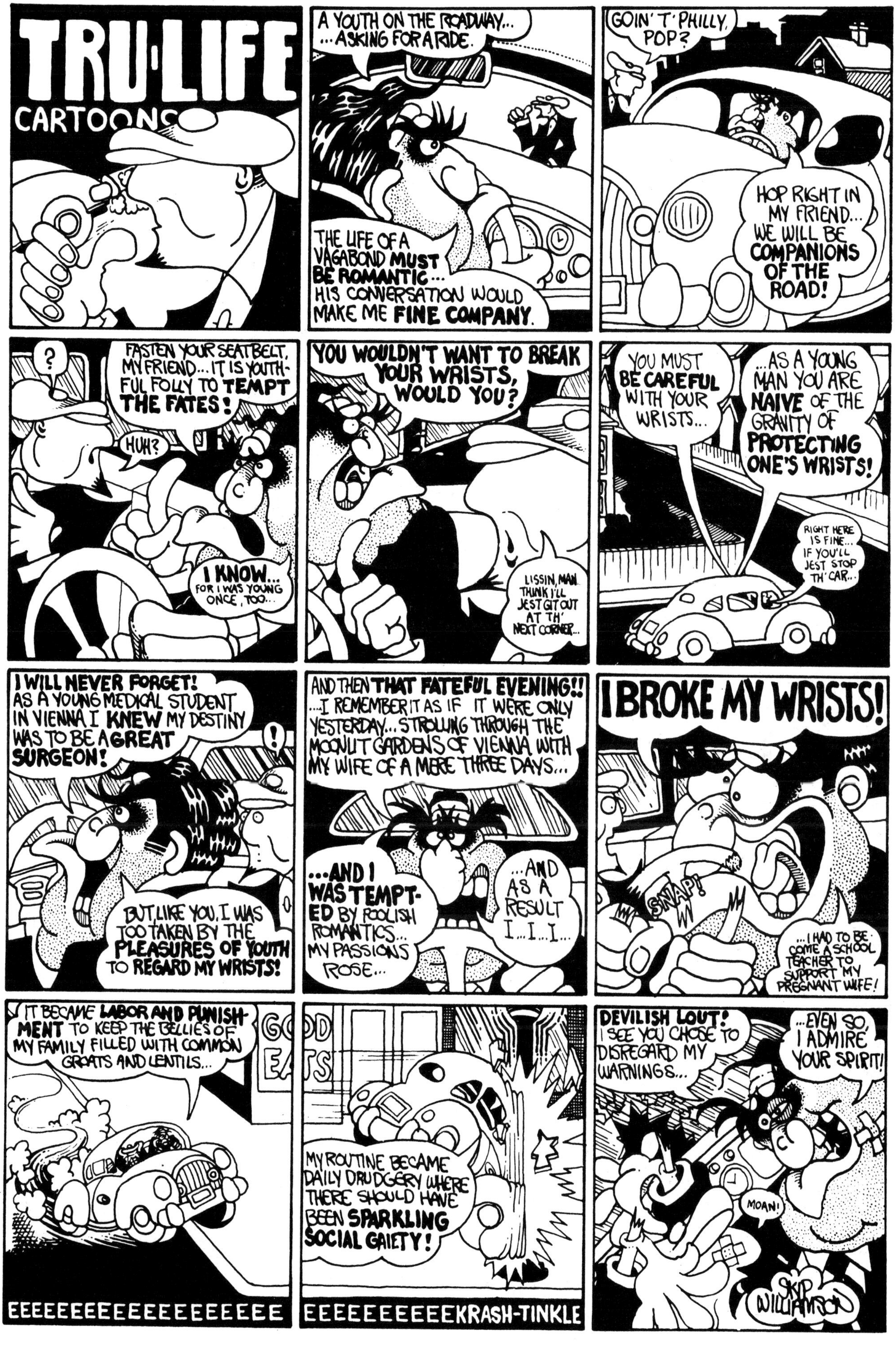
TRU·LIFE
CARTOONS
A YOUTH ON THE ROADWAY... ...ASKING FOR A RIDE.
THE LIFE OF A VAGABOND MUST BE ROMANTIC... HIS CONVERSATION WOULD MAKE ME FINE COMPANY.
GOIN' T' PHILLY, POP?
HOP RIGHT IN MY FRIEND... WE WILL BE COMPANIONS OF THE ROAD!
?
FASTEN YOUR SEATBELT, MY FRIEND... IT IS YOUTHFUL FOLLY TO TEMPT THE FATES!
HUH?
I KNOW... FOR I WAS YOUNG ONCE, TOO...
YOU WOULDN'T WANT TO BREAK YOUR WRISTS, WOULD YOU?
LISSIN, MAN. THINK I'LL JEST GIT OUT AT TH' NEXT CORNER...
YOU MUST BE CAREFUL WITH YOUR WRISTS...
...AS A YOUNG MAN YOU ARE NAIVE OF THE GRAVITY OF PROTECTING ONE'S WRISTS!
RIGHT HERE IS FINE... IF YOU'LL JEST STOP TH' CAR...
I WILL NEVER FORGET! AS A YOUNG MEDICAL STUDENT IN VIENNA I KNEW MY DESTINY WAS TO BE A GREAT SURGEON!
!
BUT, LIKE YOU, I WAS TOO TAKEN BY THE PLEASURES OF YOUTH TO REGARD MY WRISTS!
AND THEN THAT FATEFUL EVENING!! ...I REMEMBER IT AS IF IT WERE ONLY YESTERDAY... STROLLING THROUGH THE MOONLIT GARDENS OF VIENNA WITH MY WIFE OF A MERE THREE DAYS...
...AND I WAS TEMPTED BY FOOLISH ROMANTICS... MY PASSIONS ROSE...
...AND AS A RESULT I...I...I...
I BROKE MY WRISTS!
SNAP!
...I HAD TO BECOME A SCHOOL TEACHER TO SUPPORT MY PREGNANT WIFE!
IT BECAME LABOR AND PUNISHMENT TO KEEP THE BELLIES OF MY FAMILY FILLED WITH COMMON GROATS AND LENTILS...
EEEEEEEEEEEEEEEEEE
GOOD EATS
MY ROUTINE BECAME DAILY DRUDGERY WHERE THERE SHOULD HAVE BEEN SPARKLING SOCIAL GAIETY!
EEEEEEEEEKRASH-TINKLE
DEVILISH LOUT! I SEE YOU CHOSE TO DISREGARD MY WARNINGS...
...EVEN SO, I ADMIRE YOUR SPIRIT!
MOAN!
SKIP WILLIAMSON

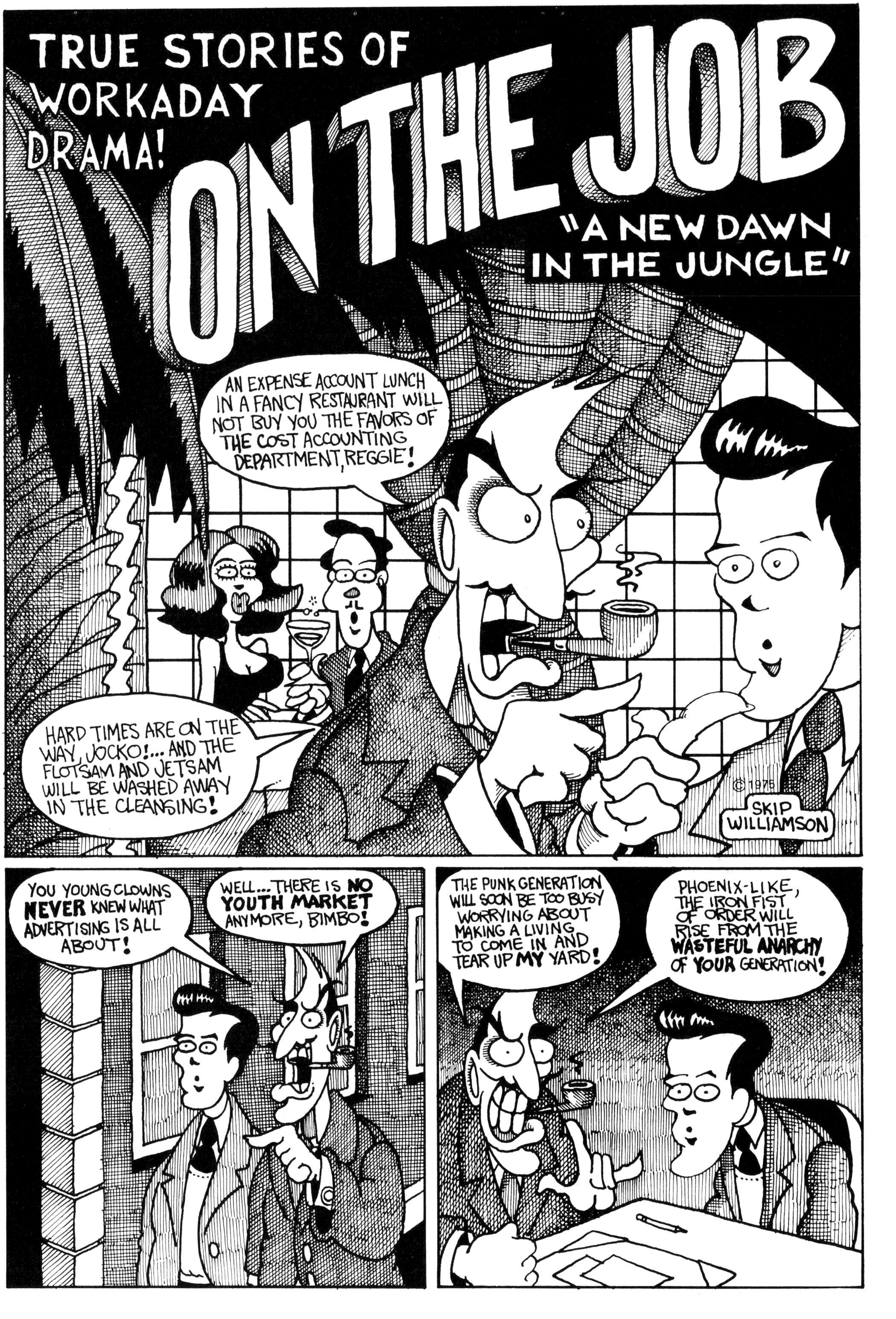
TRUE STORIES OF WORKADAY DRAMA!
ON THE JOB
"A NEW DAWN IN THE JUNGLE"
AN EXPENSE ACCOUNT LUNCH IN A FANCY RESTAURANT WILL NOT BUY YOU THE FAVORS OF THE COST ACCOUNTING DEPARTMENT, REGGIE!
HARD TIMES ARE ON THE WAY, JOCKO!... AND THE FLOTSAM AND JETSAM WILL BE WASHED AWAY IN THE CLEANSING!
© 1975
SKIP WILLIAMSON
YOU YOUNG CLOWNS NEVER KNEW WHAT ADVERTISING IS ALL ABOUT!
WELL... THERE IS NO YOUTH MARKET ANYMORE, BIMBO!
THE PUNK GENERATION WILL SOON BE TOO BUSY WORRYING ABOUT MAKING A LIVING TO COME IN AND TEAR UP MY YARD!
PHOENIX-LIKE, THE IRON FIST OF ORDER WILL RISE FROM THE WASTEFUL ANARCHY OF YOUR GENERATION!

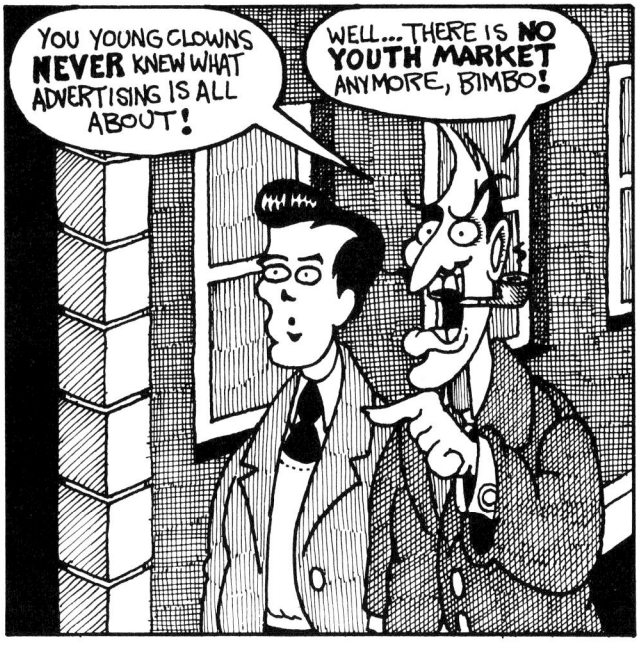

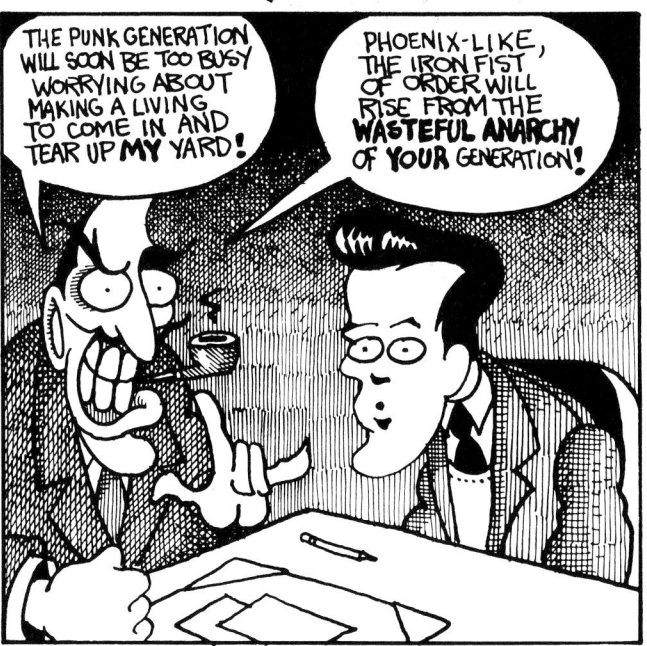

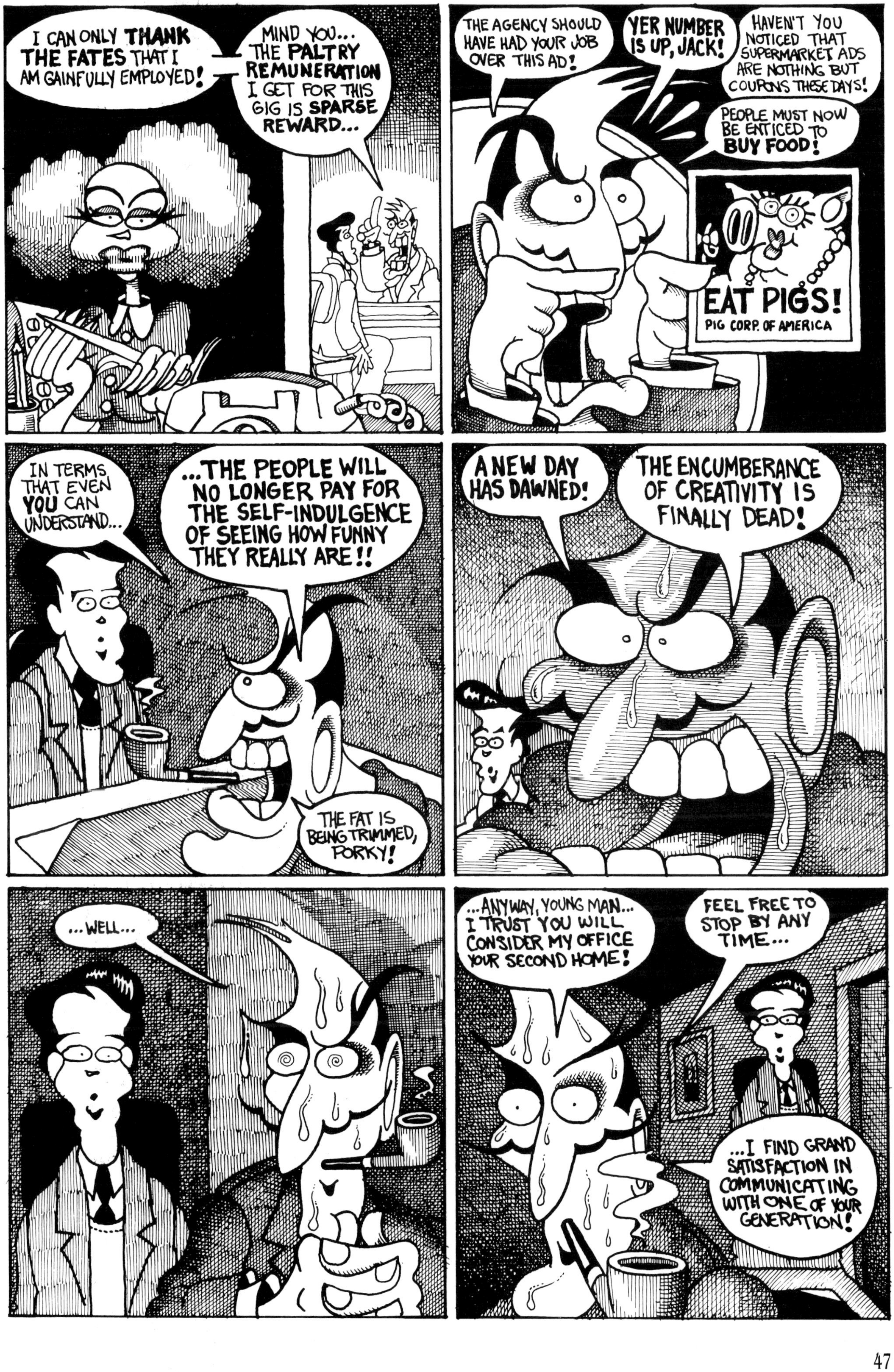
I CAN ONLY THANK THE FATES THAT I AM GAINFULLY EMPLOYED!
MIND YOU... THE PALTRY REMUNERATION I GET FOR THIS GIG IS SPARSE REWARD...
THE AGENCY SHOULD HAVE HAD YOUR JOB OVER THIS AD!
YER NUMBER IS UP, JACK!
HAVEN'T YOU NOTICED THAT SUPERMARKET ADS ARE NOTHING BUT COUPONS THESE DAYS!
PEOPLE MUST NOW BE ENTICED TO BUY FOOD!
EAT PIGS!
PIG CORP. OF AMERICA
IN TERMS THAT EVEN YOU CAN UNDERSTAND...
...THE PEOPLE WILL NO LONGER PAY FOR THE SELF-INDULGENCE OF SEEING HOW FUNNY THEY REALLY ARE!!
THE FAT IS BEING TRIMMED, PORKY!
A NEW DAY HAS DAWNED!
THE ENCUMBERANCE OF CREATIVITY IS FINALLY DEAD!
...WELL...
...ANYWAY, YOUNG MAN... I TRUST YOU WILL CONSIDER MY OFFICE YOUR SECOND HOME!
FEEL FREE TO STOP BY ANY TIME...
...I FIND GRAND SATISFACTION IN COMMUNICATING WITH ONE OF YOUR GENERATION!

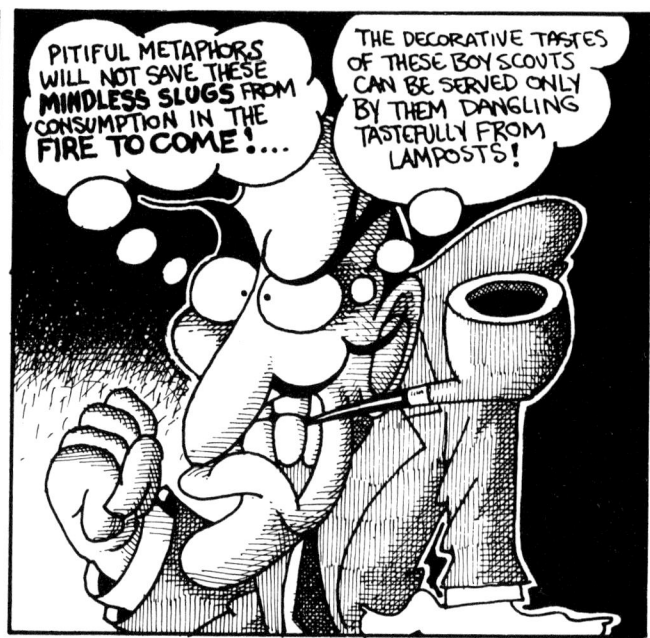

WHEN SUDDENLY, OWING TO THE LAWS OF TIME, IT'S

ACROSS TOWN...THE HOME FIRE BLAZES

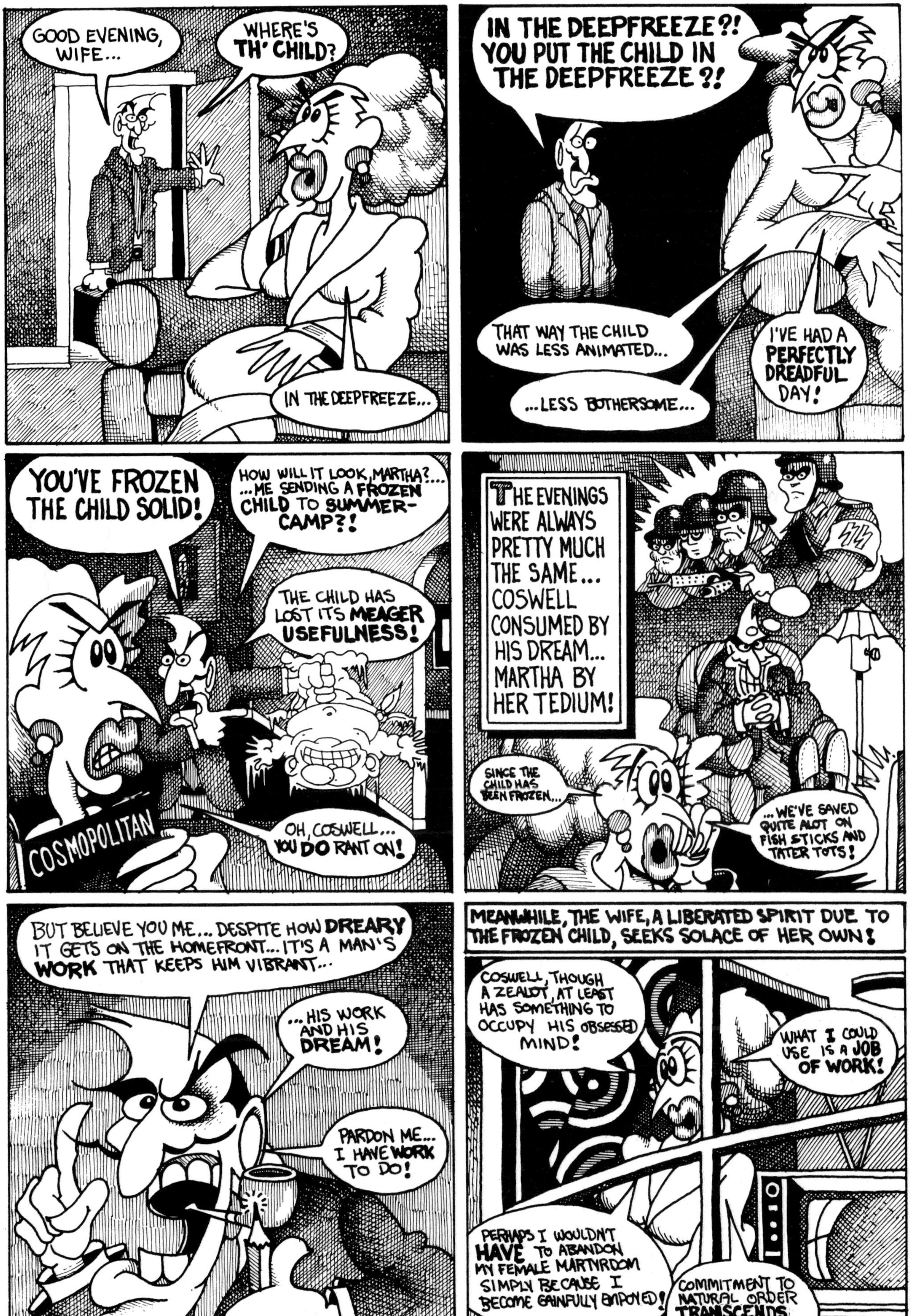
GOOD EVENING, WIFE...
WHERE'S TH' CHILD?
IN THE DEEPFREEZE...
IN THE DEEPFREEZE?! YOU PUT THE CHILD IN THE DEEPFREEZE?!
THAT WAY THE CHILD WAS LESS ANIMATED...
...LESS BOTHERSOME...
I'VE HAD A PERFECTLY DREADFUL DAY!
YOU'VE FROZEN THE CHILD SOLID!
HOW WILL IT LOOK, MARTHA?... ...ME SENDING A FROZEN CHILD TO SUMMER-CAMP?!
THE CHILD HAS LOST ITS MEAGER USEFULNESS!
COSMOPOLITAN
OH, COSWELL... YOU DO RANT ON!
THE EVENINGS WERE ALWAYS PRETTY MUCH THE SAME... COSWELL CONSUMED BY HIS DREAM... MARTHA BY HER TEDIUM!
SINCE THE CHILD HAS BEEN FROZEN...
...WE'VE SAVED QUITE ALOT ON FISH STICKS AND TATER TOTS!
BUT BELIEVE YOU ME... DESPITE HOW DREARY IT GETS ON THE HOMEFRONT... IT'S A MAN'S WORK THAT KEEPS HIM VIBRANT...
...HIS WORK AND HIS DREAM!
PARDON ME... I HAVE WORK TO DO!
MEANWHILE, THE WIFE, A LIBERATED SPIRIT DUE TO THE FROZEN CHILD, SEEKS SOLACE OF HER OWN!
COSWELL, THOUGH A ZEALOT, AT LEAST HAS SOMETHING TO OCCUPY HIS OBSESSED MIND!
WHAT I COULD USE IS A JOB OF WORK!
PERHAPS I WOULDN'T HAVE TO ABANDON MY FEMALE MARTYRDOM SIMPLY BECAUSE I BECOME GAINFULLY EMPLOYED!
COMMITMENT TO NATURAL ORDER TRANSCENDS GAINFUL EMPLOYMENT!

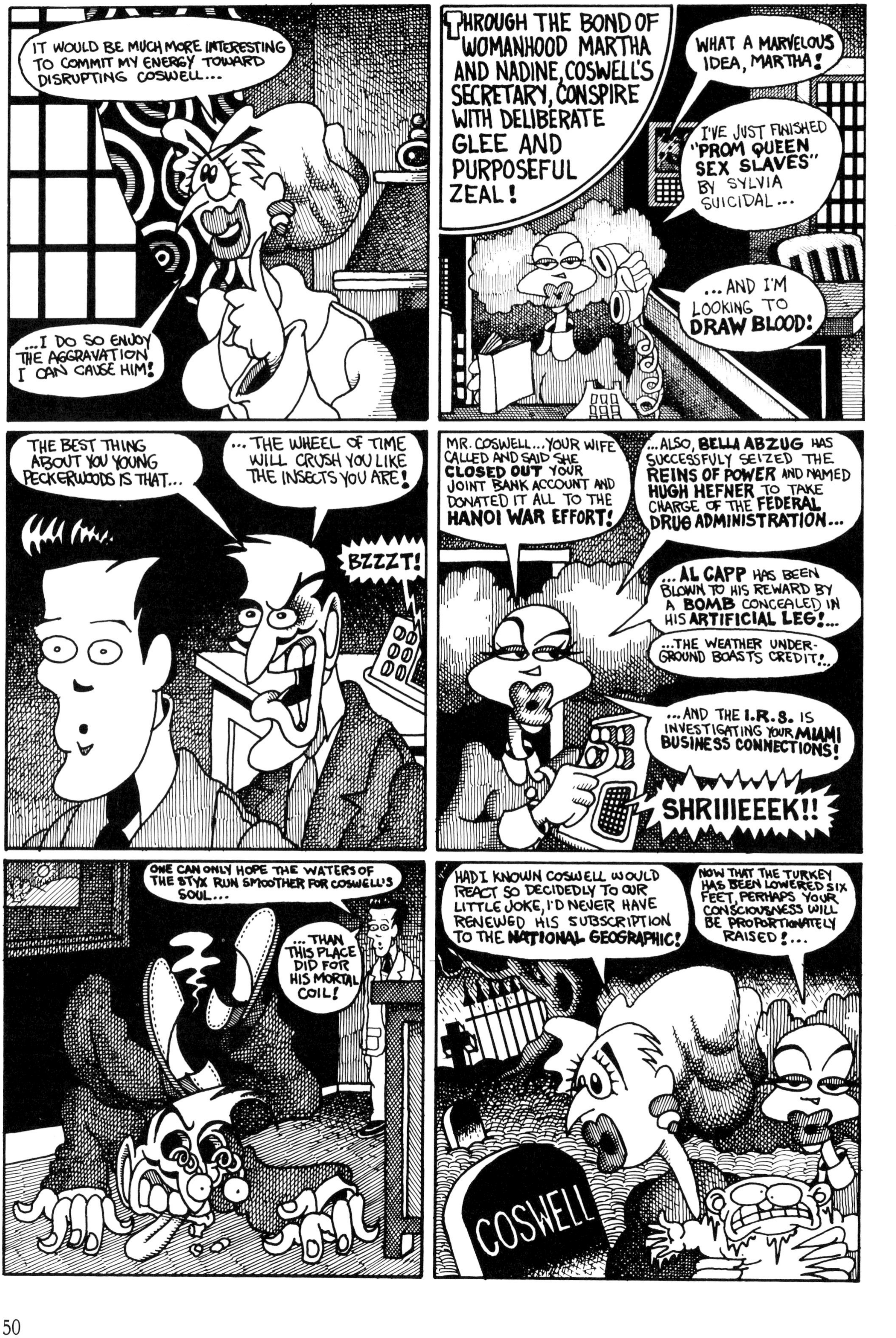

IT WOULD BE MUCH MORE INTERESTING TO COMMIT MY ENERGY TOWARD DISRUPTING COSWELL...
...I DO SO ENJOY THE AGGRAVATION I CAN CAUSE HIM!
THROUGH THE BOND OF WOMANHOOD MARTHA AND NADINE, COSWELL'S SECRETARY, CONSPIRE WITH DELIBERATE GLEE AND PURPOSEFUL ZEAL!
WHAT A MARVELOUS IDEA, MARTHA!
I'VE JUST FINISHED "PROM QUEEN SEX SLAVES" BY SYLVIA SUICIDAL...
...AND I'M LOOKING TO DRAW BLOOD!
THE BEST THING ABOUT YOU YOUNG PECKERWOODS IS THAT...
...THE WHEEL OF TIME WILL CRUSH YOU LIKE THE INSECTS YOU ARE!
BZZZT!
MR. COSWELL...YOUR WIFE CALLED AND SAID SHE CLOSED OUT YOUR JOINT BANK ACCOUNT AND DONATED IT ALL TO THE HANOI WAR EFFORT!
...ALSO, BELLA ABZUG HAS SUCCESSFULY SEIZED THE REINS OF POWER AND NAMED HUGH HEFNER TO TAKE CHARGE OF THE FEDERAL DRUG ADMINISTRATION...
...AL CAPP HAS BEEN BLOWN TO HIS REWARD BY A BOMB CONCEALED IN HIS ARTIFICIAL LEG!...
...THE WEATHER UNDERGROUND BOASTS CREDIT!...
...AND THE I.R.S. IS INVESTIGATING YOUR MIAMI BUSINESS CONNECTIONS!
SHRIIIEEEK!!
ONE CAN ONLY HOPE THE WATERS OF THE STYX RUN SMOOTHER FOR COSWELL'S SOUL...
...THAN THIS PLACE DID FOR HIS MORTAL COIL!
HAD I KNOWN COSWELL WOULD REACT SO DECIDEDLY TO OUR LITTLE JOKE, I'D NEVER HAVE RENEWED HIS SUBSCRIPTION TO THE NATIONAL GEOGRAPHIC!
NOW THAT THE TURKEY HAS BEEN LOWERED SIX FEET, PERHAPS YOUR CONSCIOUSNESS WILL BE PROPORTIONATELY RAISED!...
COSWELL

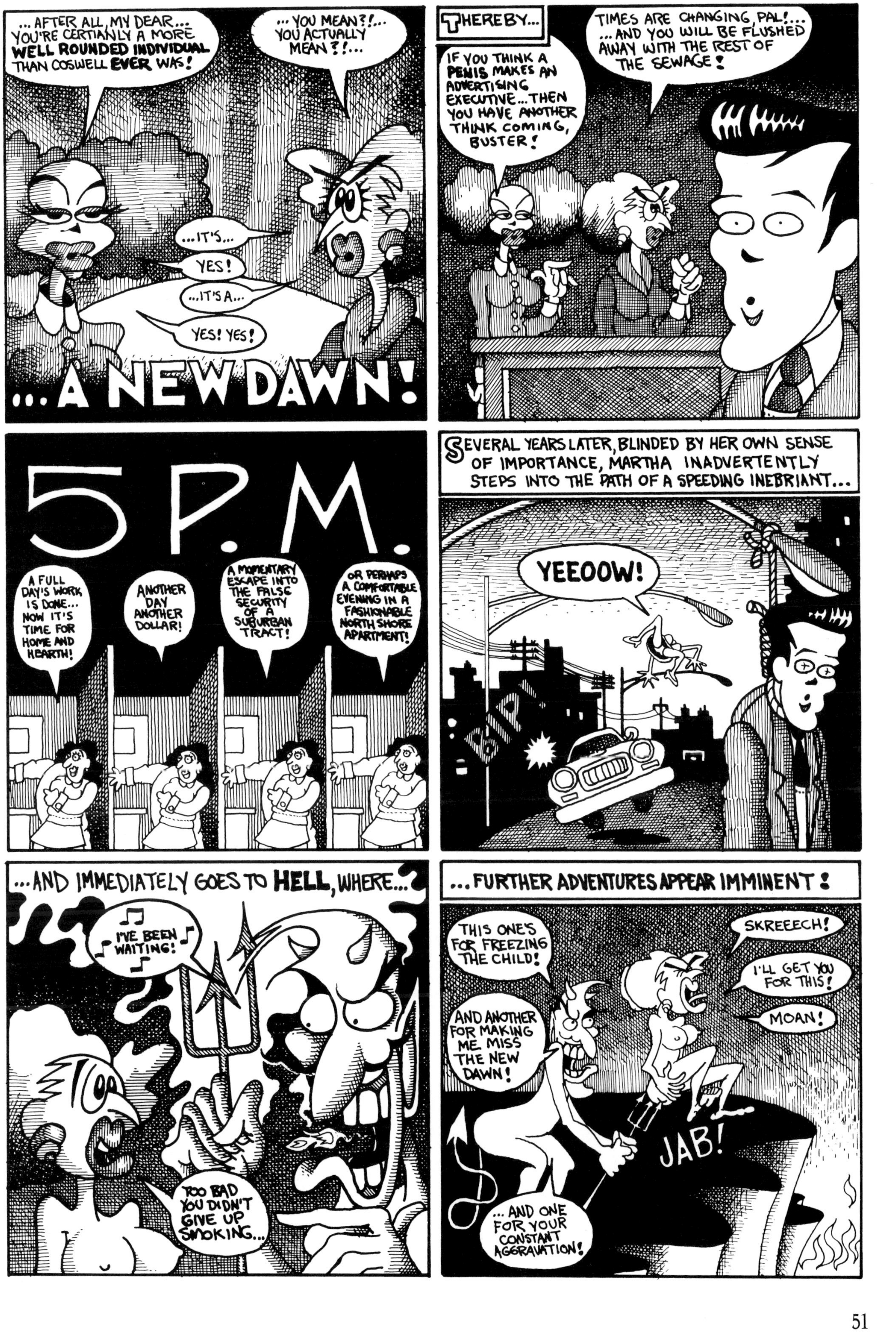
...AFTER ALL, MY DEAR... YOU'RE CERTIANLY A MORE WELL ROUNDED INDIVIDUAL THAN COSWELL EVER WAS!
...YOU MEAN?!... YOU ACTUALLY MEAN?!...
...IT'S...
YES!
...IT'S A...
YES! YES!
...A NEW DAWN!
THEREBY...
IF YOU THINK A PENIS MAKES AN ADVERTISING EXECUTIVE...THEN YOU HAVE ANOTHER THINK COMING, BUSTER!
TIMES ARE CHANGING, PAL!... ...AND YOU WILL BE FLUSHED AWAY WITH THE REST OF THE SEWAGE!
5 P.M.
A FULL DAY'S WORK IS DONE... NOW IT'S TIME FOR HOME AND HEARTH!
ANOTHER DAY ANOTHER DOLLAR!
A MOMENTARY ESCAPE INTO THE FALSE SECURITY OF A SUBURBAN TRACT!
OR PERHAPS A COMFORTABLE EVENING IN A FASHIONABLE NORTH SHORE APARTMENT!
SEVERAL YEARS LATER, BLINDED BY HER OWN SENSE OF IMPORTANCE, MARTHA INADVERTENTLY STEPS INTO THE PATH OF A SPEEDING INEBRIANT...
YEEOOW!
...AND IMMEDIATELY GOES TO HELL, WHERE...?
I'VE BEEN WAITING!
TOO BAD YOU DIDN'T GIVE UP SMOKING...
...FURTHER ADVENTURES APPEAR IMMINENT!
THIS ONE'S FOR FREEZING THE CHILD!
SKREEECH!
I'LL GET YOU FOR THIS!
MOAN!
AND ANOTHER FOR MAKING ME MISS THE NEW DAWN!
JAB!
...AND ONE FOR YOUR CONSTANT AGGRAVATION!

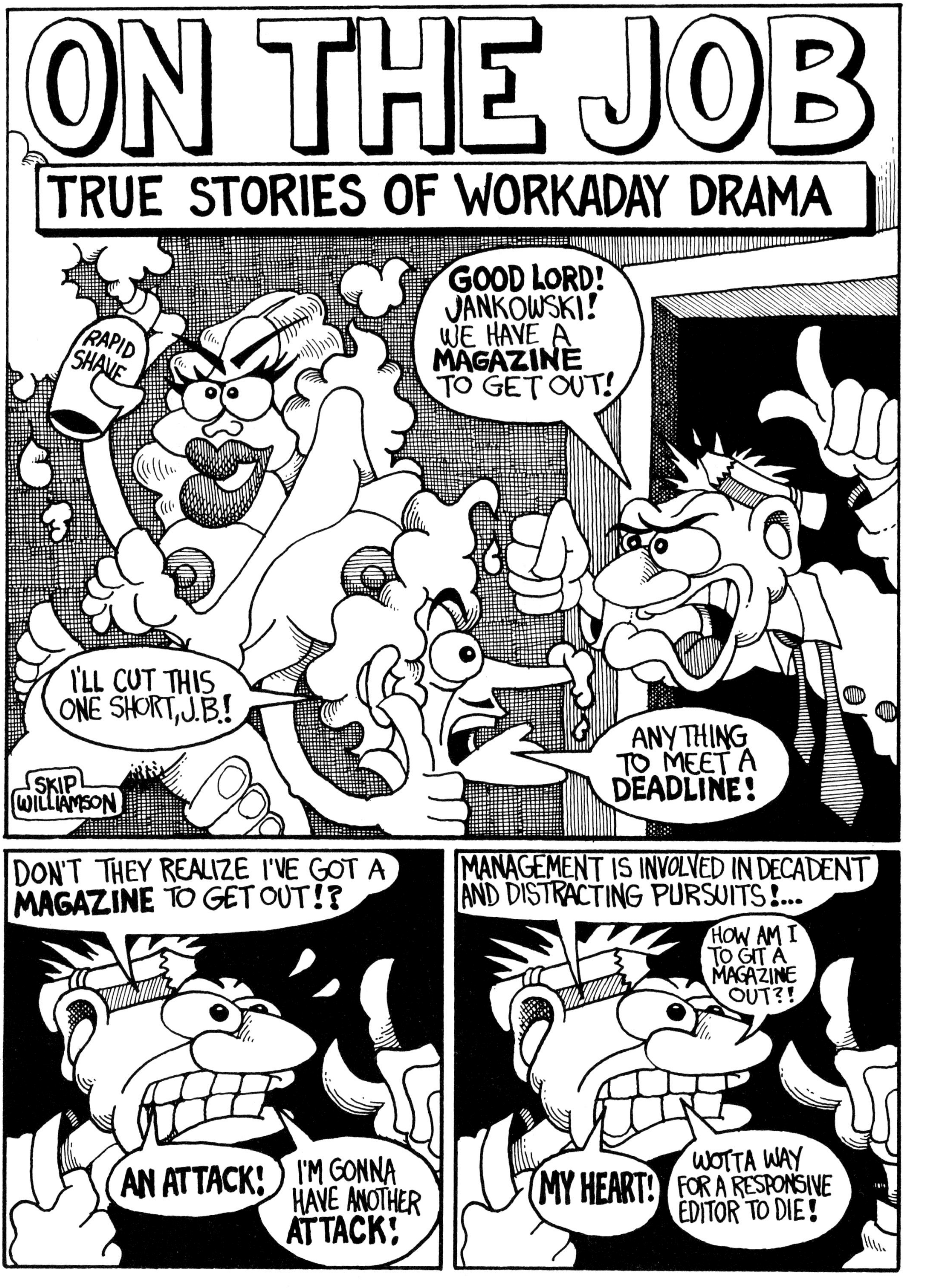
ON THE JOB
TRUE STORIES OF WORKADAY DRAMA
RAPID SHAVE
GOOD LORD! JANKOWSKI! WE HAVE A MAGAZINE TO GET OUT!
I'LL CUT THIS ONE SHORT, J.B.!
ANYTHING TO MEET A DEADLINE!
SKIP WILLIAMSON
DON'T THEY REALIZE I'VE GOT A MAGAZINE TO GET OUT!?
AN ATTACK!
I'M GONNA HAVE ANOTHER ATTACK!
MANAGEMENT IS INVOLVED IN DECADENT AND DISTRACTING PURSUITS!...
HOW AM I TO GIT A MAGAZINE OUT?!
MY HEART!
WOTTA WAY FOR A RESPONSIVE EDITOR TO DIE!

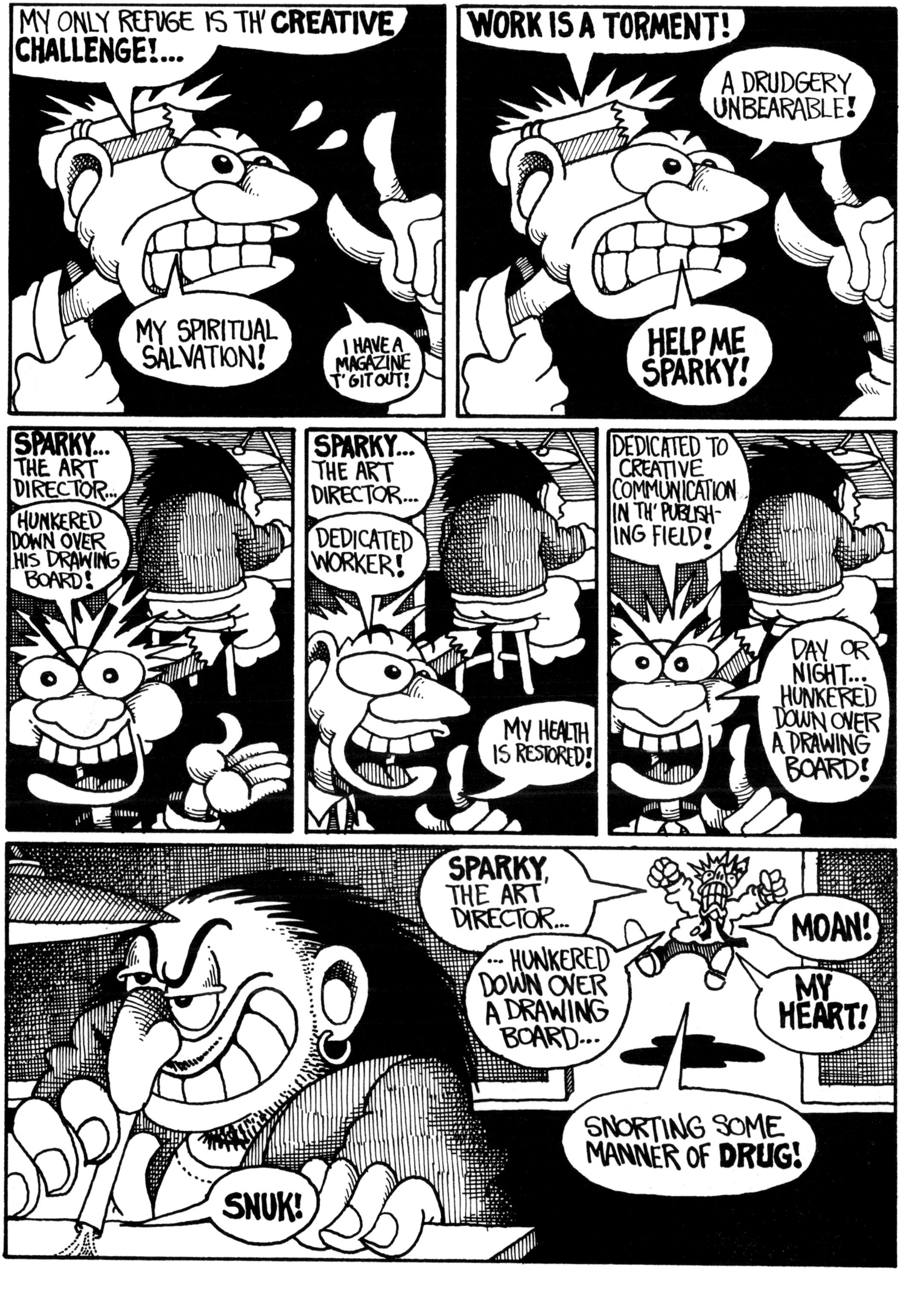
MY ONLY REFUGE IS TH' CREATIVE CHALLENGE!...
MY SPIRITUAL SALVATION!
I HAVE A MAGAZINE T' GIT OUT!
WORK IS A TORMENT!
A DRUDGERY UNBEARABLE!
HELP ME SPARKY!
SPARKY... THE ART DIRECTOR...
HUNKERED DOWN OVER HIS DRAWING BOARD!
SPARKY... THE ART DIRECTOR...
DEDICATED WORKER!
MY HEALTH IS RESTORED!
DEDICATED TO CREATIVE COMMUNICATION IN TH' PUBLISHING FIELD!
DAY OR NIGHT... HUNKERED DOWN OVER A DRAWING BOARD!
SPARKY, THE ART DIRECTOR...
... HUNKERED DOWN OVER A DRAWING BOARD...
MOAN!
MY HEART!
SNORTING SOME MANNER OF DRUG!
SNUK!

LATER...AT A STAFF MEETING...

WE GOT DEADLINES TO MEET!

HOW ARE THINGS IN ACCOUNTING, SYBIL?

TWEEK

DIVINE, DWAYNE!

I SENSE IMPENDING DOOM!

WE'LL CUT THIS ONE SHORT, J-B!

THERE MUST BE SOME SALVATION TO THIS TREACHERY!

IS THERE NO HONOR?

...NO INTEGRITY?

PERHAPS ON A HIGHER ECHELON!

PERHAPS AT TH' VERY APEX THERE IS PRINCIPLE!

ENTER THE PUBLISHER...

YOU'VE SPENT MONEY ON YACHTS AND LIMOUSINES!

CONTRIBUTORS HAVEN'T BEEN PAID FOR SIX MONTHS!

DON'T WORRY J.B.!

I GOT IT WIRED!

ME AN' MY BUSINESS ASSOCIATES WILL TAKE CARE OF EVERYTHING!

IT'S IN TH' BAG!

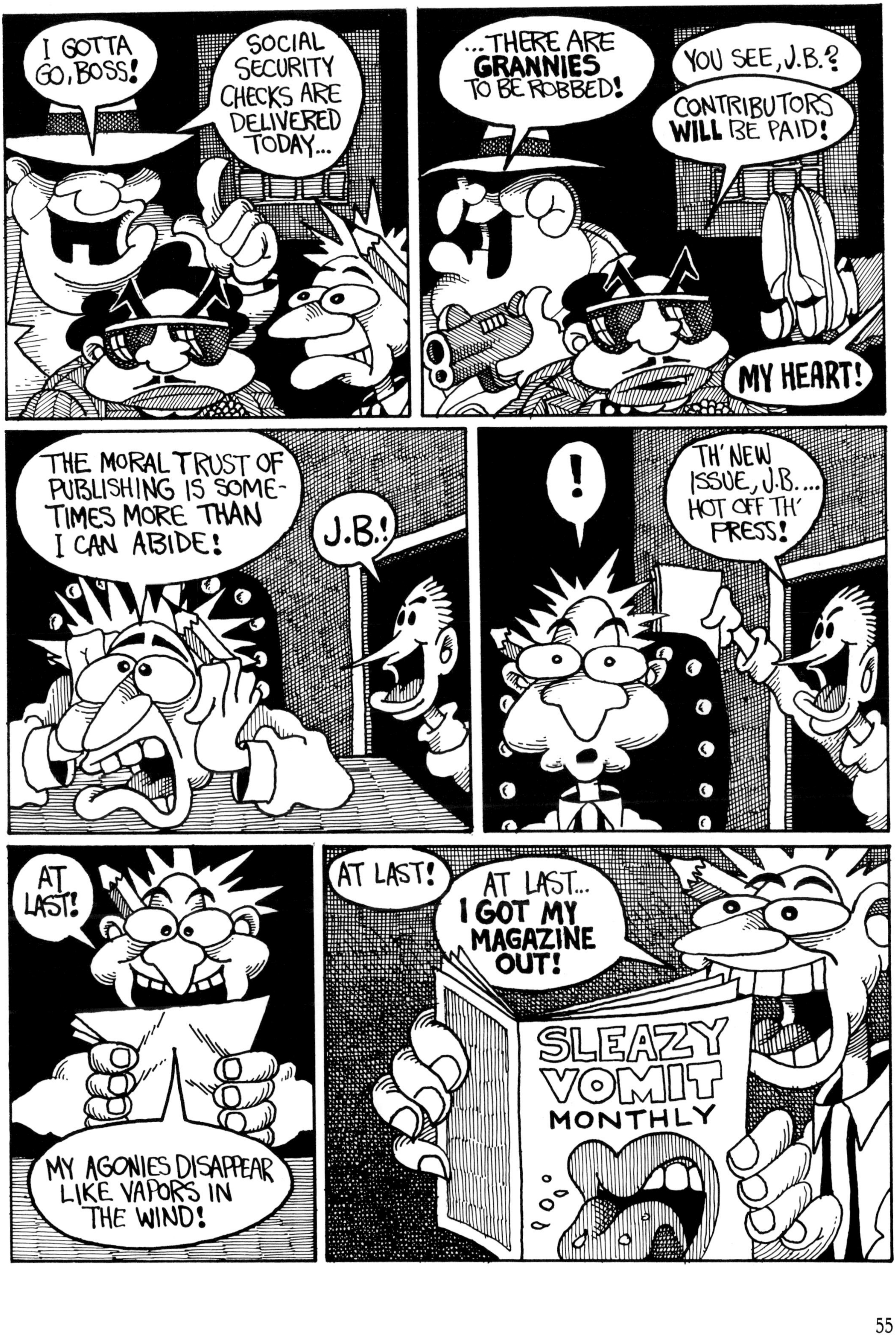
I GOTTA GO, BOSS!
SOCIAL SECURITY CHECKS ARE DELIVERED TODAY...
...THERE ARE GRANNIES TO BE ROBBED!
YOU SEE, J.B.?
CONTRIBUTORS WILL BE PAID!
MY HEART!
THE MORAL TRUST OF PUBLISHING IS SOMETIMES MORE THAN I CAN ABIDE!
J.B.!
!
TH' NEW ISSUE, J.B.... HOT OFF TH' PRESS!
AT LAST!
MY AGONIES DISAPPEAR LIKE VAPORS IN THE WIND!
AT LAST!
AT LAST... I GOT MY MAGAZINE OUT!
SLEAZY VOMIT MONTHLY

SKIP WILLIAMSON

SKIP WILLIAMSON'S
PSYCHEDELIC COMIX, INC.
PRESENTS
THOSE LOVABLE WEIRD·OS

SAM   LARRY   RINGO

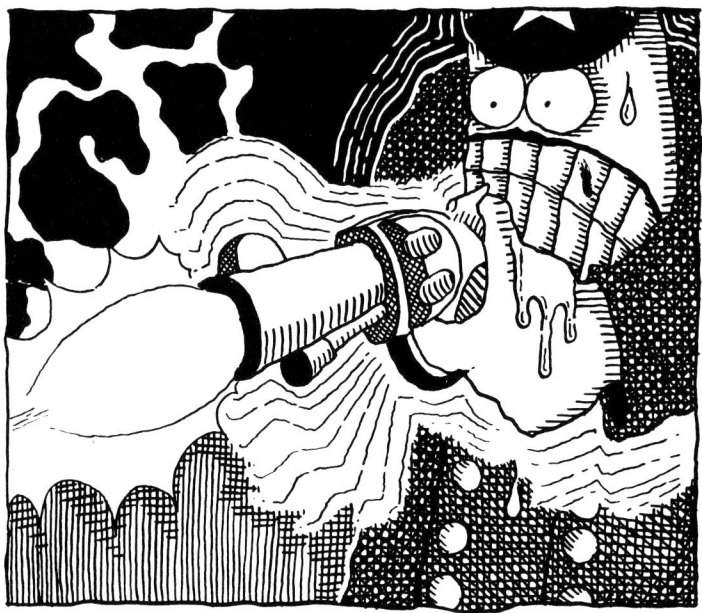

59

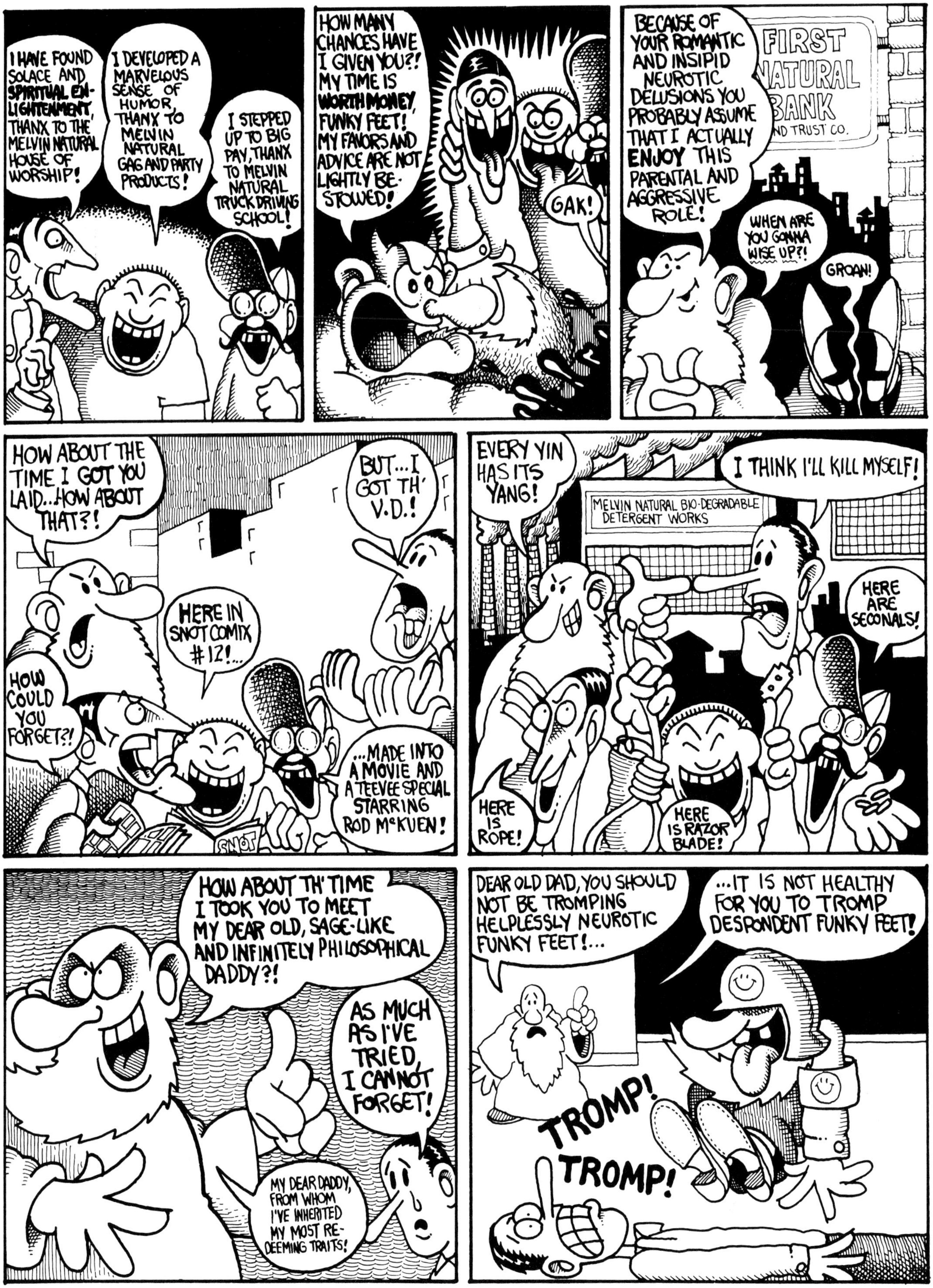
I HAVE FOUND SOLACE AND SPIRITUAL ENLIGHTENMENT, THANX TO THE MELVIN NATURAL HOUSE OF WORSHIP!
I DEVELOPED A MARVELOUS SENSE OF HUMOR, THANX TO MELVIN NATURAL GAG AND PARTY PRODUCTS!
I STEPPED UP TO BIG PAY, THANX TO MELVIN NATURAL TRUCK DRIVING SCHOOL!
HOW MANY CHANCES HAVE I GIVEN YOU?! MY TIME IS WORTH MONEY, FUNKY FEET! MY FAVORS AND ADVICE ARE NOT LIGHTLY BE-STOWED!
GAK!
BECAUSE OF YOUR ROMANTIC AND INSIPID NEUROTIC DELUSIONS YOU PROBABLY ASSUME THAT I ACTUALLY ENJOY THIS PARENTAL AND AGGRESSIVE ROLE!
FIRST NATURAL BANK AND TRUST CO.
WHEN ARE YOU GONNA WISE UP?!
GROAN!
HOW ABOUT THE TIME I GOT YOU LAID...HOW ABOUT THAT?!
BUT...I GOT TH' V.D.!
HERE IN SNOT COMIX #12!...
HOW COULD YOU FORGET?!
...MADE INTO A MOVIE AND A TEEVEE SPECIAL STARRING ROD McKUEN!
SNOT
EVERY YIN HAS ITS YANG!
I THINK I'LL KILL MYSELF!
MELVIN NATURAL BIO-DEGRADABLE DETERGENT WORKS
HERE ARE SECONALS!
HERE IS ROPE!
HERE IS RAZOR BLADE!
HOW ABOUT TH' TIME I TOOK YOU TO MEET MY DEAR OLD, SAGE-LIKE AND INFINITELY PHILOSOPHICAL DADDY?!
AS MUCH AS I'VE TRIED, I CANNOT FORGET!
MY DEAR DADDY, FROM WHOM I'VE INHERITED MY MOST RE-DEEMING TRAITS!
DEAR OLD DAD, YOU SHOULD NOT BE TROMPING HELPLESSLY NEUROTIC FUNKY FEET!...
...IT IS NOT HEALTHY FOR YOU TO TROMP DESPONDENT FUNKY FEET!
TROMP!
TROMP!

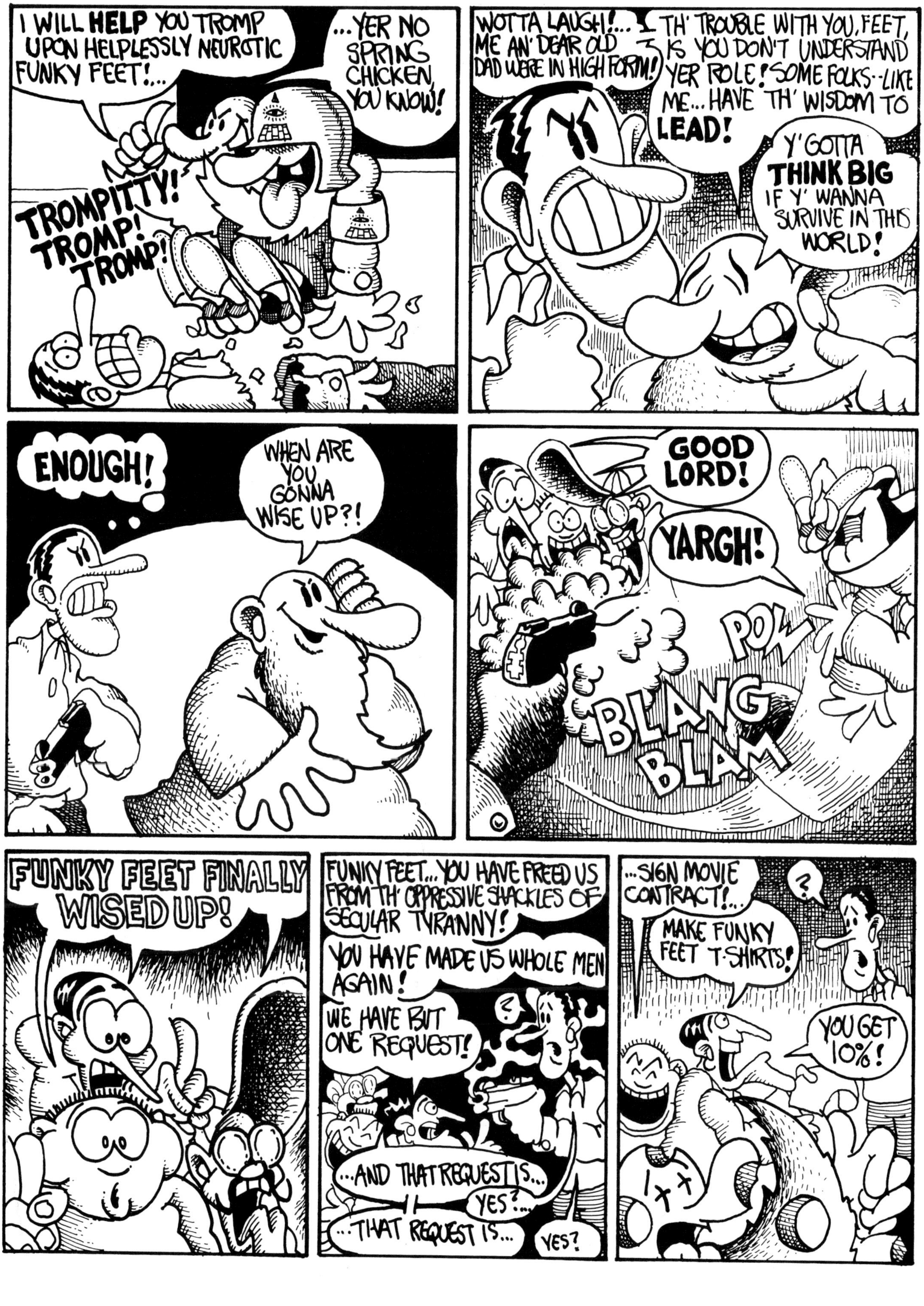
I WILL HELP YOU TROMP UPON HELPLESSLY NEUROTIC FUNKY FEET!...
...YER NO SPRING CHICKEN, YOU KNOW!
TROMPITTY! TROMP! TROMP!
WOTTA LAUGH!... ME AN' DEAR OLD DAD WERE IN HIGH FORM!
TH' TROUBLE WITH YOU, FEET, IS YOU DON'T UNDERSTAND YER ROLE! SOME FOLKS--LIKE ME... HAVE TH' WISDOM TO LEAD!
Y'GOTTA THINK BIG IF Y' WANNA SURVIVE IN THIS WORLD!
ENOUGH!
WHEN ARE YOU GONNA WISE UP?!
GOOD LORD!
YARGH!
POW
BLANG
BLAM
FUNKY FEET FINALLY WISED UP!
FUNKY FEET... YOU HAVE FREED US FROM TH' OPPRESSIVE SHACKLES OF SECULAR TYRANNY!
YOU HAVE MADE US WHOLE MEN AGAIN!
WE HAVE BUT ONE REQUEST!
?
...AND THAT REQUEST IS...
YES?...
...THAT REQUEST IS...
YES?
...SIGN MOVIE CONTRACT!...
?
MAKE FUNKY FEET T-SHIRTS!
YOU GET 10%!

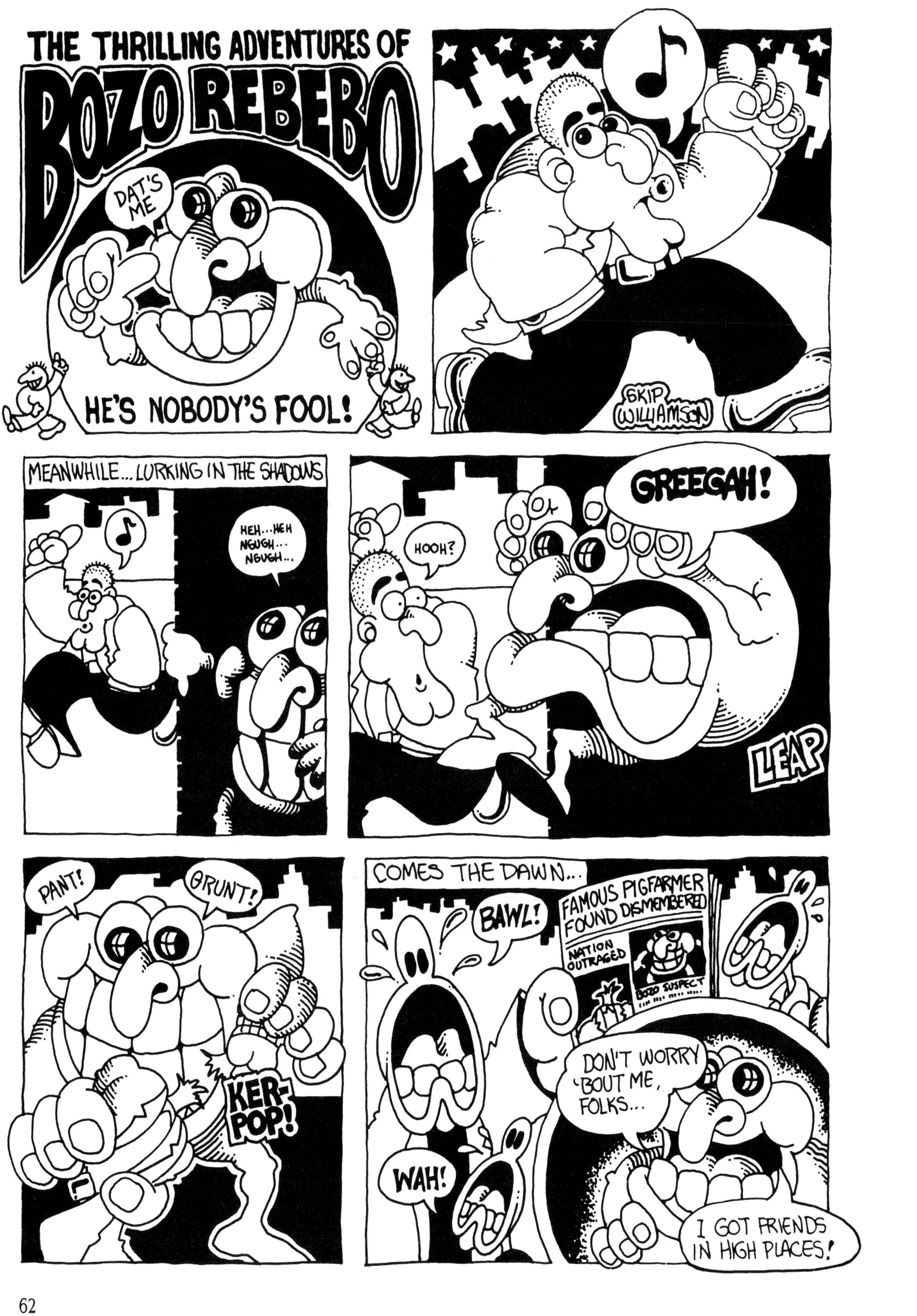
THE THRILLING ADVENTURES OF
BOZO REBEBO
DAT'S ME
HE'S NOBODY'S FOOL!
SKIP WILLIAMSON
MEANWHILE... LURKING IN THE SHADOWS
HEH...HEH NGUGH... NGUGH...
HOOH?
GREEGAH!
LEAP
PANT!
GRUNT!
KER-POP!
COMES THE DAWN...
BAWL!
FAMOUS PIGFARMER FOUND DISMEMBERED
NATION OUTRAGED
BOZO SUSPECT
WAH!
DON'T WORRY 'BOUT ME, FOLKS...
I GOT FRIENDS IN HIGH PLACES!

GENERATION AFTER GENERATION OF HEARTWARMING ESPIONAGE

DOMESTIC INTRIGUE

HOW DID THINGS GO AT SCHOOL TODAY, JUNIOR?

AW...TH' KIDS ARE STILL RAZZIN' ME 'CAUSE YOU'RE A NAZI SPY, DAD!

THIS IS AMERICA, SON...WHERE A MAN CAN PURSUE THE INDULGENCES OF HIS MANIA!

TH' LITTLE BUGGER'S RIGHT, FRITZ!...

MY BRIDGE CLUB IS FURIOUS!

THEY WANT TO KNOW WHAT YOU HAVE DONE WITH THE GOLDFEINS AND THE GREENFARBS?!

ATOMIC SECRETS CLASSIFIED

SAAAYY! LOOK AT THIS NEWS ITEM!

THIS PUTS A WHOLE NEW SLANT ON THINGS!

EAT YER TATERTOTS!

GERMANY SURRENDERS — DAILY FABRICATION

I SUPPOSE I'LL JUST HAVE TO JOIN THE REPUBLICAN PARTY!

WITH ENTERPRISING VERVE, DAD FINDS EMPLOYMENT WITH THE PHONE COMPANY AND DOMESTIC ORDER RULES THE ROOST UNTIL SUDDENLY...SOME YEARS LATER!...

FRITZ! TH' CHILD HAS GROWN A BEARD AND TAKEN TO READING GREGORY CORSO!

GOOD LORD!

...AND THE BOSS IS COMING TO DINNER TONIGHT!

FRITZ! A TAINT OF THIS NATURE COULD CRUSH YOUR POLITICAL ASPIRATIONS!

SOMETIMES JUNIOR'S TOO BRIGHT FOR HIS OWN GOOD!

FETCH ME THE PINKING SHEARS AND SUMMON THE CHILD!

NOW THE CHILD IS NOT SO BRIGHT...

HE IS MORE FUNCTION- AL...HIS GLARING IDEALISM IS DISCONNECTED...HE IS MORE DIMMLY LIT...

...HE HAS A THREE-WAY BULB!

SKIP WILLIAMSON

by DAVID STANDISH & JERRY SULLIVAN -- ILLUSTRATED BY SKIP WILLIAMSON

DICK DISGUSTING'S NEW-WAVE NATURE NOTES

MR. DISGUSTING WAS FORMERLY OF THE FORKS AND IS PRESENTLY LEAD SINGER FOR BLOODY HOLLY. BUT DICK WAS INTO NATURE *BEFORE* HE WAS A JUNKIE AND A PUNK IDOL IN ALL THE BEST SOHO LOFTS. BACK IN SIOUX FALLS, WHEN HIS NAME WAS STILL BILLY DISGUSTING, HE WAS BUT ONE MERIT BADGE AWAY FROM BEING AN EAGLE SCOUT THE NIGHT LOU REED PLAYED TOWN AND HE MET LOU AND -- WELL, THE REST IS HISTORY!

DICK'S DOO-DOO CORNER

BEAVERS EAT SHIT!
THE TREE BARK THAT BEAVERS EAT IN WINTER IS SO UN-NUTRITIOUS THAT THEY HAVE TO EAT IT *TWICE!*

CANNIBAL SON DEVOURS MOM!
IF YOU THINK YOUR KIDS ARE TERRORS, HOW ABOUT POOR *MICROMALTHUS DEBILIS*? THE NEWBORN SONS OF THESE PUT-UPON MOTHER BEETLES HANG ON THE MATERNAL SHELL FOR A FEW DAYS AFTER BIRTH. THEN THEY CRAWL INTO MAMA'S GENITAL APERTURE WHERE THEY CHEW AND SWALLOW UNTIL THERE'S NOTHING LEFT BUT MOM'S EXO-SKELETON. PUTS YOUR KID'S DRUG PROBLEM IN PERSPECTIVE, DOESN'T IT?

CUTAWAY VIEW

DEER EAT FISH!!

THE *MUTINUS CANINUS* FUNGUS OF ENGLAND LOOKS *EXACTLY* LIKE A BIG HARD DOG'S DICK!

A MODERN INSTANCE: MEGAPODES, WILDFOWL FROM AUSTRALIA, DO NOT BUILD NESTS! MOM LAYS HER EGGS IN A PILE OF ROTTING PLANTS DAD HAS ASSEMBL- ED FOR HER, THEN MOM SPLITS FOR GOOD, ANOTHER RUNAWAY HOUSE- WIFE, LEAVING DAD IN CHARGE OF IN- CUBATION--SORT OF. THE HEAT OF THE DECAYING VEGETATION DOES THE INCUBATION. WHEN THE BABIES HATCH, DAD ABANDONS THEM, TOO.

SKIP WILLMSON

LITTLE DAVEY STANDISH OF LAKEWOOD, OHIO, WHILE FISHING IN THE POLLUTED ROCKY RIVER, WHERE THERE ARE VERY FEW FISH, CAUGHT THE SAME SMALL- MOUTH BASS *13* TIMES!

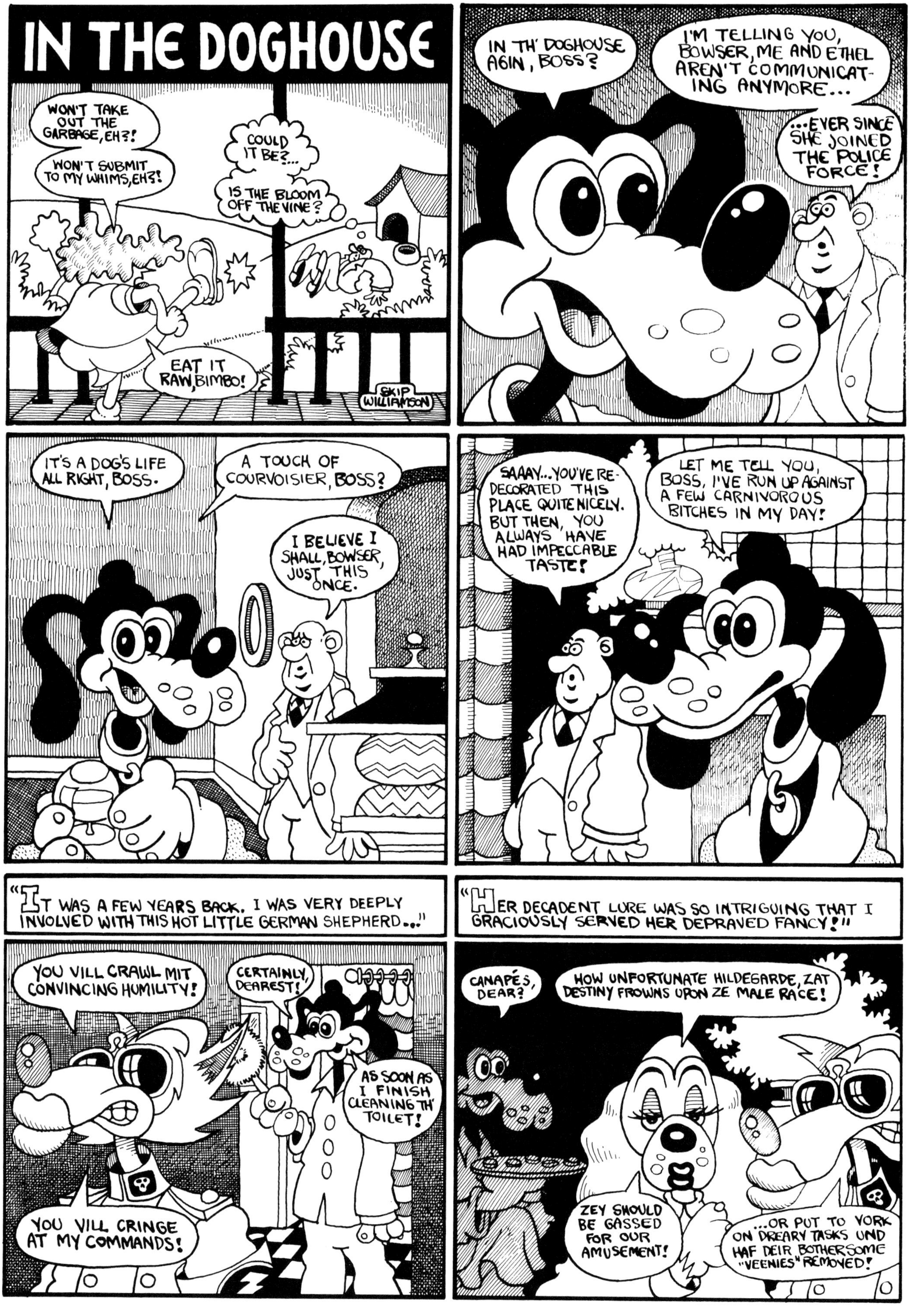
IN THE DOGHOUSE
WON'T TAKE OUT THE GARBAGE, EH?!
WON'T SUBMIT TO MY WHIMS, EH?!
COULD IT BE?...
IS THE BLOOM OFF THE VINE?
EAT IT RAW, BIMBO!
SKIP WILLIAMSON
IN TH' DOGHOUSE AGIN, BOSS?
I'M TELLING YOU, BOWSER, ME AND ETHEL AREN'T COMMUNICATING ANYMORE...
...EVER SINCE SHE JOINED THE POLICE FORCE!
IT'S A DOG'S LIFE ALL RIGHT, BOSS.
A TOUCH OF COURVOISIER, BOSS?
I BELIEVE I SHALL, BOWSER, JUST THIS ONCE.
SAAAY... YOU'VE REDECORATED THIS PLACE QUITE NICELY. BUT THEN, YOU ALWAYS HAVE HAD IMPECCABLE TASTE!
LET ME TELL YOU, BOSS, I'VE RUN UP AGAINST A FEW CARNIVOROUS BITCHES IN MY DAY!
"IT WAS A FEW YEARS BACK. I WAS VERY DEEPLY INVOLVED WITH THIS HOT LITTLE GERMAN SHEPHERD..."
"HER DECADENT LURE WAS SO INTRIGUING THAT I GRACIOUSLY SERVED HER DEPRAVED FANCY!"
YOU VILL CRAWL MIT CONVINCING HUMILITY!
CERTAINLY, DEAREST!
AS SOON AS I FINISH CLEANING TH' TOILET!
YOU VILL CRINGE AT MY COMMANDS!
CANAPÉS, DEAR?
HOW UNFORTUNATE HILDEGARDE, ZAT DESTINY FROWNS UPON ZE MALE RACE!
ZEY SHOULD BE GASSED FOR OUR AMUSEMENT!
...OR PUT TO VORK ON DREARY TASKS UND HAF DEIR BOTHERSOME "VEENIES" REMOVED!

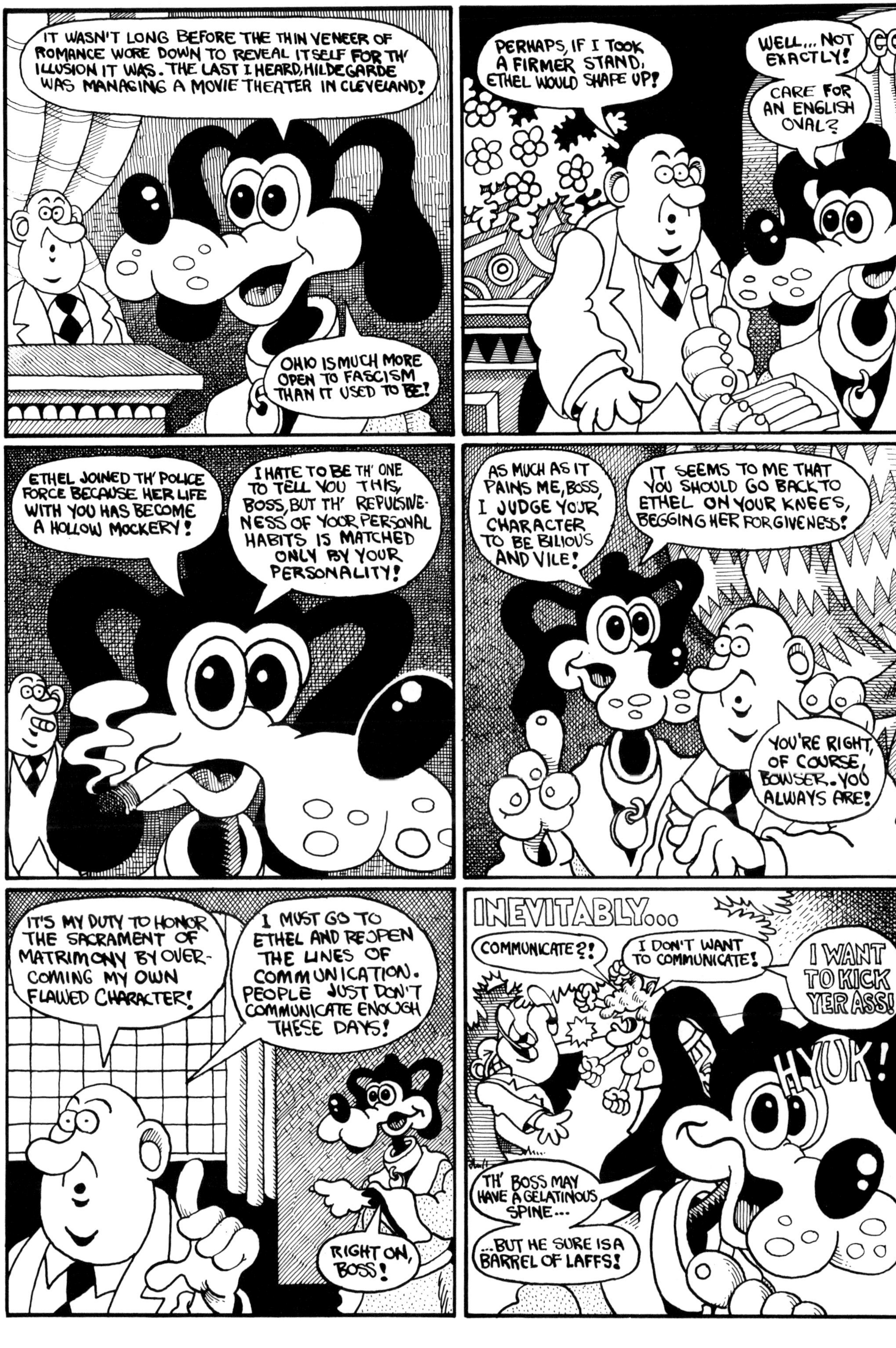
IT WASN'T LONG BEFORE THE THIN VENEER OF ROMANCE WORE DOWN TO REVEAL ITSELF FOR TH' ILLUSION IT WAS. THE LAST I HEARD, HILDEGARDE WAS MANAGING A MOVIE THEATER IN CLEVELAND!
OHIO IS MUCH MORE OPEN TO FASCISM THAN IT USED TO BE!
PERHAPS, IF I TOOK A FIRMER STAND, ETHEL WOULD SHAPE UP!
WELL... NOT EXACTLY!
CARE FOR AN ENGLISH OVAL?
ETHEL JOINED TH' POLICE FORCE BECAUSE HER LIFE WITH YOU HAS BECOME A HOLLOW MOCKERY!
I HATE TO BE TH' ONE TO TELL YOU THIS, BOSS, BUT TH' REPULSIVENESS OF YOUR PERSONAL HABITS IS MATCHED ONLY BY YOUR PERSONALITY!
AS MUCH AS IT PAINS ME, BOSS, I JUDGE YOUR CHARACTER TO BE BILIOUS AND VILE!
IT SEEMS TO ME THAT YOU SHOULD GO BACK TO ETHEL ON YOUR KNEES, BEGGING HER FORGIVENESS!
YOU'RE RIGHT, OF COURSE, BOWSER. YOU ALWAYS ARE!
IT'S MY DUTY TO HONOR THE SACRAMENT OF MATRIMONY BY OVERCOMING MY OWN FLAWED CHARACTER!
I MUST GO TO ETHEL AND REOPEN THE LINES OF COMMUNICATION. PEOPLE JUST DON'T COMMUNICATE ENOUGH THESE DAYS!
RIGHT ON, BOSS!
INEVITABLY...
COMMUNICATE?!
I DON'T WANT TO COMMUNICATE!
I WANT TO KICK YER ASS!
HYUK!
TH' BOSS MAY HAVE A GELATINOUS SPINE...
...BUT HE SURE IS A BARREL OF LAFFS!

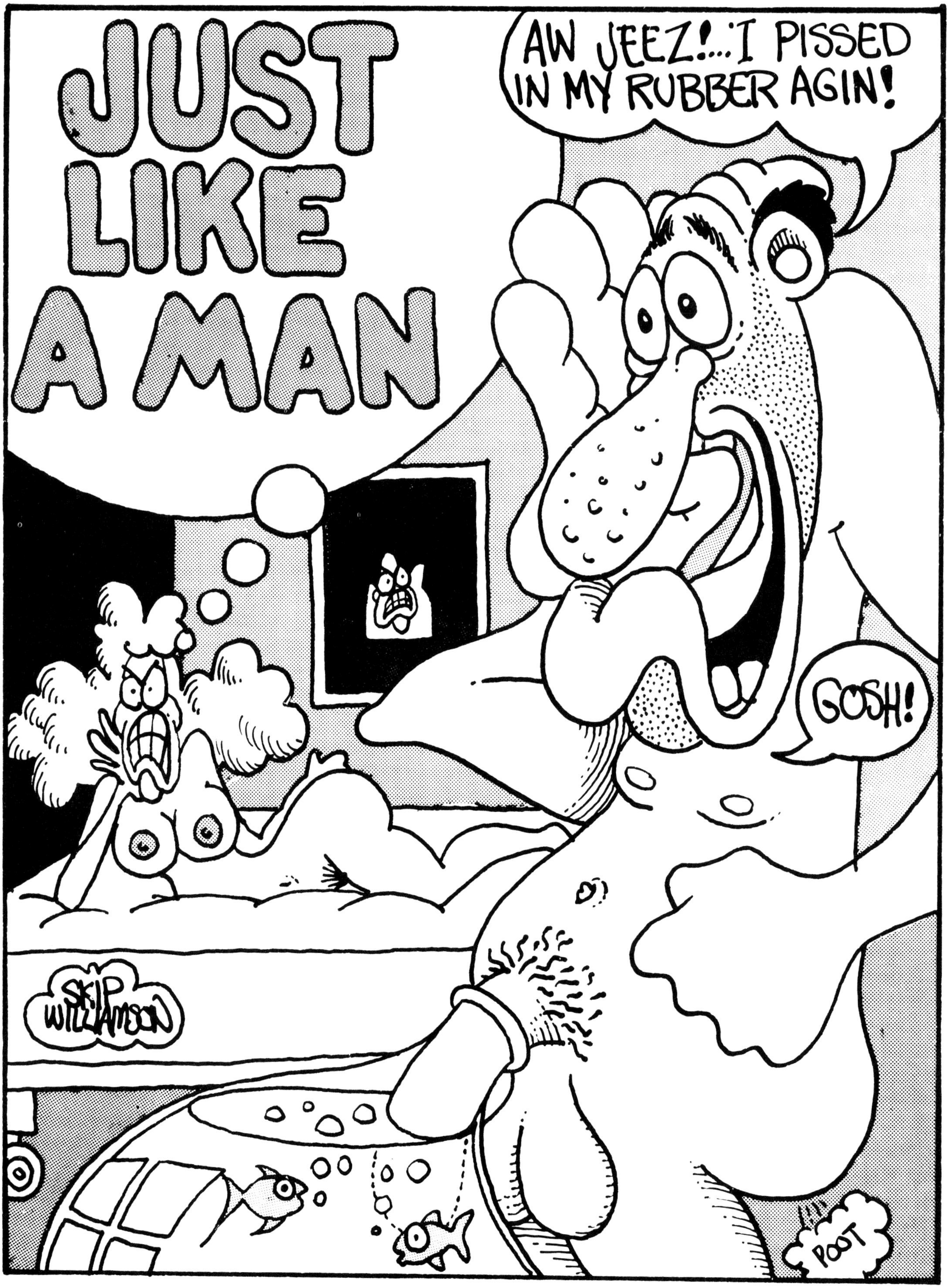
JUST LIKE A MAN
AW JEEZ!...I PISSED IN MY RUBBER AGIN!
GOSH!
SKIP WILLIAMSON
POOT

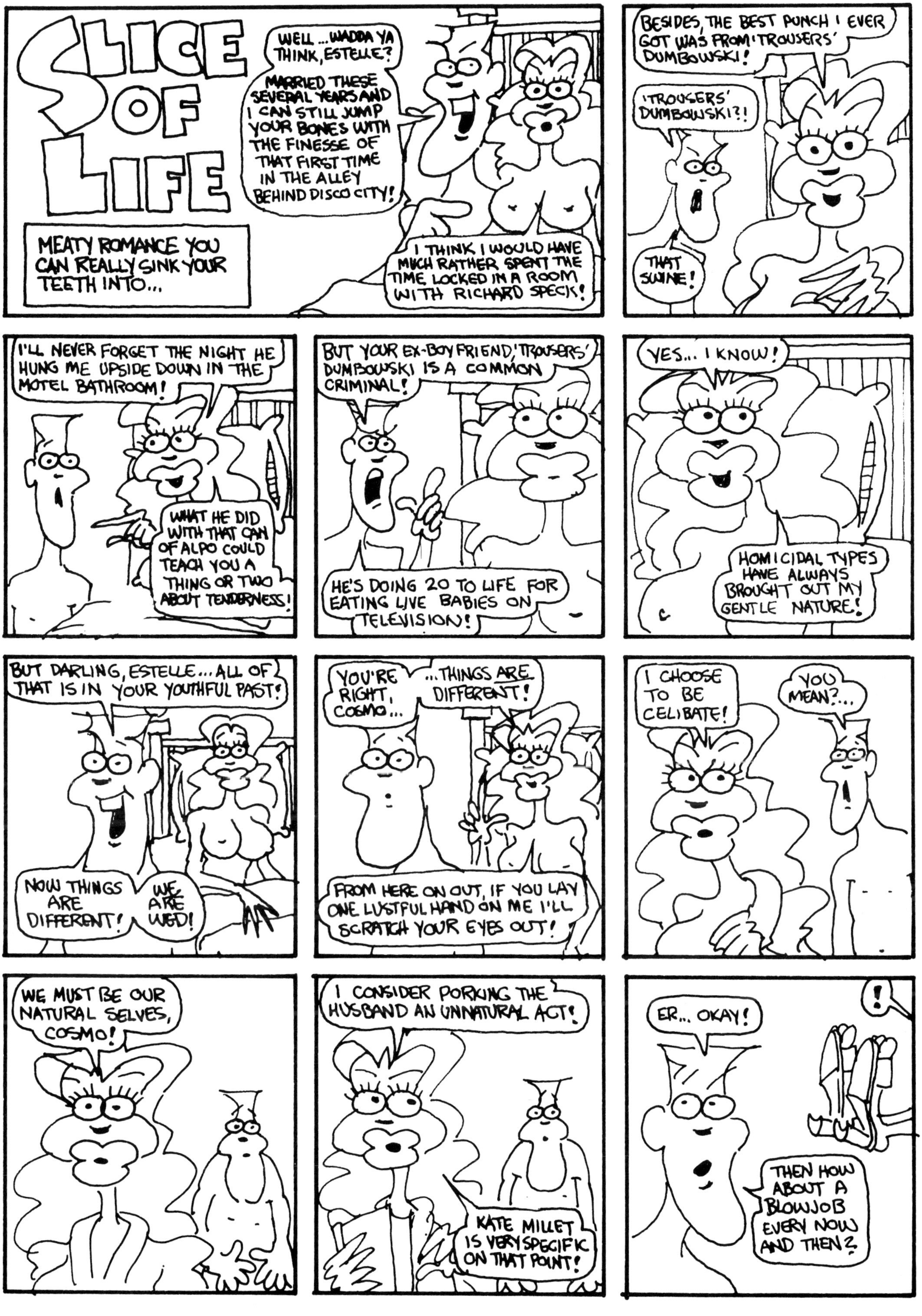
SLICE OF LIFE
MEATY ROMANCE YOU CAN REALLY SINK YOUR TEETH INTO...
WELL...WADDA YA THINK, ESTELLE?
MARRIED THESE SEVERAL YEARS AND I CAN STILL JUMP YOUR BONES WITH THE FINESSE OF THAT FIRST TIME IN THE ALLEY BEHIND DISCO CITY!
I THINK I WOULD HAVE MUCH RATHER SPENT THE TIME LOCKED IN A ROOM WITH RICHARD SPECK!
BESIDES, THE BEST PUNCH I EVER GOT WAS FROM 'TROUSERS' DUMBOWSKI!
'TROUSERS' DUMBOWSKI?!
THAT SWINE!
I'LL NEVER FORGET THE NIGHT HE HUNG ME UPSIDE DOWN IN THE MOTEL BATHROOM!
WHAT HE DID WITH THAT CAN OF ALPO COULD TEACH YOU A THING OR TWO ABOUT TENDERNESS!
BUT YOUR EX-BOY FRIEND, 'TROUSERS' DUMBOWSKI IS A COMMON CRIMINAL!
HE'S DOING 20 TO LIFE FOR EATING LIVE BABIES ON TELEVISION!
YES... I KNOW!
HOMICIDAL TYPES HAVE ALWAYS BROUGHT OUT MY GENTLE NATURE!
BUT DARLING, ESTELLE... ALL OF THAT IS IN YOUR YOUTHFUL PAST!
NOW THINGS ARE DIFFERENT!
WE ARE WED!
YOU'RE RIGHT, COSMO...
...THINGS ARE DIFFERENT!
FROM HERE ON OUT, IF YOU LAY ONE LUSTFUL HAND ON ME I'LL SCRATCH YOUR EYES OUT!
I CHOOSE TO BE CELIBATE!
YOU MEAN?...
WE MUST BE OUR NATURAL SELVES, COSMO!
I CONSIDER PORKING THE HUSBAND AN UNNATURAL ACT!
KATE MILLET IS VERY SPECIFIC ON THAT POINT!
ER... OKAY!
!
THEN HOW ABOUT A BLOWJOB EVERY NOW AND THEN?

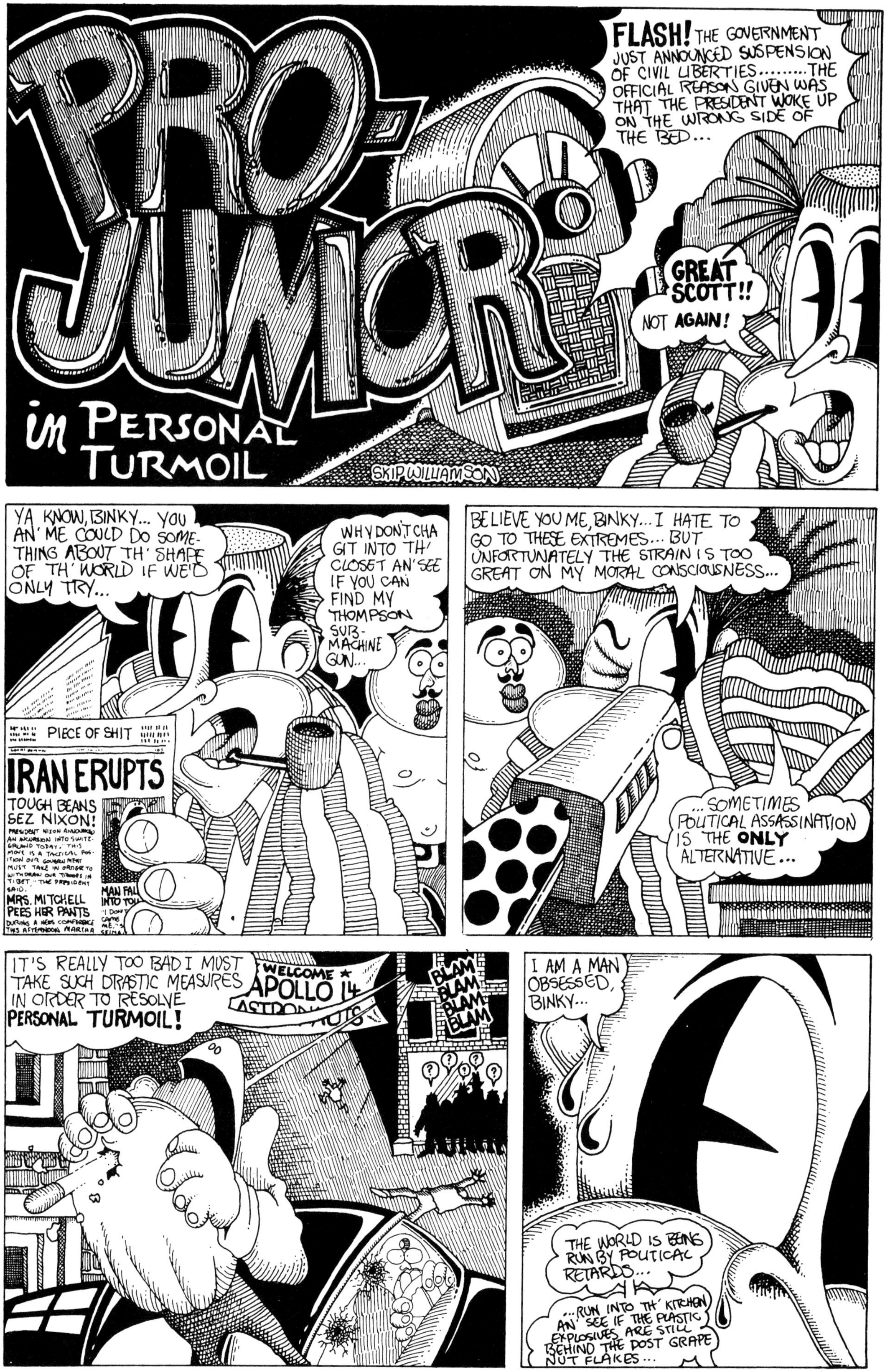
PRO-JUNIOR
in PERSONAL TURMOIL
SKIP WILLIAMSON
FLASH! THE GOVERNMENT JUST ANNOUNCED SUSPENSION OF CIVIL LIBERTIES.........THE OFFICIAL REASON GIVEN WAS THAT THE PRESIDENT WOKE UP ON THE WRONG SIDE OF THE BED...
GREAT SCOTT!!
NOT AGAIN!
YA KNOW, BINKY... YOU AN' ME COULD DO SOMETHING ABOUT TH' SHAPE OF TH' WORLD IF WE'D ONLY TRY...
WHY DON'T CHA GIT INTO TH' CLOSET AN' SEE IF YOU CAN FIND MY THOMPSON SUB-MACHINE GUN...
PIECE OF SHIT
IRAN ERUPTS
TOUGH BEANS SEZ NIXON!
PRESIDENT NIXON ANNOUNCED AN INCURSION INTO SWITZERLAND TODAY. "THIS MOVE IS A TACTICAL POSITION OUR GOVERNMENT MUST TAKE IN ORDER TO WITHDRAW OUR TROOPS IN TIBET," THE PRESIDENT SAID.
MRS. MITCHELL PEES HER PANTS
DURING A NEWS CONFERENCE THIS AFTERNOON MARTHA
MAN FAL
INTO TOU
BELIEVE YOU ME, BINKY... I HATE TO GO TO THESE EXTREMES... BUT UNFORTUNATELY THE STRAIN IS TOO GREAT ON MY MORAL CONSCIOUSNESS...
...SOMETIMES POLITICAL ASSASSINATION IS THE ONLY ALTERNATIVE...
IT'S REALLY TOO BAD I MUST TAKE SUCH DRASTIC MEASURES IN ORDER TO RESOLVE PERSONAL TURMOIL!
WELCOME APOLLO 14
BLAM BLAM BLAM BLAM
I AM A MAN OBSESSED, BINKY...
THE WORLD IS BEING RUN BY POLITICAL RETARDS...
...RUN INTO TH' KITCHEN AN' SEE IF THE PLASTIC EXPLOSIVES ARE STILL BEHIND THE POST GRAPE NUT FLAKES...

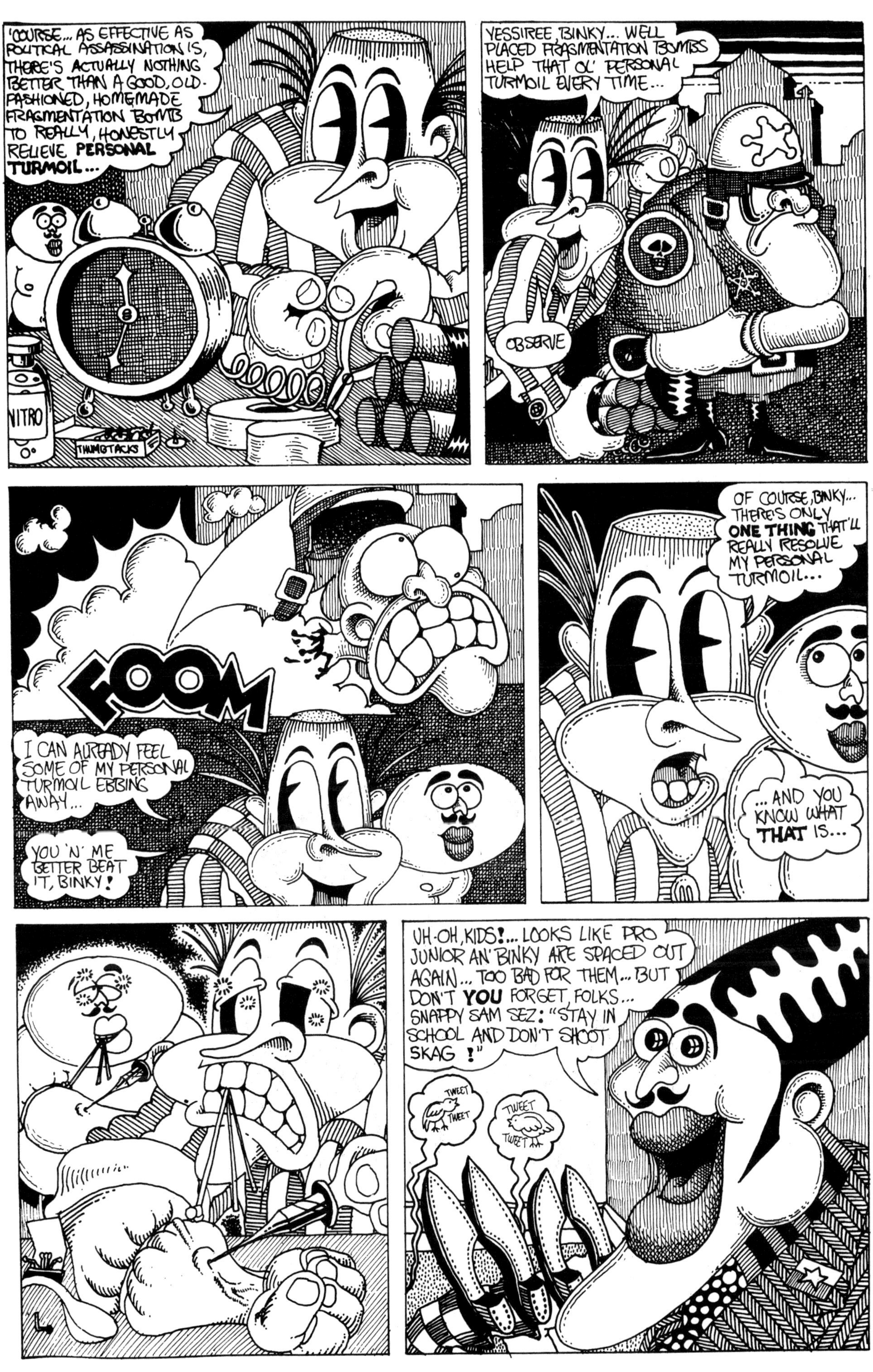
'COURSE... AS EFFECTIVE AS POLITICAL ASSASSINATION IS, THERE'S ACTUALLY NOTHING BETTER THAN A GOOD, OLD-FASHIONED, HOMEMADE FRAGMENTATION BOMB TO REALLY, HONESTLY RELIEVE PERSONAL TURMOIL...
NITRO
THUMBTACKS
YESSIREE, BINKY... WELL PLACED FRAGMENTATION BOMBS HELP THAT OL' PERSONAL TURMOIL EVERY TIME...
OBSERVE
FOOM
I CAN ALREADY FEEL SOME OF MY PERSONAL TURMOIL EBBING AWAY...
YOU 'N' ME BETTER BEAT IT, BINKY!
OF COURSE, BINKY... THERE'S ONLY ONE THING THAT'LL REALLY RESOLVE MY PERSONAL TURMOIL...
...AND YOU KNOW WHAT THAT IS...
UH-OH, KIDS!... LOOKS LIKE PRO JUNIOR AN' BINKY ARE SPACED OUT AGAIN... TOO BAD FOR THEM... BUT DON'T YOU FORGET, FOLKS... SNAPPY SAM SEZ: "STAY IN SCHOOL AND DON'T SHOOT SKAG!"
TWEET TWEET
TWEET TWEET

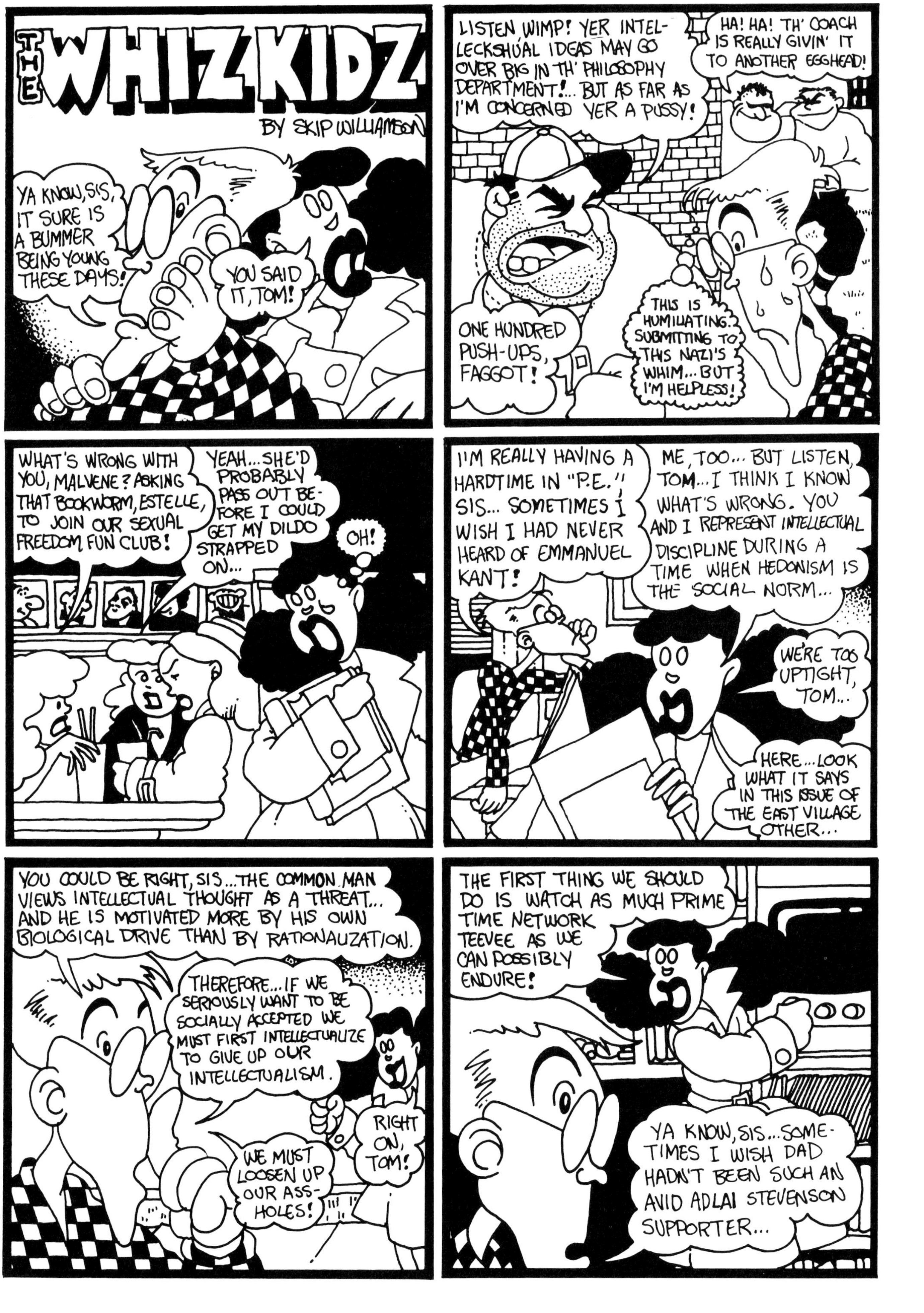
THE WHIZ KIDZ
BY SKIP WILLIAMSON
YA KNOW, SIS, IT SURE IS A BUMMER BEING YOUNG THESE DAYS!
YOU SAID IT, TOM!
LISTEN WIMP! YER INTEL-LECKSHUAL IDEAS MAY GO OVER BIG IN TH' PHILOSOPHY DEPARTMENT!... BUT AS FAR AS I'M CONCERNED YER A PUSSY!
HA! HA! TH' COACH IS REALLY GIVIN' IT TO ANOTHER EGGHEAD!
ONE HUNDRED PUSH-UPS, FAGGOT!
THIS IS HUMILIATING.. SUBMITTING TO THIS NAZI'S WHIM... BUT I'M HELPLESS!
WHAT'S WRONG WITH YOU, MALVENE? ASKING THAT BOOKWORM, ESTELLE, TO JOIN OUR SEXUAL FREEDOM FUN CLUB!
YEAH... SHE'D PROBABLY PASS OUT BE-FORE I COULD GET MY DILDO STRAPPED ON...
OH!
I'M REALLY HAVING A HARDTIME IN "P.E.," SIS... SOMETIMES I WISH I HAD NEVER HEARD OF EMMANUEL KANT!
ME, TOO... BUT LISTEN, TOM... I THINK I KNOW WHAT'S WRONG. YOU AND I REPRESENT INTELLECTUAL DISCIPLINE DURING A TIME WHEN HEDONISM IS THE SOCIAL NORM...
WE'RE TOO UPTIGHT, TOM...
HERE... LOOK WHAT IT SAYS IN THIS ISSUE OF THE EAST VILLAGE OTHER...
YOU COULD BE RIGHT, SIS... THE COMMON MAN VIEWS INTELLECTUAL THOUGHT AS A THREAT... AND HE IS MOTIVATED MORE BY HIS OWN BIOLOGICAL DRIVE THAN BY RATIONALIZATION.
THEREFORE... IF WE SERIOUSLY WANT TO BE SOCIALLY ACCEPTED WE MUST FIRST INTELLECTUALIZE TO GIVE UP OUR INTELLECTUALISM.
WE MUST LOOSEN UP OUR ASS-HOLES!
RIGHT ON, TOM!
THE FIRST THING WE SHOULD DO IS WATCH AS MUCH PRIME TIME NETWORK TEEVEE AS WE CAN POSSIBLY ENDURE!
YA KNOW, SIS... SOME-TIMES I WISH DAD HADN'T BEEN SUCH AN AVID ADLAI STEVENSON SUPPORTER...

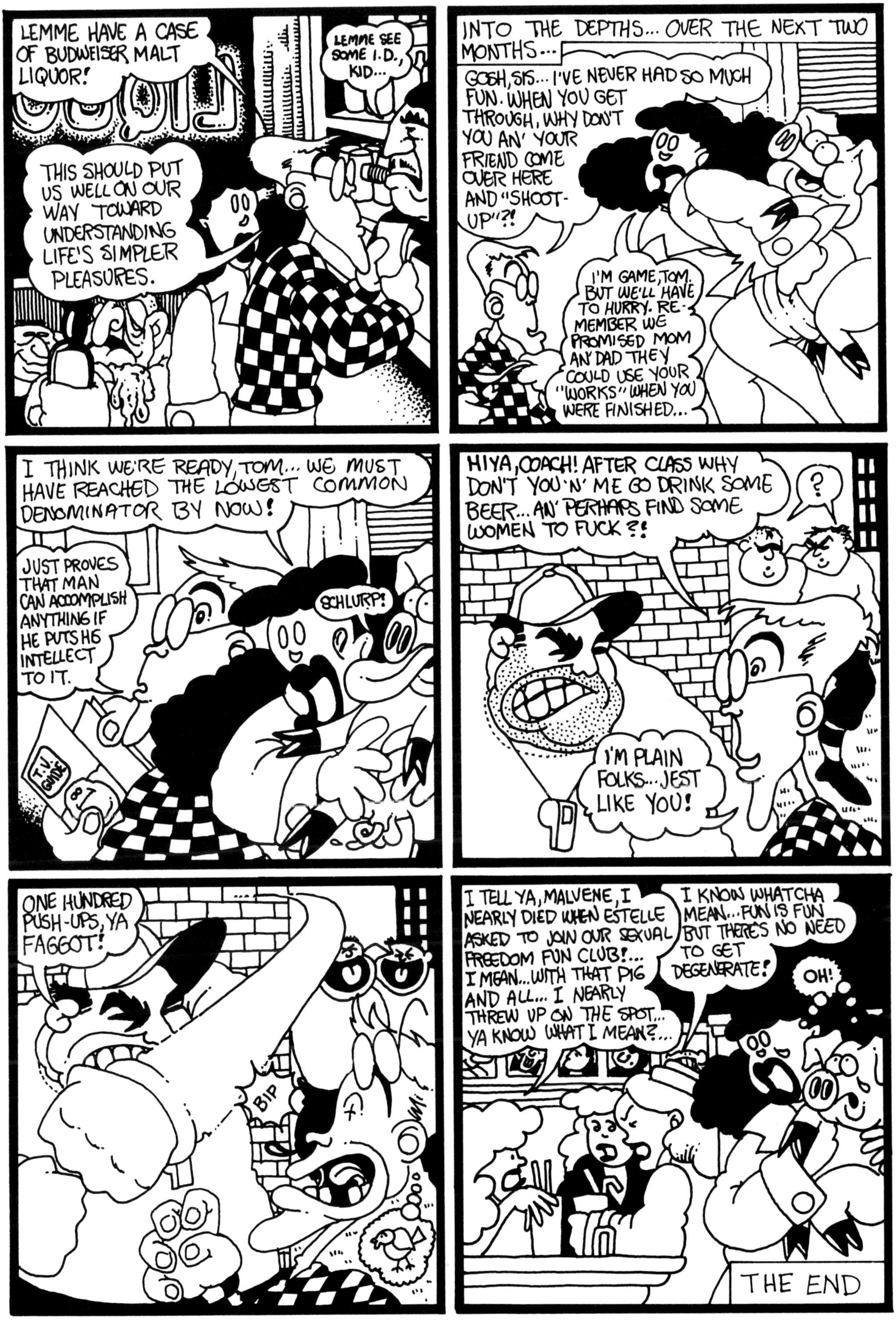
LEMME HAVE A CASE OF BUDWEISER MALT LIQUOR!
LEMME SEE SOME I.D., KID...
THIS SHOULD PUT US WELL ON OUR WAY TOWARD UNDERSTANDING LIFE'S SIMPLER PLEASURES.
INTO THE DEPTHS... OVER THE NEXT TWO MONTHS...
GOSH, SIS... I'VE NEVER HAD SO MUCH FUN. WHEN YOU GET THROUGH, WHY DON'T YOU AN' YOUR FRIEND COME OVER HERE AND "SHOOT-UP"?!
I'M GAME, TOM. BUT WE'LL HAVE TO HURRY. REMEMBER WE PROMISED MOM AN' DAD THEY COULD USE YOUR "WORKS" WHEN YOU WERE FINISHED...
I THINK WE'RE READY, TOM... WE MUST HAVE REACHED THE LOWEST COMMON DENOMINATOR BY NOW!
JUST PROVES THAT MAN CAN ACCOMPLISH ANYTHING IF HE PUTS HIS INTELLECT TO IT.
SCHLURP!
T.V. GUIDE
HIYA, COACH! AFTER CLASS WHY DON'T YOU 'N' ME GO DRINK SOME BEER... AN' PERHAPS FIND SOME WOMEN TO FUCK?!
?
I'M PLAIN FOLKS... JEST LIKE YOU!
ONE HUNDRED PUSH-UPS, YA FAGGOT!
BIP
I TELL YA, MALVENE, I NEARLY DIED WHEN ESTELLE ASKED TO JOIN OUR SEXUAL FREEDOM FUN CLUB!... I MEAN... WITH THAT PIG AND ALL... I NEARLY THREW UP ON THE SPOT... YA KNOW WHAT I MEAN?...
I KNOW WHATCHA MEAN... FUN IS FUN BUT THERE'S NO NEED TO GET DEGENERATE!
OH!
THE END

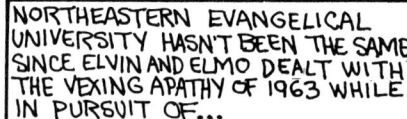

HIGHER EDUCATION

© 1970 BY SKIP WILLIAMSON

NORTHEASTERN EVANGELICAL UNIVERSITY HASN'T BEEN THE SAME SINCE ELVIN AND ELMO DEALT WITH THE VEXING APATHY OF 1963 WHILE IN PURSUIT OF...

GIT THAT SHEEPSKIN, BOY... NOBODY KIN TAKE THAT AWAY FROM YOU!

WHO WOULD WANT IT!?

I DREAMT I WUS WALKIN' IN WORLD WAR THREE... WENT TO TH' DOCTOR TH' VERY NEXT DAY T' SEE WHUT KINDA WORDS HE COULD SAY... SAID IT WUZ A BAD DREAM... I WOULDN'T WORRY ABOUT IT NONE...

JEEZUS CHRIST, ELMO! THAT'S RILLY TERRIBLE SINGIN'!... WHY DON'CHA PUT DAVE BRUBECK BACK ON TH' BOX?!

GOLLY, ELVIN... LISSEN T' WHUT THIS GUY'S SINGIN' ABOUT... IMPENDING SOCIAL CHANGE, WARMONGERS, RACIAL STRIFE, INJUSTICE, FREEDOM...

I AIN'T INTERESTED, ELMO! I GIT ENOUGH OF THAT PHILOSOPHICAL SHIT IN MY HUMANITIES COURSE!

WHY CAN'TCHA JUST BE THANKFUL YOU WERE BORN WHITE! ...AN' ENJOY TH' DEBAUCHERIES AVAILABLE AS STANDARD FARE...

I'M AMAZED YOU SURVIVED TO THIS AGE.

ACROSS CAMPUS AUTHORITIES BROOD...

THESE TWO DISTURB ME!

THE MEASURE OF AN ADMINISTRATOR IS HIS COMPASSION AND REASON.

BUT THESE STUDENTS ARE POTENTIAL TROUBLE-MAKERS!

ONCE YOU WERE YOUNG WITH POTENTIAL, DEAN...

HOWEVER, THE BUSINESS OF EDUCATION HAS MORE IMMEDIATE DEMANDS!

STILL... I RELISH THE DAY I WILL BE AFFORDED THE OPPORTUNITY TO DEAL WITH THOSE TWO AS JUSTICE DEMANDS!

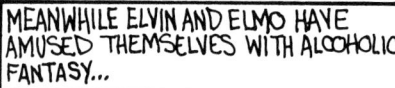

MEANWHILE ELVIN AND ELMO HAVE AMUSED THEMSELVES WITH ALCOHOLIC FANTASY...

Y' KNOW, ELVIN, TH' SOLEMN NONSENSE OF EDUCATION IS GETTIN' ME DOWN!

WE MUST ABANDON FORMAL RITUAL IN ORDER TO ESTABLISH OUR IDENTITY!

WE MUST TASTE THE SWEETNESS OF "ACADEMIC FREEDOM!"

THUS WAS EVANGELICAL'S LITERARY CRITICISM CLASS RUDELY DISRUPTED.

OBSERVE, PROFESSOR... ...AN EXAMPLE OF "LOW COMEDY"... ...IN THE CHAUCERIAN MODE!

RETRIBUTION!

NORTHCENTRAL EVANGELICAL SHALL NO LONGER KEEP THESE TWO FROM VISITING SCENIC VIETNAM!

PERHAPS SUCH A MORAL MISSION WILL BUILD VIRTUE IN THESE RUFFIANS...

SHOOTING ORIENTALS IN THE SOUTH PACIFIC CERTAINLY DID ME A WORLD OF GOOD!

"Right now I'd like to do an original composition which deals with the basic existential-istic thought and parallels between the work of Kafka, Tillich, and Buber in relation to the 'I-Thou' concept, and which has just been recorded by The Rolling Stones..."

THE THRILLING ADVENTURES OF...
BOZO REBEBO

ORDER IN TH' COURT! ORDER IN TH' COURT!!!!

TH' STATE VS. BOZO REBEBO...HOWDOYA PLEAD?...

NOT GUILTY, YER HONOR?

CONTEMPT OF COURT! CONTEMPT OF COURT!!

YOU ARE CHARGED WITH DISMEMBERING AN ABNORMAL NUMBER OF INNOCENT BYSTANDERS...

BUT...BUT... THERE'S BEEN A TERRIBLE MISTAKE!

I WARN YOU, REBEBO...TH' SWORD OF JUSTICE IS SWIFT! MINORITY CRIMINALS WILL FIND NO SYMPATHY IN THIS COURT!

LISSEN, YER HONOR...YOU GOT ME ALL WRONG!...I WAS IN PITTSBURG WHEN THIS ALL HAPPENED...

YOU MUST BE MISTAKEING ME FER...

...MY TWIN COUSIN, BEBO REBONO!

NO...JUDGE NO...I AIN'T GUILTY EITHER

NOT ME... I WAS IN BALTIMORE

OBVIOUSLY YOU HAVE ERRED...

IN REALITY IT WAS...

...MY UNCLE, BOHUNK REDONDO...THAT'S WHO IT WAS...

NO...NOT ME... IT WAS REBO LABONZO

NO... NO... IT WAS BOHOP REBEBOP!

NO...

NO... NOT ME

NO

NO

NO...NOT ME...

I DIDN'T...NOT ME...

I DIDN'T...NOT ME...

ORDERINACOURT! ORDERINACOURT! ORDERINACOURT!

DO NOT TOY WITH TH' SCALES OF JUSTICE, REBEBO!

THIS JUDICIAL SYSTEM WILL NOT TOLERATE YOUR ANARCHY, REBONO!

BUT THIS IS A MISCARRIAGE OF JUSTICE, YER HONOR! IT'S ALL COMING BACK TO ME NOW...I WASN'T IN PITTSBURG AT ALL...

ACK! ACK! CHOKE! ACK!

I WAS IN TOLEDO!

ACK!

ACK! ACK! CHOKE

YOU'RE A FOOL!...YOU'LL BE JUDGED, REDONDO! BY A JURY OF YOUR PEERS!

BY A JURY OF SOLID, UPSTANDING CITIZENS!

NOT GUILTY

JUSTICE SERVED...BOZO GOES ABOUT HIS DAILY BUSINESS...

HEY KID! LOOK WHAT I JUST DID TO THIS CUTE LITTLE KITTY CAT!

SKIP WILLIAMSON

CLASS WAR COMIX

These drawings were executed in Judge Julius Hoffman's courtroom in 1969 during the conspiracy trial of the Chicago Seven. Seating was limited to those with chic credentials (like Jules Feiffer, sketching an assignment for the *Village Voice*) or to the families of the defendants. I was admitted as Abbie Hoffman's sister.

WILLIAM KUNSTLER

JERRY RUBIN

BOBBY SEALE

FEDERAL MARSHALL PRESTON

TOM FORAN

LEE WEINER

TOM HAYDEN

ABBIE HOFFMAN

LEONARD WEINGLASS

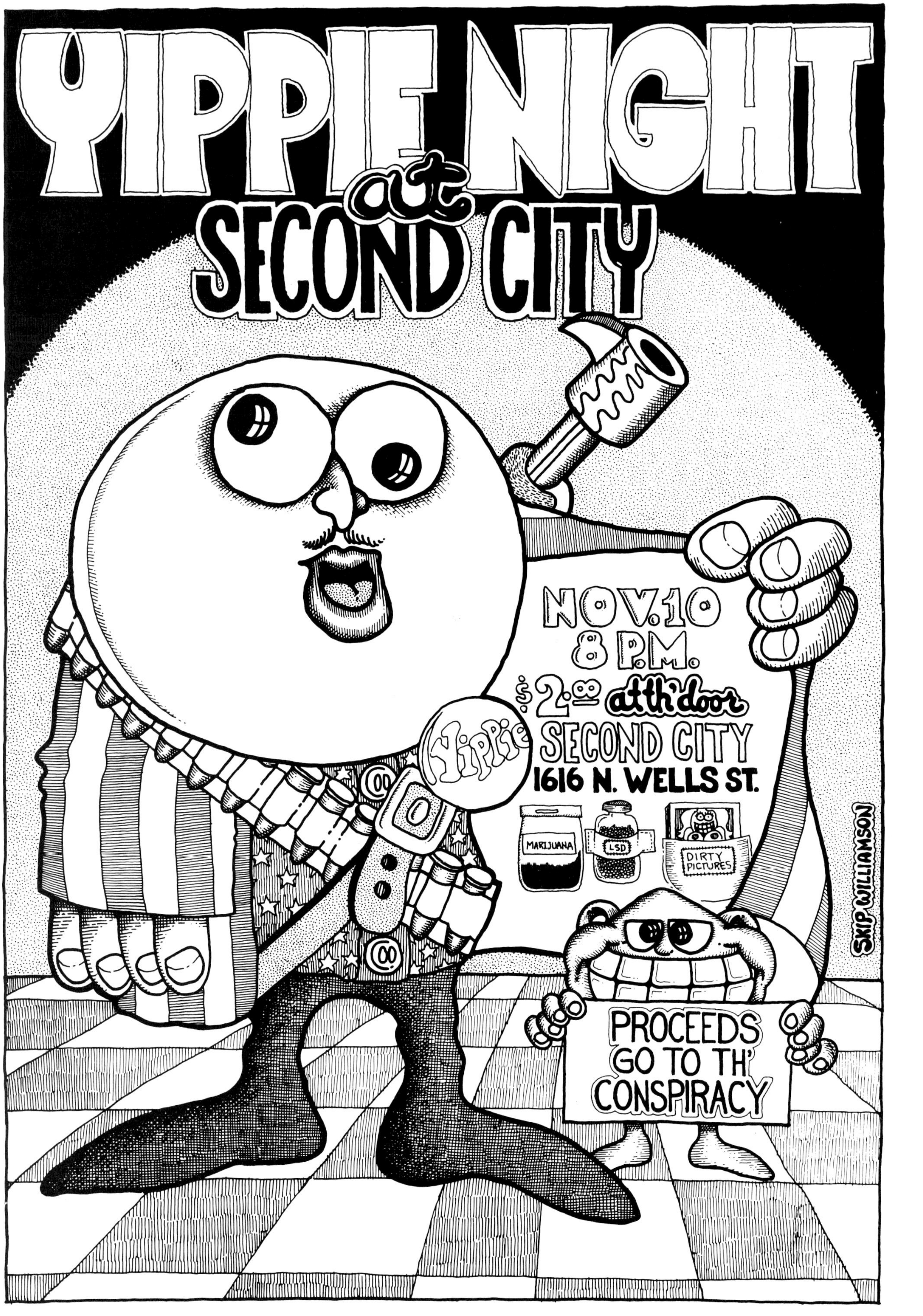
YIPPIE NIGHT
at
SECOND CITY
NOV. 10
8 P.M.
$2.00 at th' door
SECOND CITY
1616 N. WELLS ST.
Yippie
MARIJUANA
LSD
DIRTY PICTURES
PROCEEDS GO TO TH' CONSPIRACY
SKIP WILLIAMSON

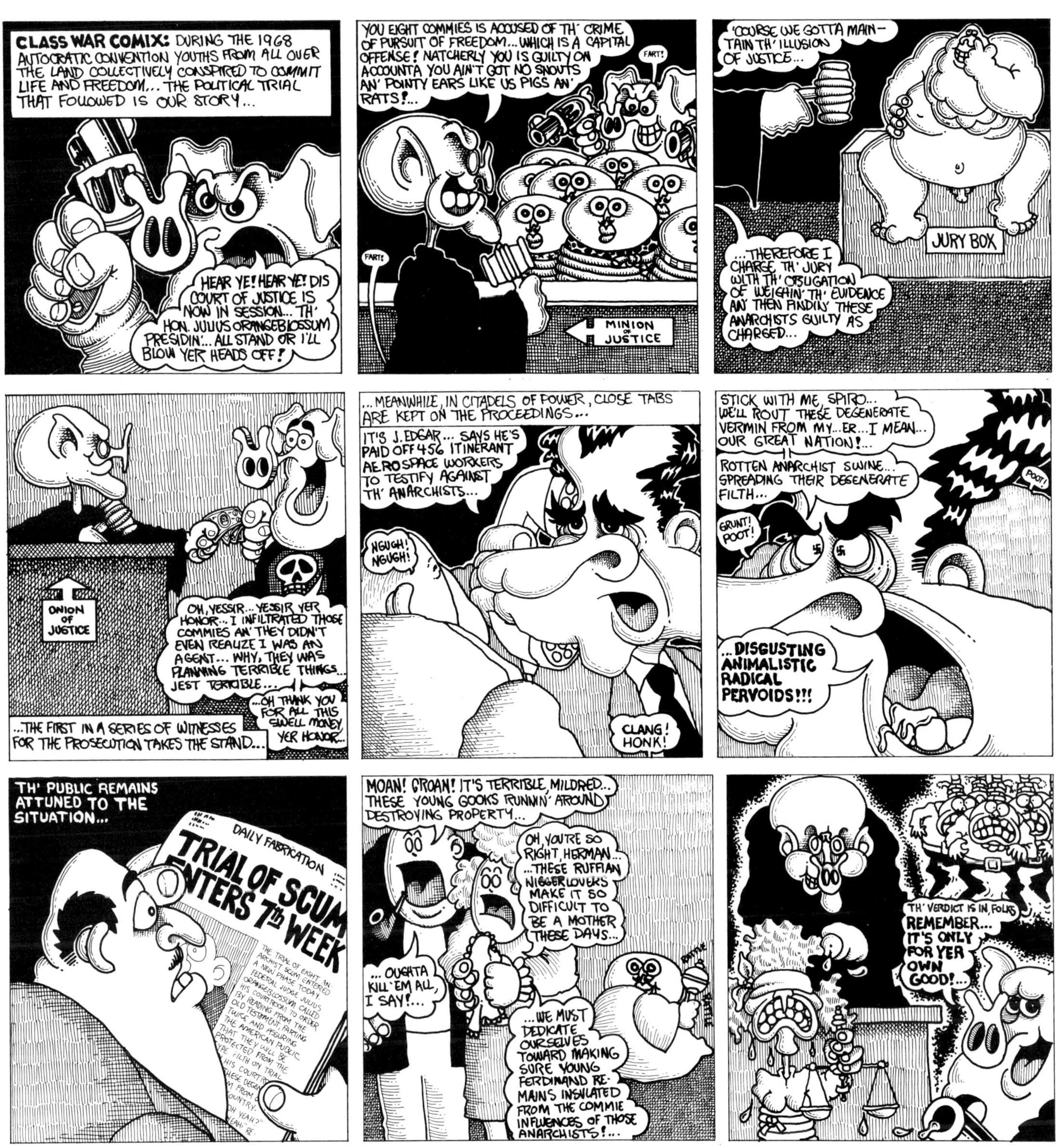
CLASS WAR COMIX: DURING THE 1968 AUTOCRATIC CONVENTION YOUTHS FROM ALL OVER THE LAND COLLECTIVELY CONSPIRED TO COMMIT LIFE AND FREEDOM... THE POLITICAL TRIAL THAT FOLLOWED IS OUR STORY...
HEAR YE! HEAR YE! DIS COURT OF JUSTICE IS NOW IN SESSION... TH' HON. JULIUS ORANGEBLOSSUM PRESIDIN'... ALL STAND OR I'LL BLOW YER HEADS OFF!
YOU EIGHT COMMIES IS ACCUSED OF TH' CRIME OF PURSUIT OF FREEDOM... WHICH IS A CAPITAL OFFENSE! NATCHERLY YOU IS GUILTY ON ACCOUNTA YOU AIN'T GOT NO SNOUTS AN' POINTY EARS LIKE US PIGS AN' RATS!...
FART!
FART!
MINION OF JUSTICE
'COURSE WE GOTTA MAIN-TAIN TH' ILLUSION OF JUSTICE...
...THEREFORE I CHARGE TH' JURY WITH TH' OBLIGATION OF WEIGHIN' TH' EVIDENCE AN' THEN FINDIN' THESE ANARCHISTS GUILTY AS CHARGED...
JURY BOX
ONION OF JUSTICE
OH, YESSIR... YESSIR YER HONOR... I INFILTRATED THOSE COMMIES AN' THEY DIDN'T EVEN REALIZE I WAS AN AGENT... WHY, THEY WAS PLANNING TERRIBLE THINGS... JEST TERRIBLE...
...OH THANK YOU FOR ALL THIS SWELL MONEY YER HONOR...
...THE FIRST IN A SERIES OF WITNESSES FOR THE PROSECUTION TAKES THE STAND...
...MEANWHILE, IN CITADELS OF POWER, CLOSE TABS ARE KEPT ON THE PROCEEDINGS...
IT'S J. EDGAR... SAYS HE'S PAID OFF 456 ITINERANT AEROSPACE WORKERS TO TESTIFY AGAINST TH' ANARCHISTS...
NGUGH! NGUGH!
CLANG! HONK!
STICK WITH ME, SPIRO... WE'LL ROUT THESE DEGENERATE VERMIN FROM MY... ER... I MEAN... OUR GREAT NATION!...
ROTTEN ANARCHIST SWINE... SPREADING THEIR DEGENERATE FILTH...
POOT!
GRUNT! POOT!
...DISGUSTING ANIMALISTIC RADICAL PERVOIDS!!!
TH' PUBLIC REMAINS ATTUNED TO THE SITUATION...
DAILY FABRICATION
TRIAL OF SCUM ENTERS 7th WEEK
MOAN! GROAN! IT'S TERRIBLE, MILDRED... THESE YOUNG GOOKS RUNNIN' AROUND DESTROYING PROPERTY...
OH, YOU'RE SO RIGHT, HERMAN... ...THESE RUFFIAN NIGGERLOVERS MAKE IT SO DIFFICULT TO BE A MOTHER THESE DAYS...
...OUGHTA KILL 'EM ALL, I SAY!...
...WE MUST DEDICATE OURSELVES TOWARD MAKING SURE YOUNG FERDINAND RE-MAINS INSULATED FROM THE COMMIE INFLUENCES OF THOSE ANARCHISTS!...
TH' VERDICT IS IN, FOLKS REMEMBER... IT'S ONLY FOR YER OWN GOOD!...

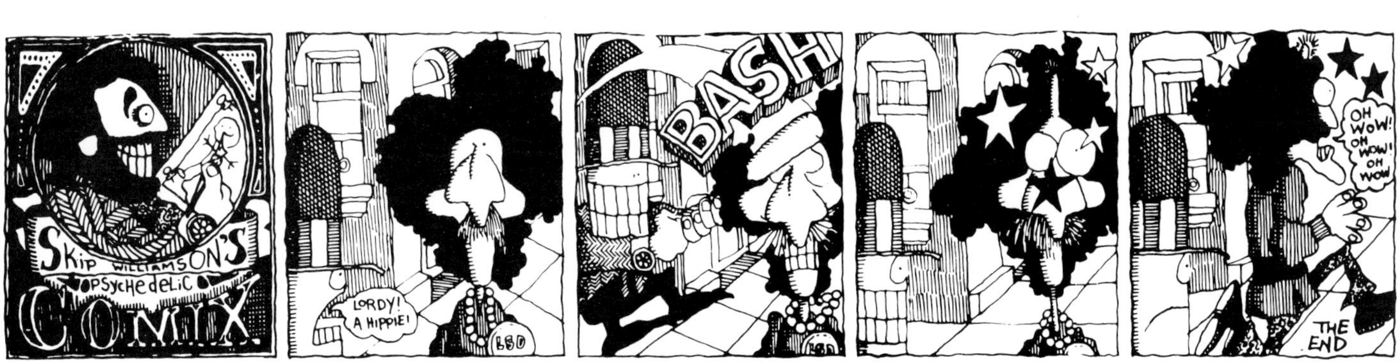
SKIP WILLIAMSON'S PSYCHEDELIC COMIX
LORDY! A HIPPIE!
BASH
OH WOW! OH WOW! OH WOW
THE END

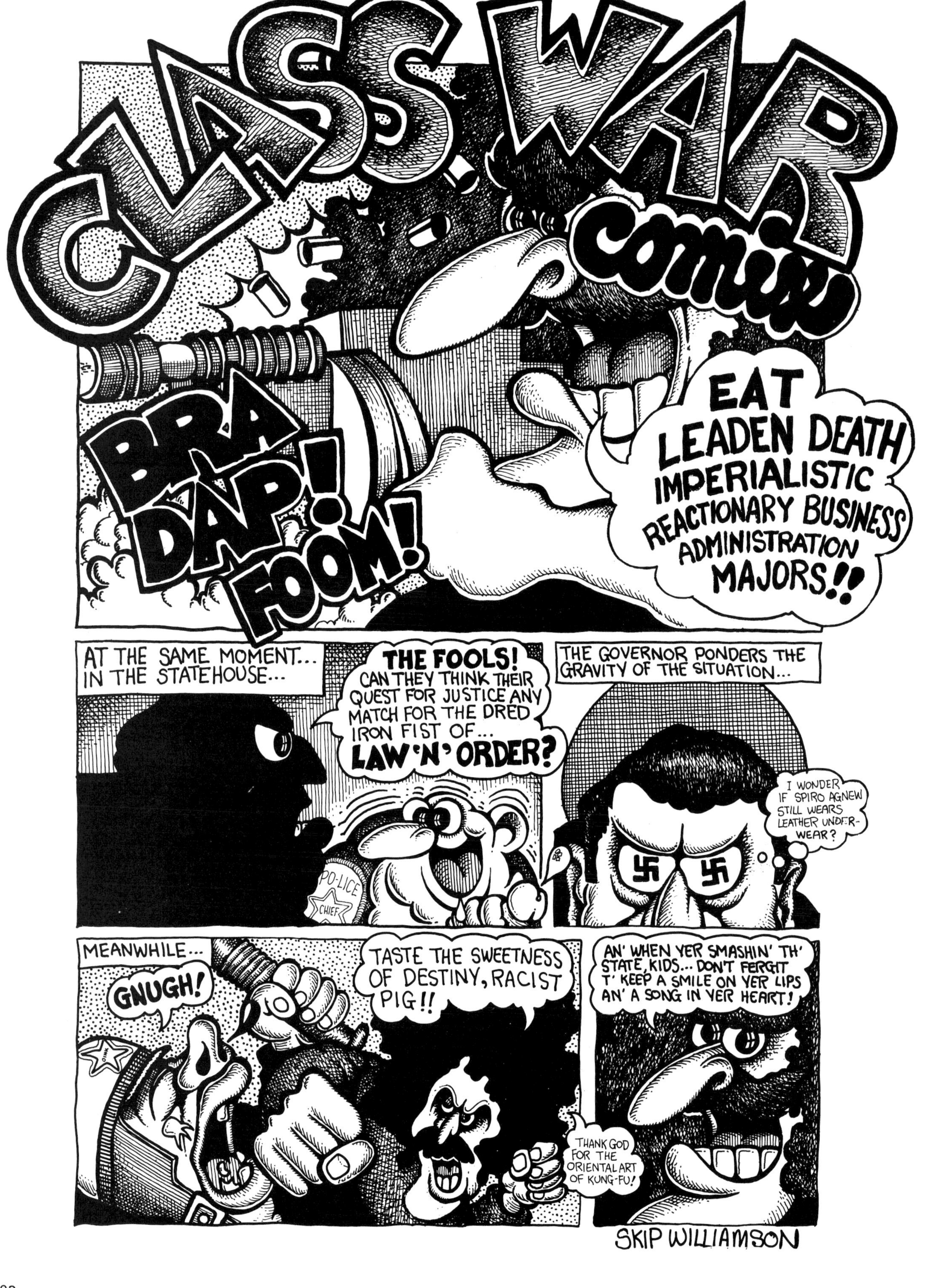
CLASS WAR comix
BRA DAP! DAP! FOOM!
EAT LEADEN DEATH IMPERIALISTIC REACTIONARY BUSINESS ADMINISTRATION MAJORS!!
AT THE SAME MOMENT... IN THE STATEHOUSE...
THE FOOLS! CAN THEY THINK THEIR QUEST FOR JUSTICE ANY MATCH FOR THE DRED IRON FIST OF... LAW 'N' ORDER?
PO-LICE CHIEF
THE GOVERNOR PONDERS THE GRAVITY OF THE SITUATION...
I WONDER IF SPIRO AGNEW STILL WEARS LEATHER UNDER-WEAR?
MEANWHILE...
GNUGH!
TASTE THE SWEETNESS OF DESTINY, RACIST PIG!!
THANK GOD FOR THE ORIENTAL ART OF KUNG-FU!
AN' WHEN YER SMASHIN' TH' STATE, KIDS... DON'T FERGIT T' KEEP A SMILE ON YER LIPS AN' A SONG IN YER HEART!
SKIP WILLIAMSON

COVERS FOR UNDERGROUND PRESS PUBLICATIONS DURING THE LATE '60s AND EARLY '70s.

Below, left: Cover for the *Chicago Seed* demonstrating the worthiness of Yippie politics.
Below, right: Cover for the *Chicago Seed* featuring anti-war message.

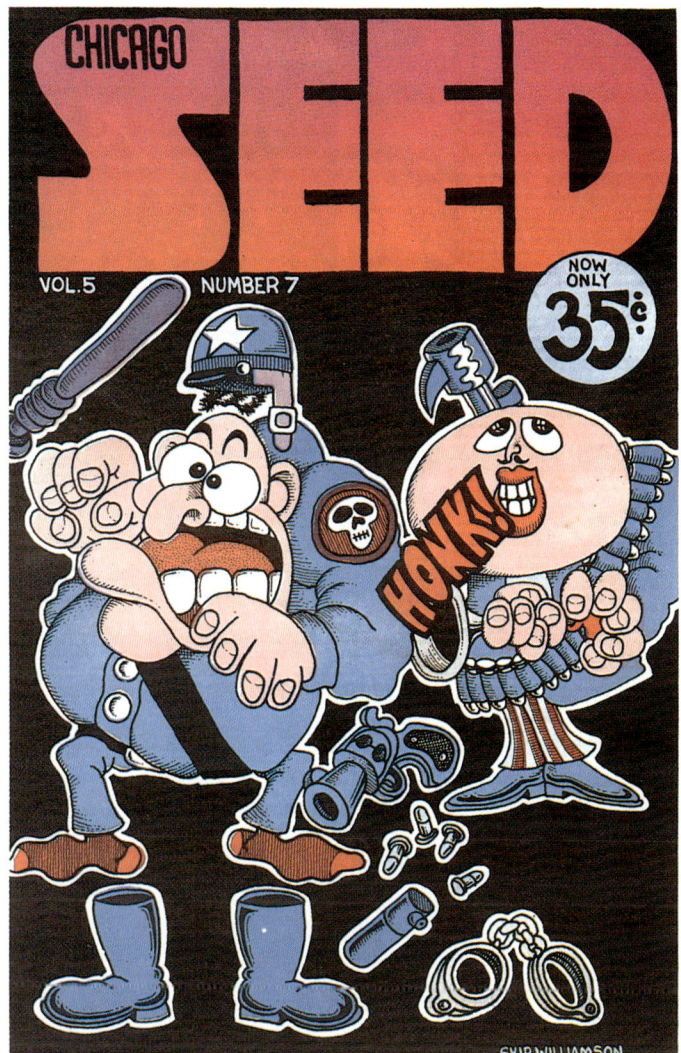

Below, left: Cover for the *Chicago Seed* spotlighting reverse zero tolerance.

Below, middle: *Bijou Funnies* cover with Smoot and his peer group.
Below, right: *Bijou Funnies* cover. A portrait of the artist and family meting out justice to a landlord.

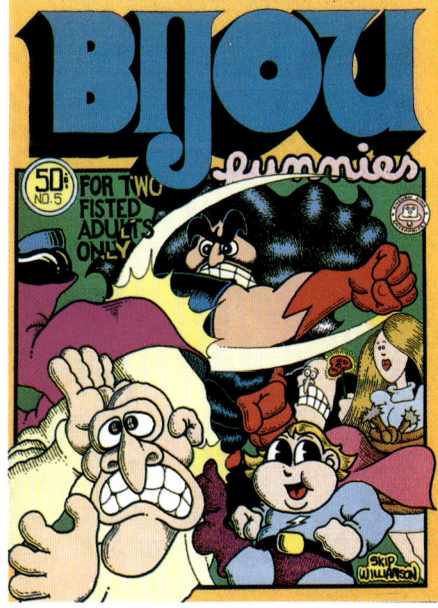

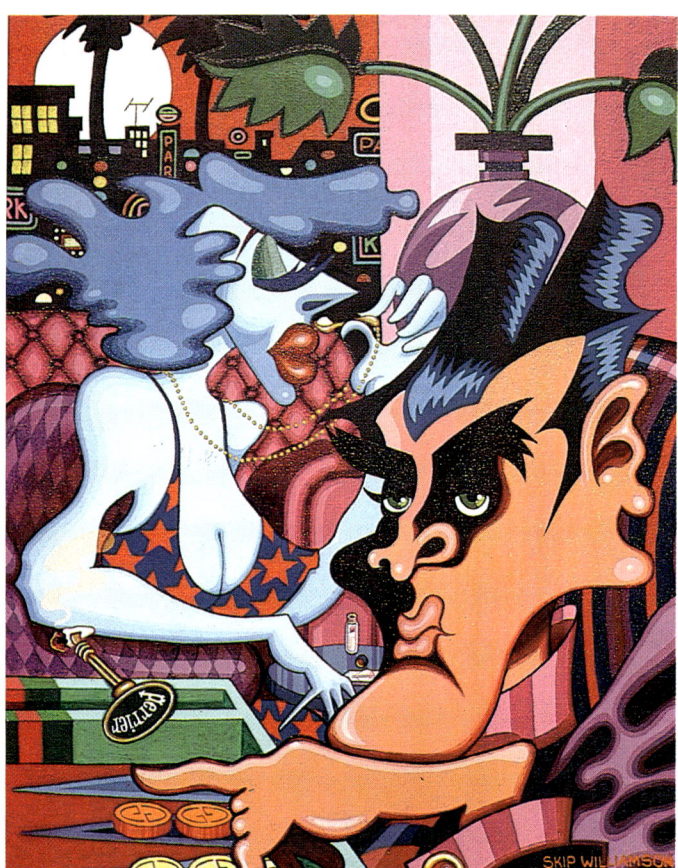

Lost Angeles.

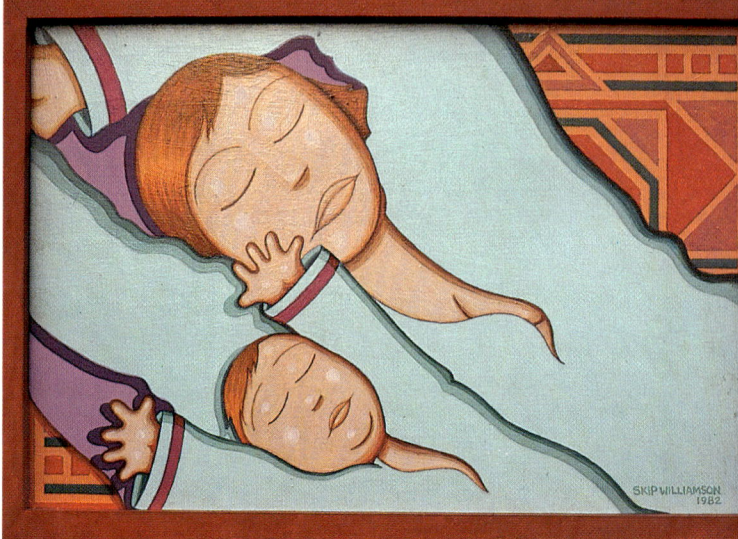

Hattie & Molly.

The Udder Degenerates.

TV Dinner.

The Masses/Intellectuals.

Cartune.

84

Cafe Society.

Ben Ochio.

Perquisites.

Aliens Must Register.

Mr. Ed.

The Skokie Swift.

SOMEDAY, WHEN I GROW UP, THIS WILL ALL BE YOURS.

Christie & Hugh Hefner.

Slim Whitman & His Fame.

Not the Beatles.

All-American Hot Dog.

Business Mouse.

The Rolling Stones Meet Heinrich Kley.

Meltdown.

Computer Camp.

Invest.

Mixed Metaphors.

Nixon from Mars.

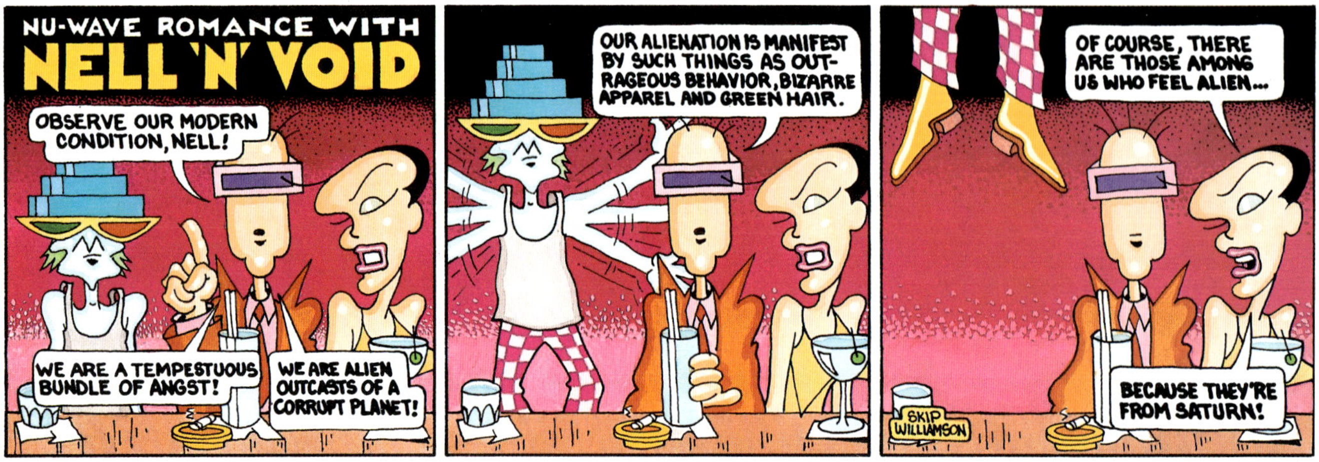
NU-WAVE ROMANCE WITH
NELL 'N' VOID
OBSERVE OUR MODERN CONDITION, NELL!
WE ARE A TEMPESTUOUS BUNDLE OF ANGST!
WE ARE ALIEN OUTCASTS OF A CORRUPT PLANET!
OUR ALIENATION IS MANIFEST BY SUCH THINGS AS OUTRAGEOUS BEHAVIOR, BIZARRE APPAREL AND GREEN HAIR.
OF COURSE, THERE ARE THOSE AMONG US WHO FEEL ALIEN...
BECAUSE THEY'RE FROM SATURN!
SKIP WILLIAMSON

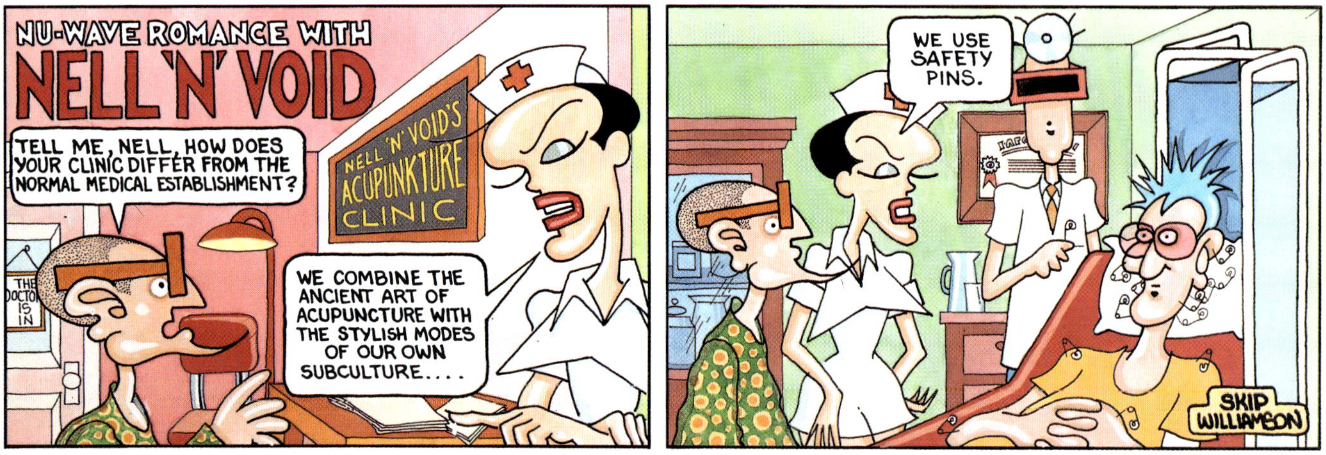
NU-WAVE ROMANCE WITH
NELL 'N' VOID
TELL ME, NELL, HOW DOES YOUR CLINIC DIFFER FROM THE NORMAL MEDICAL ESTABLISHMENT?
NELL 'N' VOID'S ACUPUNKTURE CLINIC
THE DOCTOR IS IN
WE COMBINE THE ANCIENT ART OF ACUPUNCTURE WITH THE STYLISH MODES OF OUR OWN SUBCULTURE....
WE USE SAFETY PINS.
SKIP WILLIAMSON

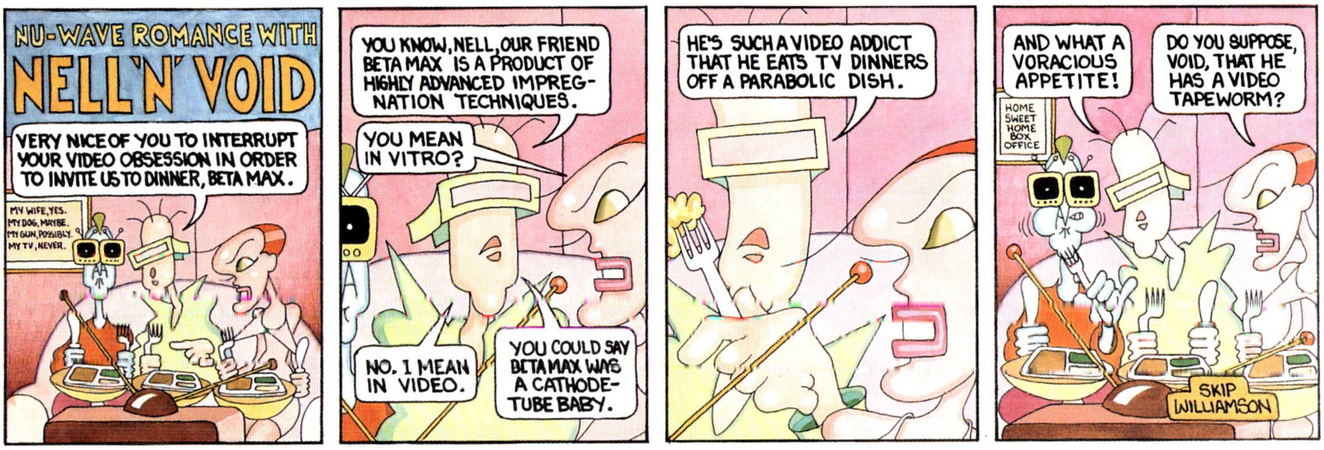
NU-WAVE ROMANCE WITH
NELL 'N' VOID
VERY NICE OF YOU TO INTERRUPT YOUR VIDEO OBSESSION IN ORDER TO INVITE US TO DINNER, BETA MAX.
MY WIFE, YES. MY DOG, MAYBE. MY GUN, POSSIBLY. MY TV, NEVER.
YOU KNOW, NELL, OUR FRIEND BETA MAX IS A PRODUCT OF HIGHLY ADVANCED IMPREGNATION TECHNIQUES.
YOU MEAN IN VITRO?
NO. I MEAN IN VIDEO.
YOU COULD SAY BETA MAX WAS A CATHODE-TUBE BABY.
HE'S SUCH A VIDEO ADDICT THAT HE EATS TV DINNERS OFF A PARABOLIC DISH.
AND WHAT A VORACIOUS APPETITE!
DO YOU SUPPOSE, VOID, THAT HE HAS A VIDEO TAPEWORM?
HOME SWEET HOME BOX OFFICE
SKIP WILLIAMSON

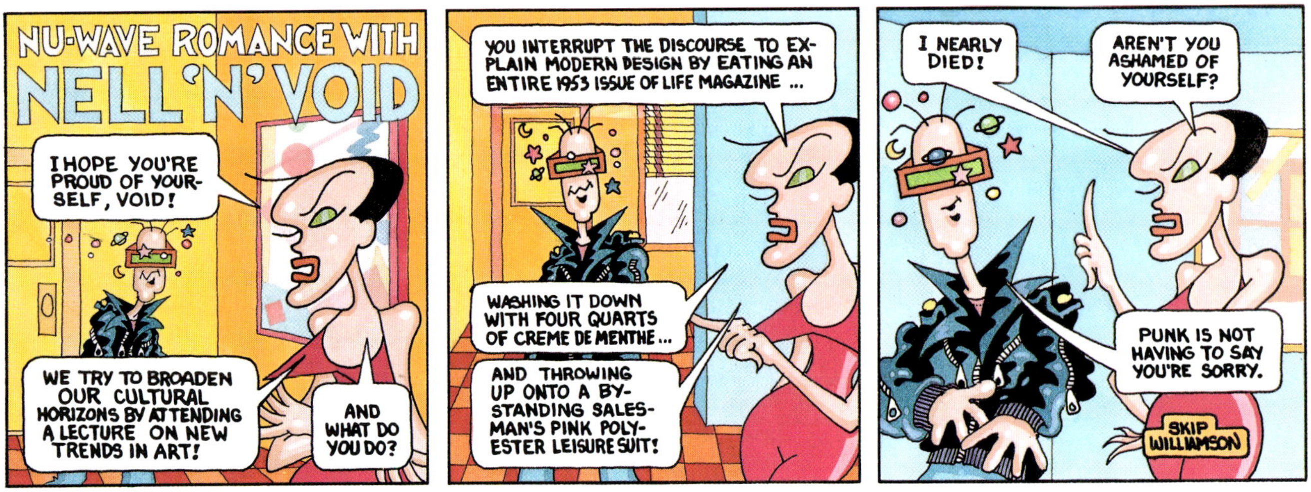
NU-WAVE ROMANCE WITH
NELL 'N' VOID
I HOPE YOU'RE PROUD OF YOURSELF, VOID!
WE TRY TO BROADEN OUR CULTURAL HORIZONS BY ATTENDING A LECTURE ON NEW TRENDS IN ART!
AND WHAT DO YOU DO?
YOU INTERRUPT THE DISCOURSE TO EXPLAIN MODERN DESIGN BY EATING AN ENTIRE 1953 ISSUE OF LIFE MAGAZINE ...
WASHING IT DOWN WITH FOUR QUARTS OF CREME DE MENTHE...
AND THROWING UP ONTO A BYSTANDING SALESMAN'S PINK POLYESTER LEISURE SUIT!
I NEARLY DIED!
AREN'T YOU ASHAMED OF YOURSELF?
PUNK IS NOT HAVING TO SAY YOU'RE SORRY.
SKIP WILLIAMSON

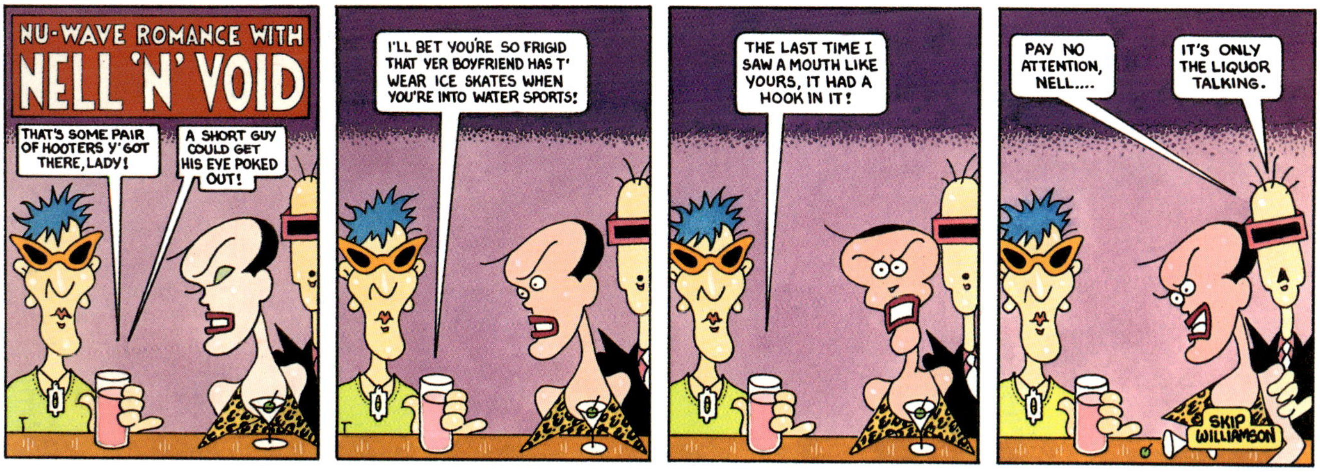
NU-WAVE ROMANCE WITH
NELL 'N' VOID
THAT'S SOME PAIR OF HOOTERS Y' GOT THERE, LADY!
A SHORT GUY COULD GET HIS EYE POKED OUT!
I'LL BET YOU'RE SO FRIGID THAT YER BOYFRIEND HAS T' WEAR ICE SKATES WHEN YOU'RE INTO WATER SPORTS!
THE LAST TIME I SAW A MOUTH LIKE YOURS, IT HAD A HOOK IN IT!
PAY NO ATTENTION, NELL....
IT'S ONLY THE LIQUOR TALKING.
SKIP WILLIAMSON

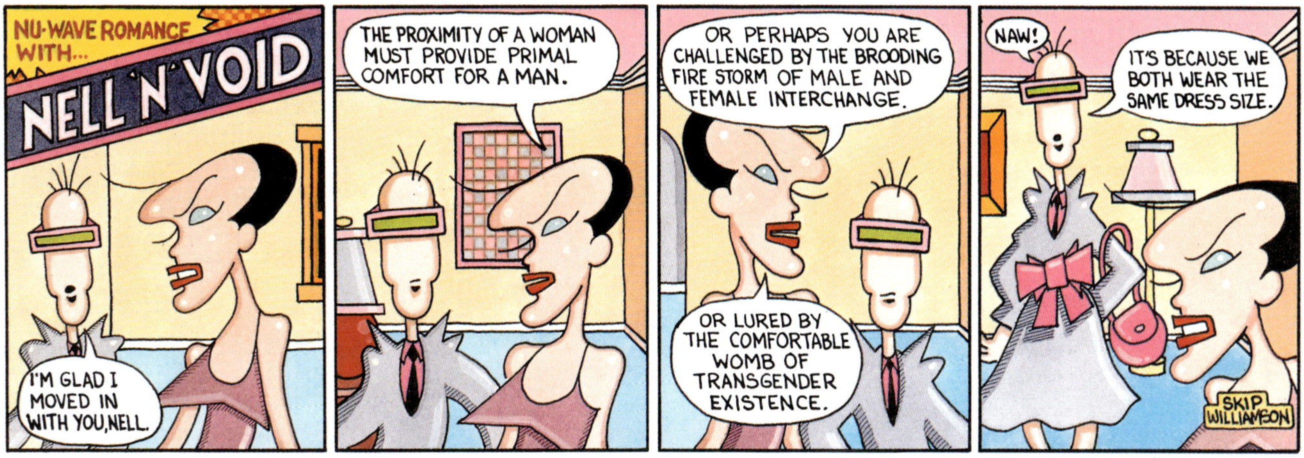
NU-WAVE ROMANCE WITH...
NELL 'N' VOID
I'M GLAD I MOVED IN WITH YOU, NELL.
THE PROXIMITY OF A WOMAN MUST PROVIDE PRIMAL COMFORT FOR A MAN.
OR PERHAPS YOU ARE CHALLENGED BY THE BROODING FIRE STORM OF MALE AND FEMALE INTERCHANGE.
OR LURED BY THE COMFORTABLE WOMB OF TRANSGENDER EXISTENCE.
NAW!
IT'S BECAUSE WE BOTH WEAR THE SAME DRESS SIZE.
SKIP WILLIAMSON

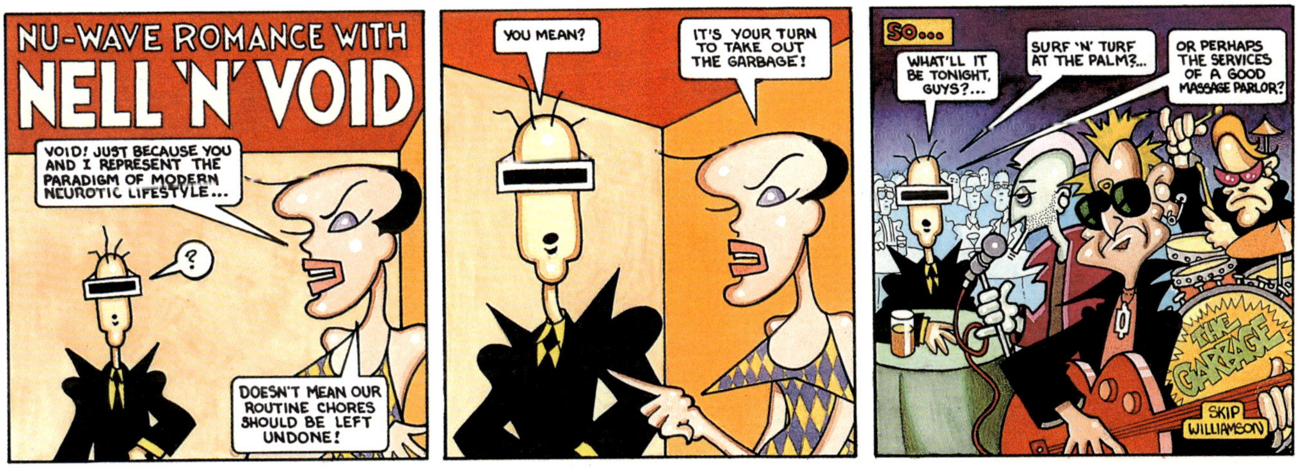
NU-WAVE ROMANCE WITH
NELL 'N' VOID
VOID! JUST BECAUSE YOU AND I REPRESENT THE PARADIGM OF MODERN NEUROTIC LIFESTYLE...
?
DOESN'T MEAN OUR ROUTINE CHORES SHOULD BE LEFT UNDONE!
YOU MEAN?
IT'S YOUR TURN TO TAKE OUT THE GARBAGE!
SO...
WHAT'LL IT BE TONIGHT, GUYS?...
SURF 'N' TURF AT THE PALM?...
OR PERHAPS THE SERVICES OF A GOOD MASSAGE PARLOR?
THE GARBAGE
SKIP WILLIAMSON

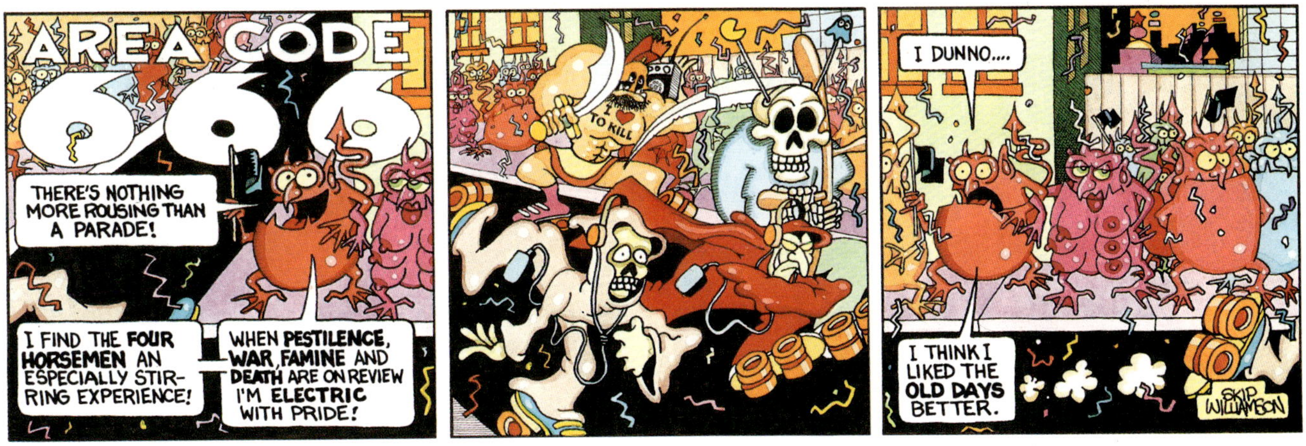
AREA CODE 666
THERE'S NOTHING MORE ROUSING THAN A PARADE!
I FIND THE FOUR HORSEMEN AN ESPECIALLY STIRRING EXPERIENCE!
WHEN PESTILENCE, WAR, FAMINE AND DEATH ARE ON REVIEW I'M ELECTRIC WITH PRIDE!
TO KILL
I DUNNO....
I THINK I LIKED THE OLD DAYS BETTER.
SKIP WILLIAMSON

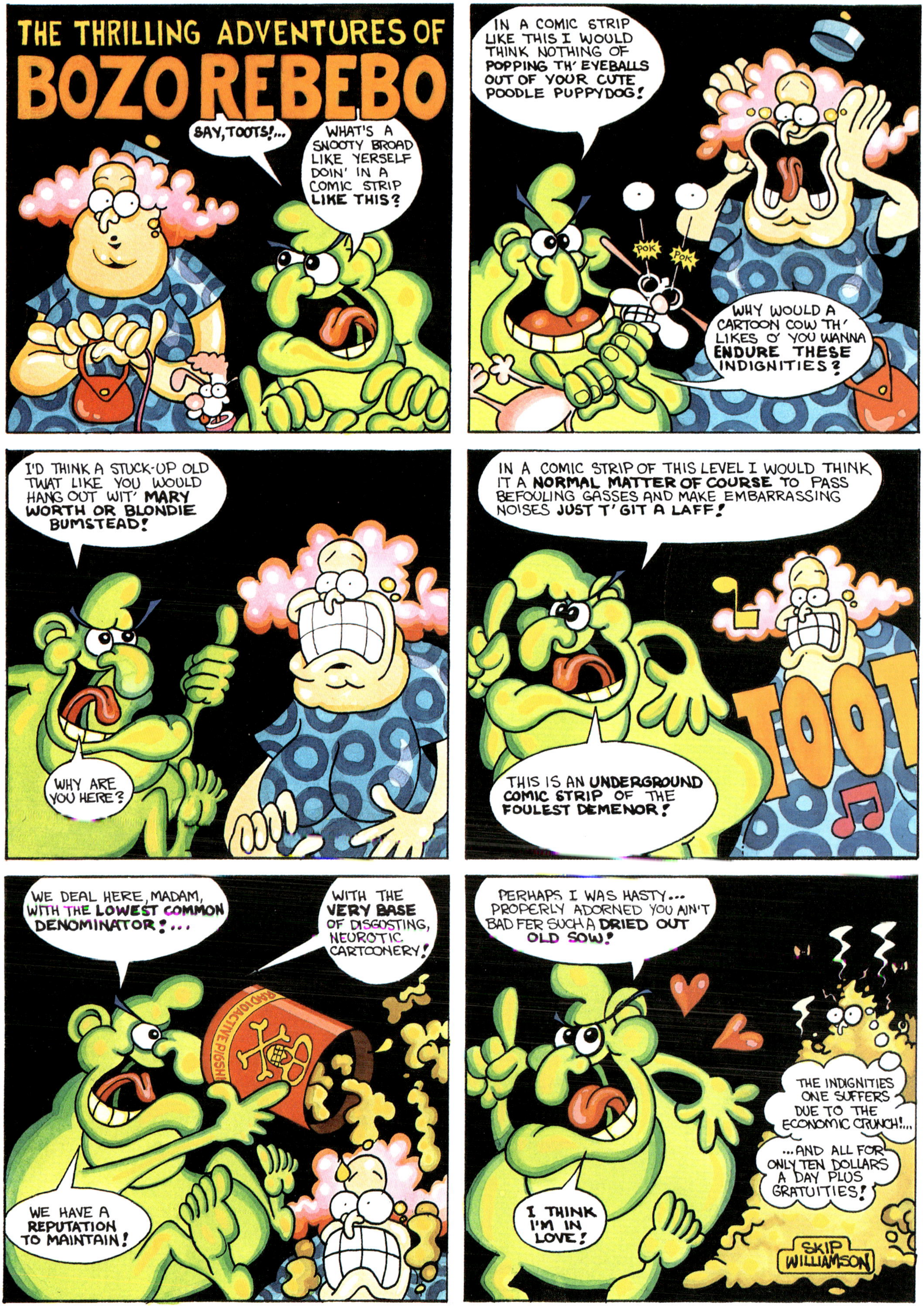
THE THRILLING ADVENTURES OF
BOZO REBEBO
SAY, TOOTS!...
WHAT'S A SNOOTY BROAD LIKE YERSELF DOIN' IN A COMIC STRIP LIKE THIS?
IN A COMIC STRIP LIKE THIS I WOULD THINK NOTHING OF POPPING TH' EYEBALLS OUT OF YOUR CUTE POODLE PUPPYDOG!
POK
POK
WHY WOULD A CARTOON COW TH' LIKES O' YOU WANNA ENDURE THESE INDIGNITIES?
I'D THINK A STUCK-UP OLD TWAT LIKE YOU WOULD HANG OUT WIT' MARY WORTH OR BLONDIE BUMSTEAD!
WHY ARE YOU HERE?
IN A COMIC STRIP OF THIS LEVEL I WOULD THINK IT A NORMAL MATTER OF COURSE TO PASS BEFOULING GASSES AND MAKE EMBARRASSING NOISES JUST T' GIT A LAFF!
TOOT
THIS IS AN UNDERGROUND COMIC STRIP OF THE FOULEST DEMENOR!
WE DEAL HERE, MADAM, WITH THE LOWEST COMMON DENOMINATOR!...
WITH THE VERY BASE OF DISGUSTING, NEUROTIC CARTOONERY!
WE HAVE A REPUTATION TO MAINTAIN!
PERHAPS I WAS HASTY... PROPERLY ADORNED YOU AIN'T BAD FER SUCH A DRIED OUT OLD SOW!
I THINK I'M IN LOVE!
THE INDIGNITIES ONE SUFFERS DUE TO THE ECONOMIC CRUNCH!...
...AND ALL FOR ONLY TEN DOLLARS A DAY PLUS GRATUITIES!
SKIP WILLIAMSON

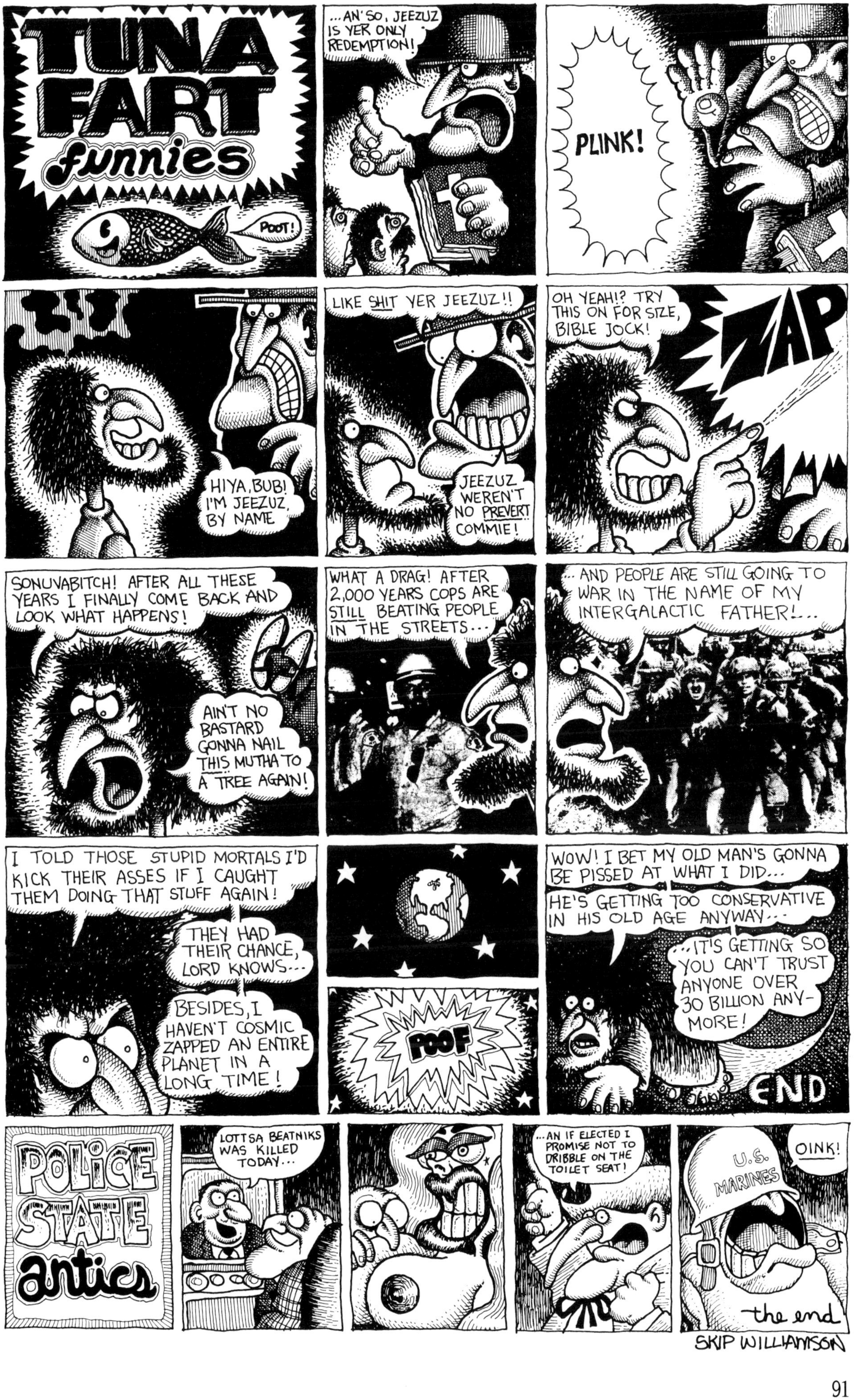
TUNA FART funnies
POOT!
...AN' SO, JEEZUZ IS YER ONLY REDEMPTION!
PLINK!
HIYA, BUB! I'M JEEZUZ, BY NAME
LIKE SHIT YER JEEZUZ!!
JEEZUZ WEREN'T NO PREVERT COMMIE!
OH YEAH!? TRY THIS ON FOR SIZE, BIBLE JOCK!
ZAP
SONUVABITCH! AFTER ALL THESE YEARS I FINALLY COME BACK AND LOOK WHAT HAPPENS!
AIN'T NO BASTARD GONNA NAIL THIS MUTHA TO A TREE AGAIN!
WHAT A DRAG! AFTER 2,000 YEARS COPS ARE STILL BEATING PEOPLE IN THE STREETS...
...AND PEOPLE ARE STILL GOING TO WAR IN THE NAME OF MY INTERGALACTIC FATHER!...
I TOLD THOSE STUPID MORTALS I'D KICK THEIR ASSES IF I CAUGHT THEM DOING THAT STUFF AGAIN!
THEY HAD THEIR CHANCE, LORD KNOWS...
BESIDES, I HAVEN'T COSMIC ZAPPED AN ENTIRE PLANET IN A LONG TIME!
POOF
WOW! I BET MY OLD MAN'S GONNA BE PISSED AT WHAT I DID...
HE'S GETTING TOO CONSERVATIVE IN HIS OLD AGE ANYWAY...
...IT'S GETTING SO YOU CAN'T TRUST ANYONE OVER 30 BILLION ANY-MORE!
END
POLICE STATE antics
LOTTSA BEATNIKS WAS KILLED TODAY...
...AN IF ELECTED I PROMISE NOT TO DRIBBLE ON THE TOILET SEAT!
U.S. MARINES
OINK!
the end
SKIP WILLIAMSON

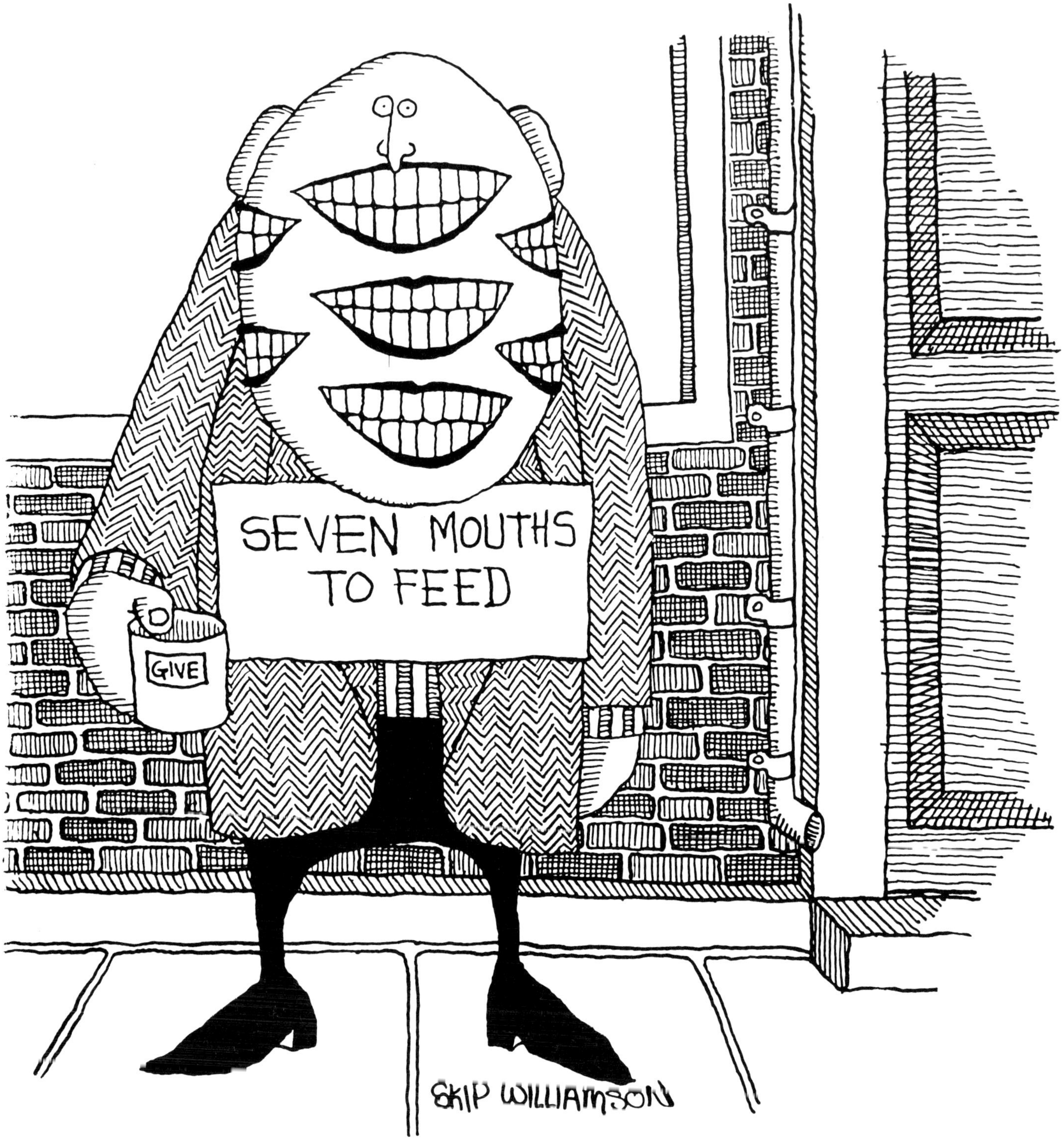
SEVEN MOUTHS TO FEED
GIVE
SKIP WILLIAMSON

"Blow it out your pooh-pooh hole!"

"Frankly, man, it sounds a little like you're trying too hard to reconcile yourself to the stated values and the implicit contradictions of contemporary middle-class Western society."

"Smuggling arms into Cuba again, eh, Rodrigues?"

"I believe I ordered a **highball**..."

"Normally we vampires suck our victim's throat...however, I'm a homosexual!"

HEF'S 119th DAYDREAM

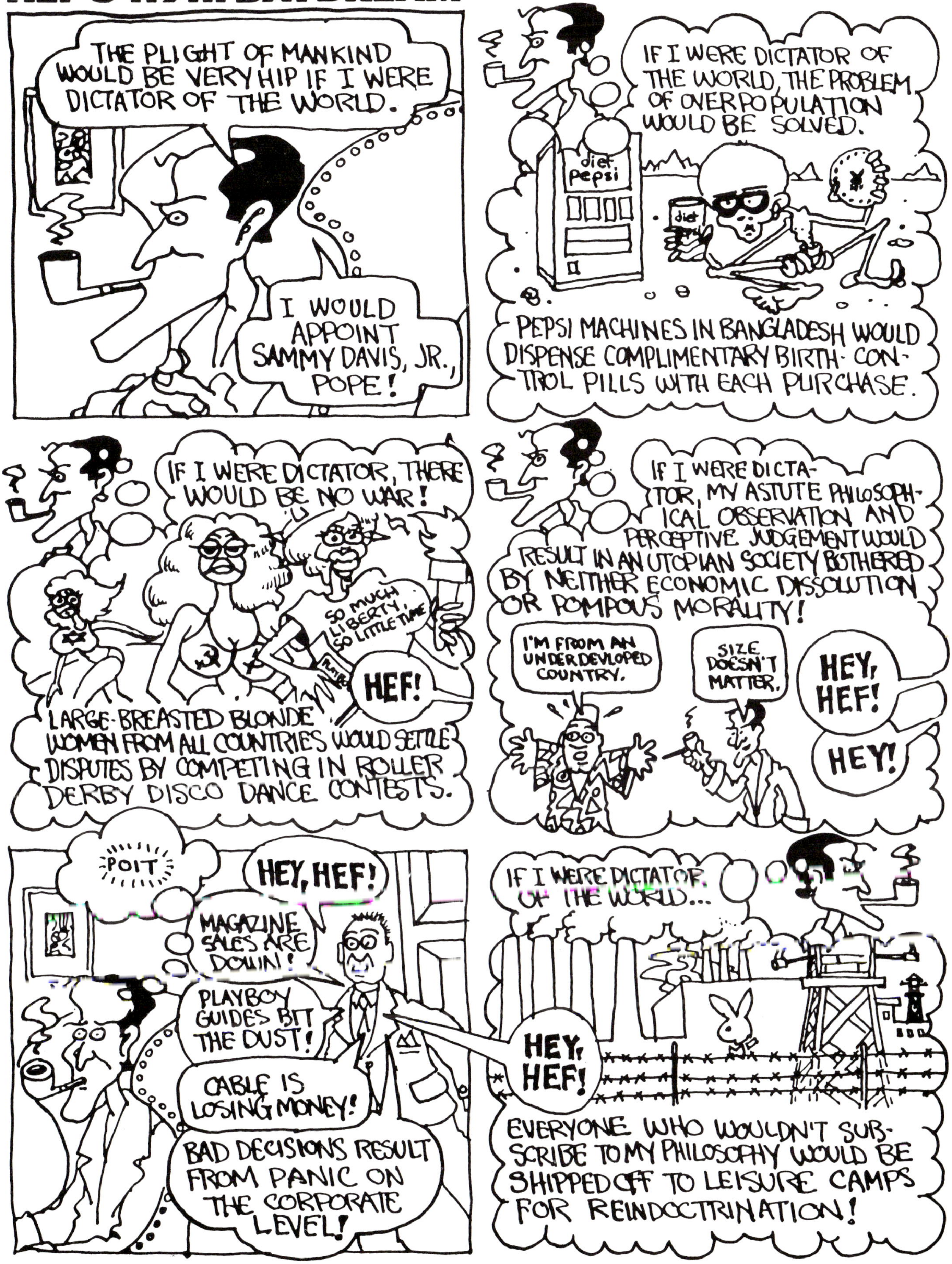
THE PLIGHT OF MANKIND WOULD BE VERY HIP IF I WERE DICTATOR OF THE WORLD.
I WOULD APPOINT SAMMY DAVIS, JR., POPE!
IF I WERE DICTATOR OF THE WORLD, THE PROBLEM OF OVERPOPULATION WOULD BE SOLVED.
diet Pepsi
PEPSI MACHINES IN BANGLADESH WOULD DISPENSE COMPLIMENTARY BIRTH-CONTROL PILLS WITH EACH PURCHASE.
IF I WERE DICTATOR, THERE WOULD BE NO WAR!
SO MUCH LIBERTY, SO LITTLE TIME
HEF!
LARGE-BREASTED BLONDE WOMEN FROM ALL COUNTRIES WOULD SETTLE DISPUTES BY COMPETING IN ROLLER DERBY DISCO DANCE CONTESTS.
IF I WERE DICTATOR, MY ASTUTE PHILOSOPHICAL OBSERVATION AND PERCEPTIVE JUDGEMENT WOULD RESULT IN AN UTOPIAN SOCIETY BOTHERED BY NEITHER ECONOMIC DISSOLUTION OR POMPOUS MORALITY!
I'M FROM AN UNDERDEVELOPED COUNTRY.
SIZE DOESN'T MATTER.
HEY, HEF!
HEY!
POIT
HEY, HEF!
MAGAZINE SALES ARE DOWN!
PLAYBOY GUIDES BIT THE DUST!
CABLE IS LOSING MONEY!
BAD DECISIONS RESULT FROM PANIC ON THE CORPORATE LEVEL!
IF I WERE DICTATOR OF THE WORLD...
HEY, HEF!
EVERYONE WHO WOULDN'T SUBSCRIBE TO MY PHILOSOPHY WOULD BE SHIPPED OFF TO LEISURE CAMPS FOR REINDOCTRINATION!

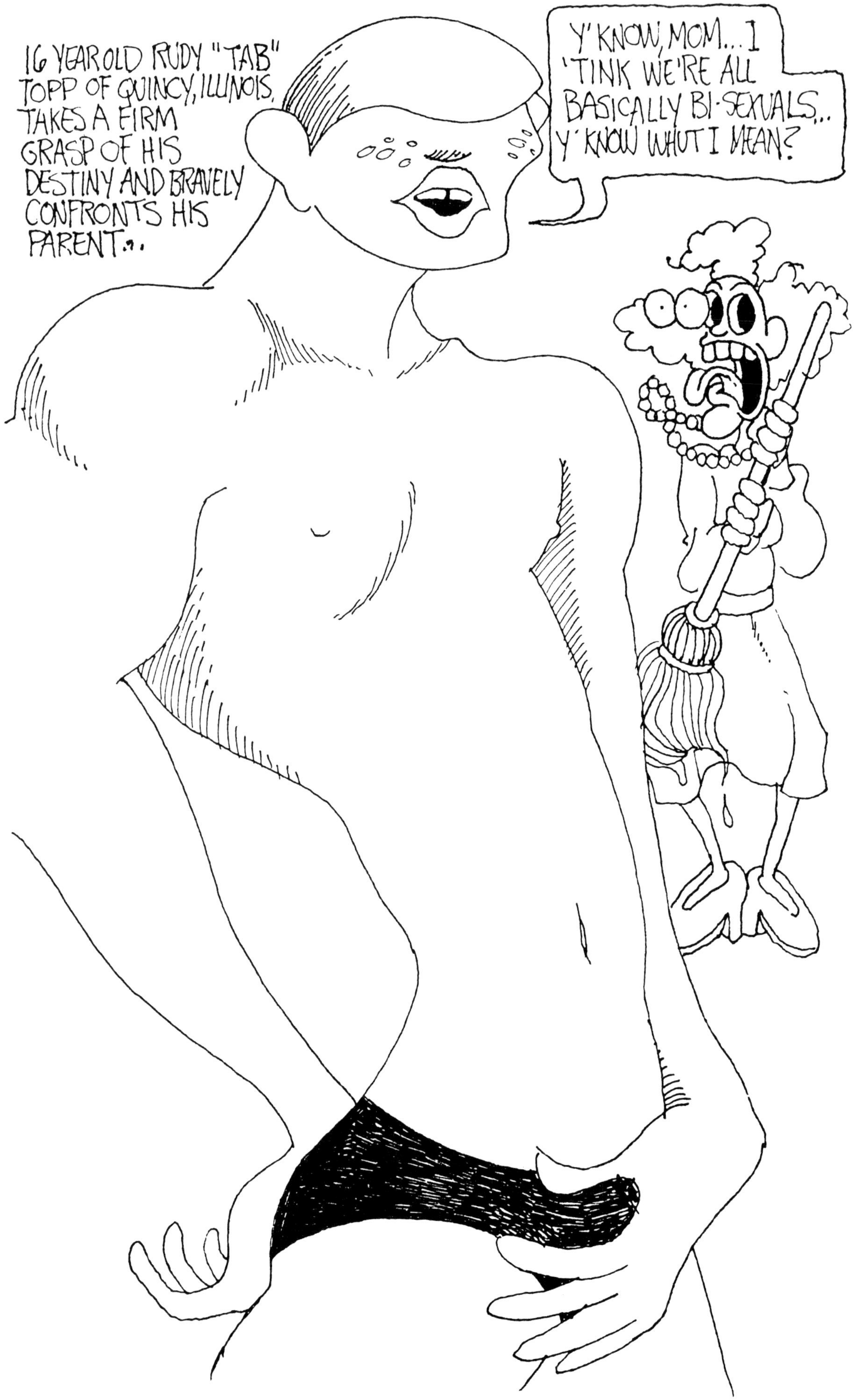
16 YEAR OLD RUDY "TAB" TOPP OF QUINCY, ILLINOIS, TAKES A FIRM GRASP OF HIS DESTINY AND BRAVELY CONFRONTS HIS PARENT...
Y'KNOW, MOM... I 'TINK WE'RE ALL BASICALLY BI-SEXUALS... Y'KNOW WHUT I MEAN?

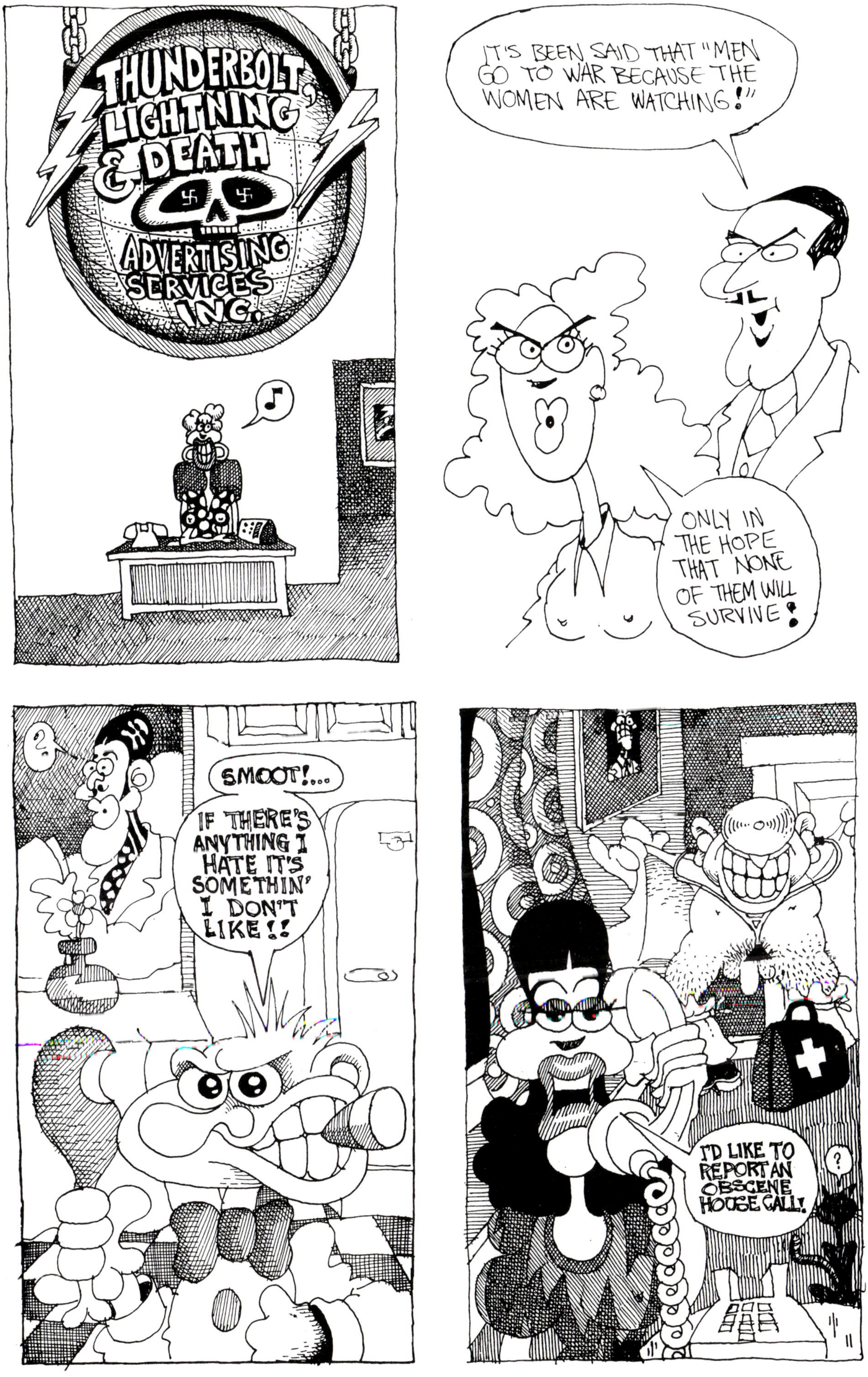
THUNDERBOLT, LIGHTNING & DEATH
ADVERTISING SERVICES INC.
IT'S BEEN SAID THAT "MEN GO TO WAR BECAUSE THE WOMEN ARE WATCHING!"
ONLY IN THE HOPE THAT NONE OF THEM WILL SURVIVE!
?
SMOOT!...
IF THERE'S ANYTHING I HATE IT'S SOMETHIN' I DON'T LIKE!!
I'D LIKE TO REPORT AN OBSCENE HOUSE CALL!
?

"You realize, of course, that this means inter-planetary conflict."

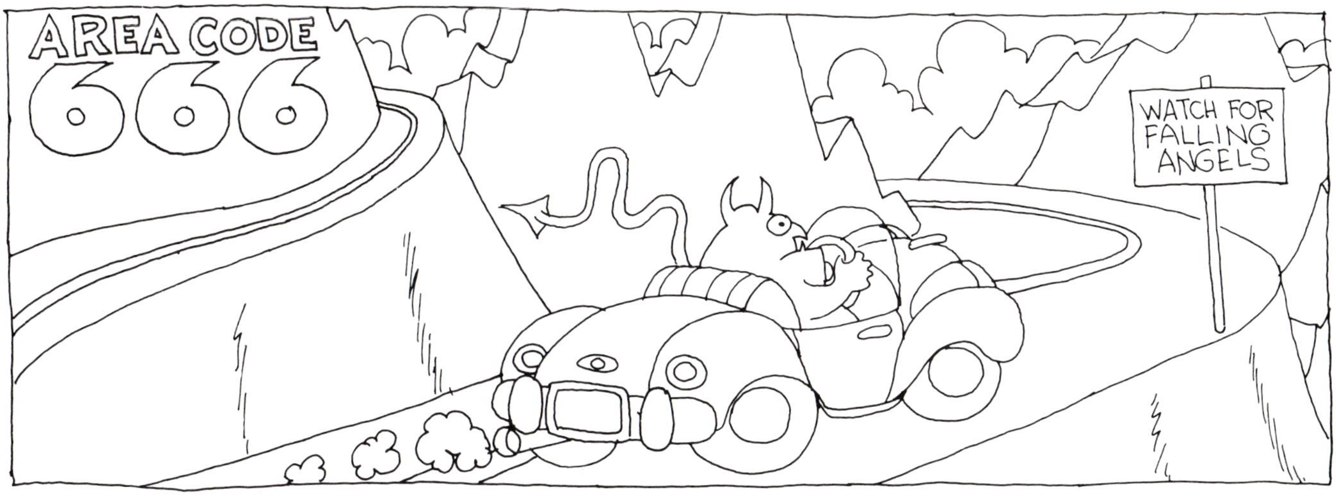
AREA CODE
666
WATCH FOR FALLING ANGELS

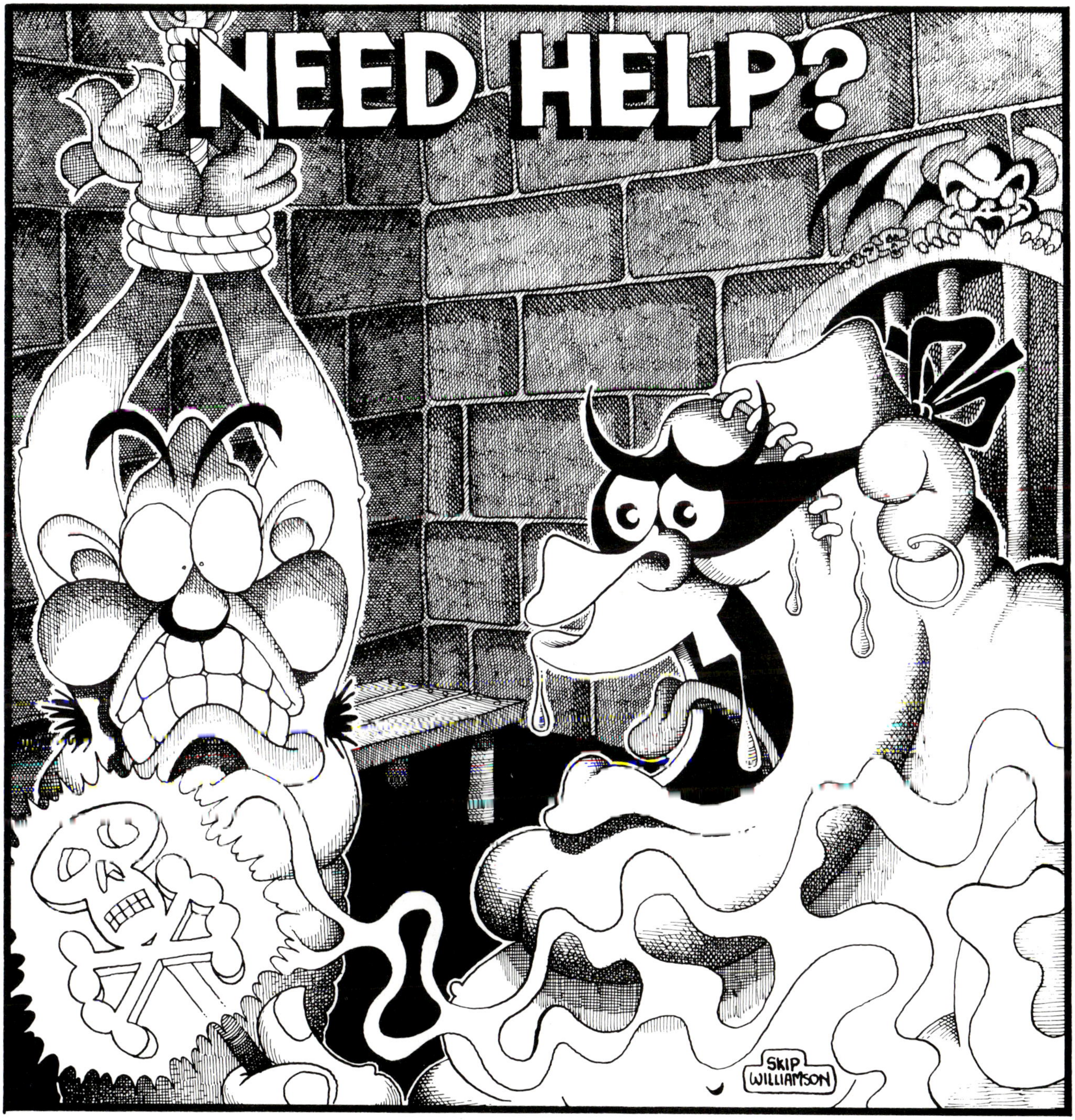
NEED HELP?
SKIP WILLIAMSON

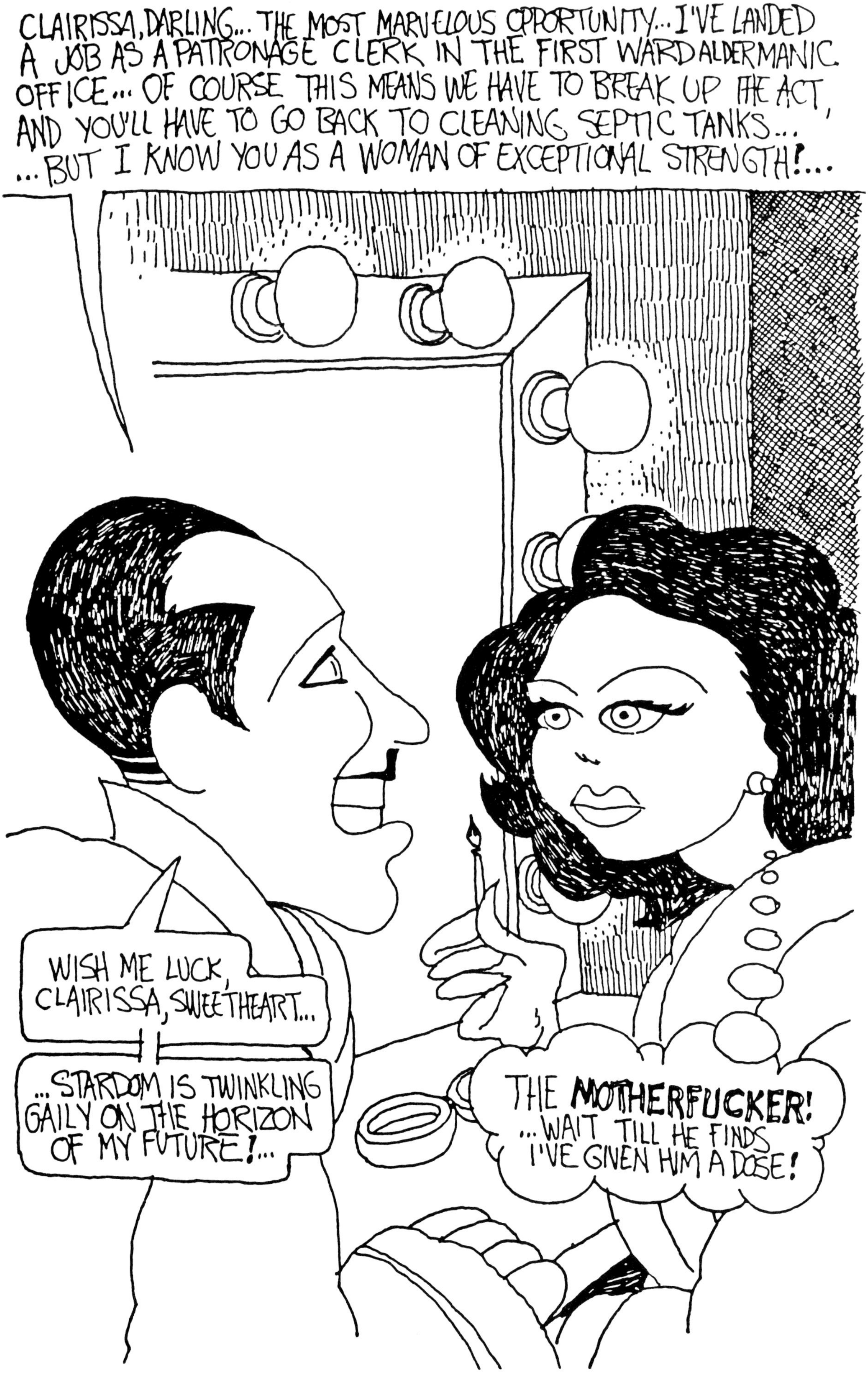
CLAIRISSA, DARLING... THE MOST MARVELOUS OPPORTUNITY... I'VE LANDED A JOB AS A PATRONAGE CLERK IN THE FIRST WARD ALDERMANIC OFFICE... OF COURSE THIS MEANS WE HAVE TO BREAK UP THE ACT, AND YOU'LL HAVE TO GO BACK TO CLEANING SEPTIC TANKS... ...BUT I KNOW YOU AS A WOMAN OF EXCEPTIONAL STRENGTH!...
WISH ME LUCK, CLAIRISSA, SWEETHEART...
...STARDOM IS TWINKLING GAILY ON THE HORIZON OF MY FUTURE!...
THE MOTHERFUCKER! ...WAIT TILL HE FINDS I'VE GIVEN HIM A DOSE!

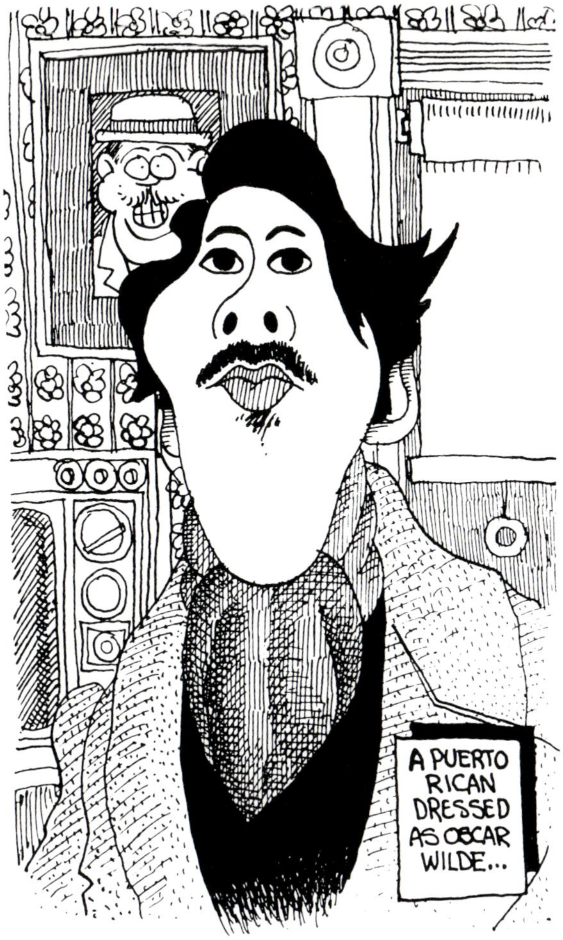
A PUERTO RICAN DRESSED AS OBCAR WILDE...

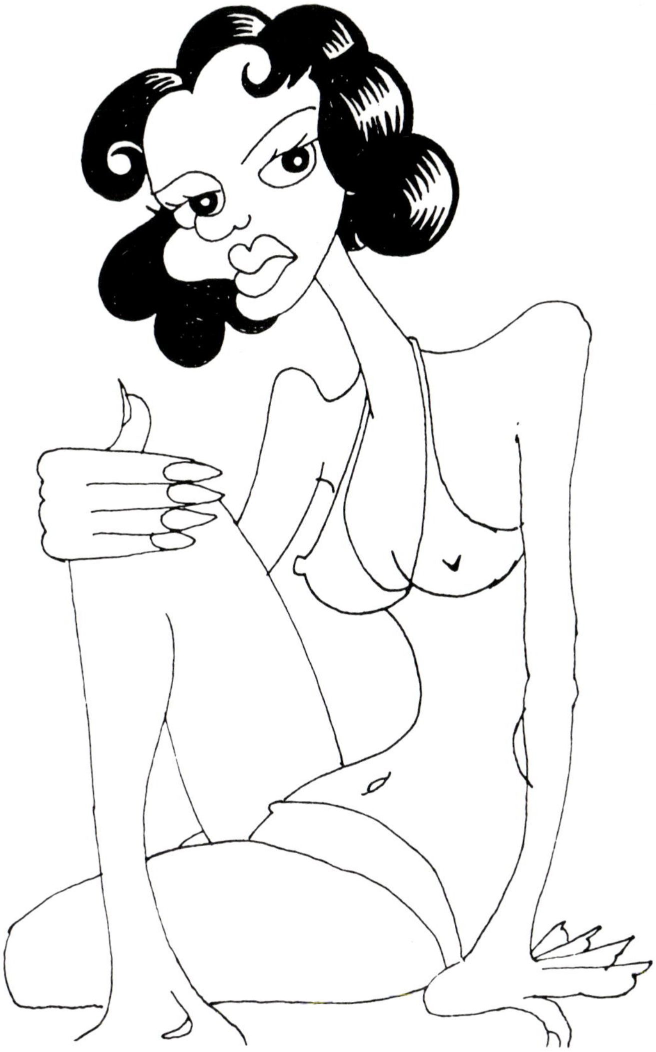

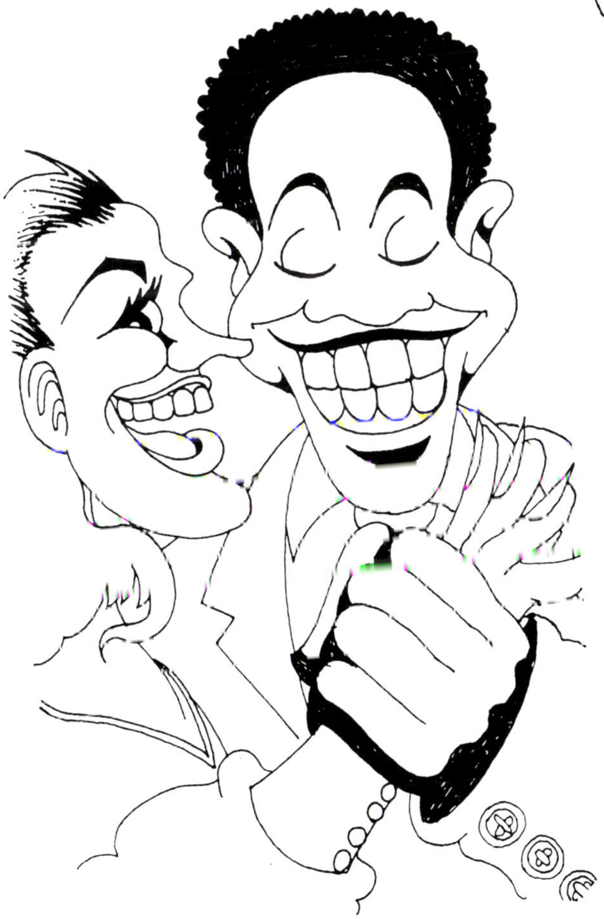

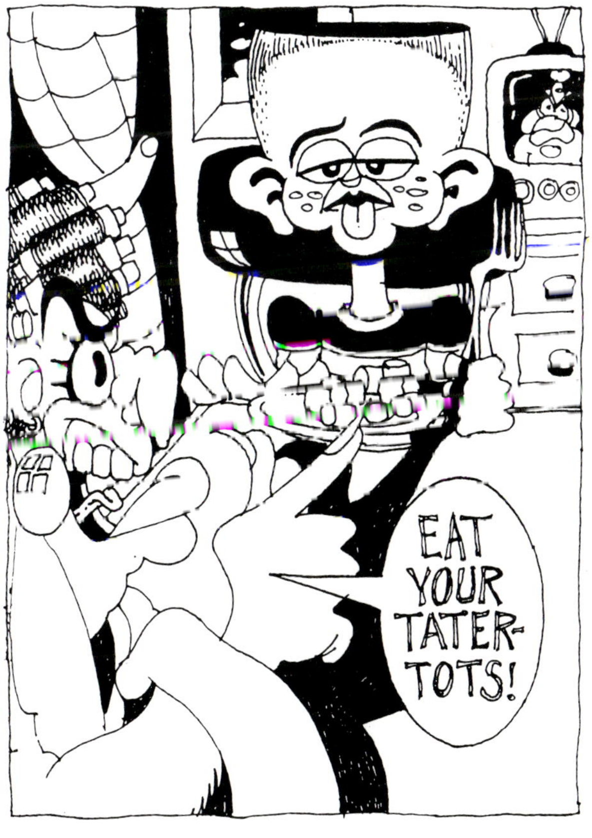
EAT YOUR TATER-TOTS!

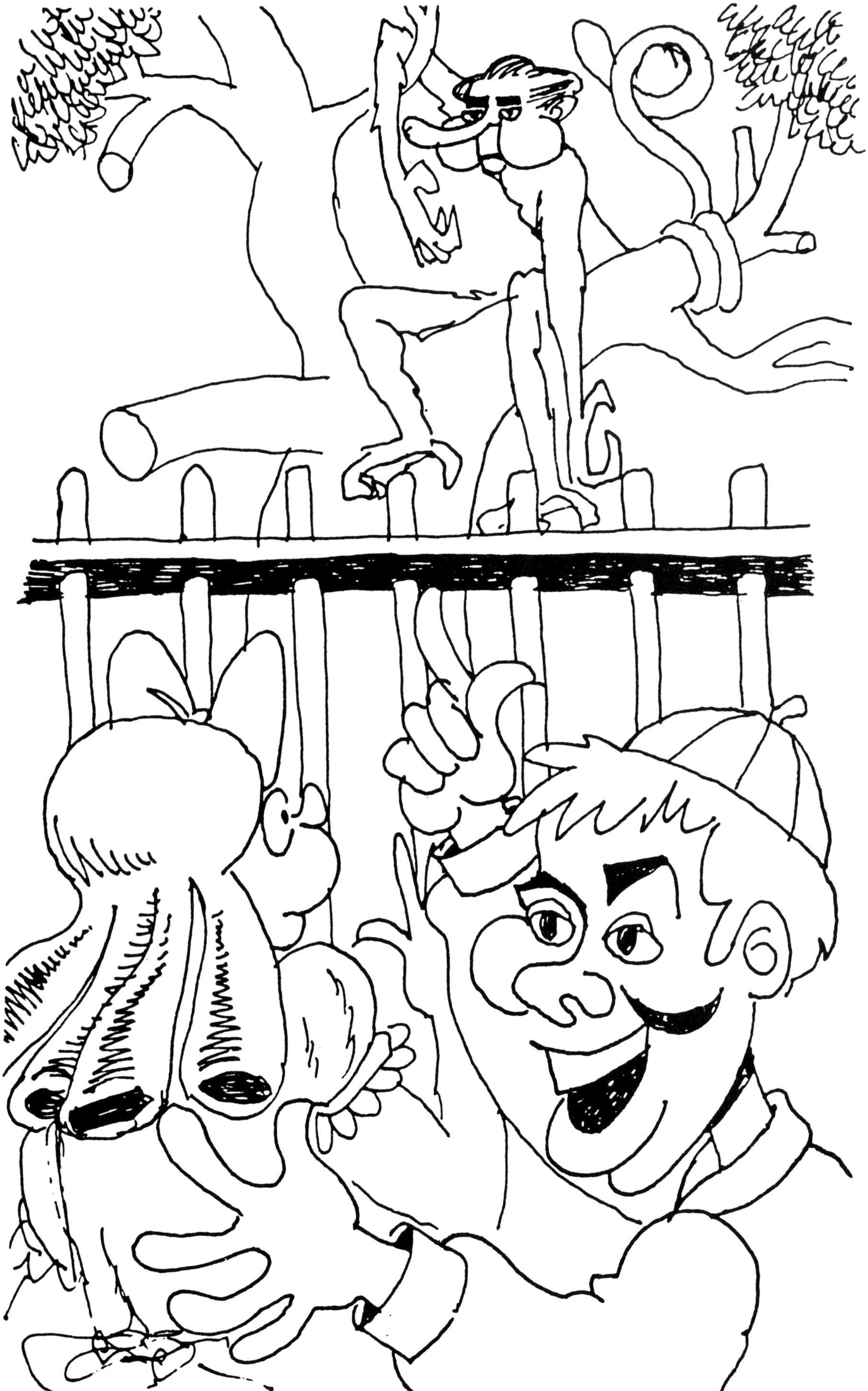

RICHARD NIXON

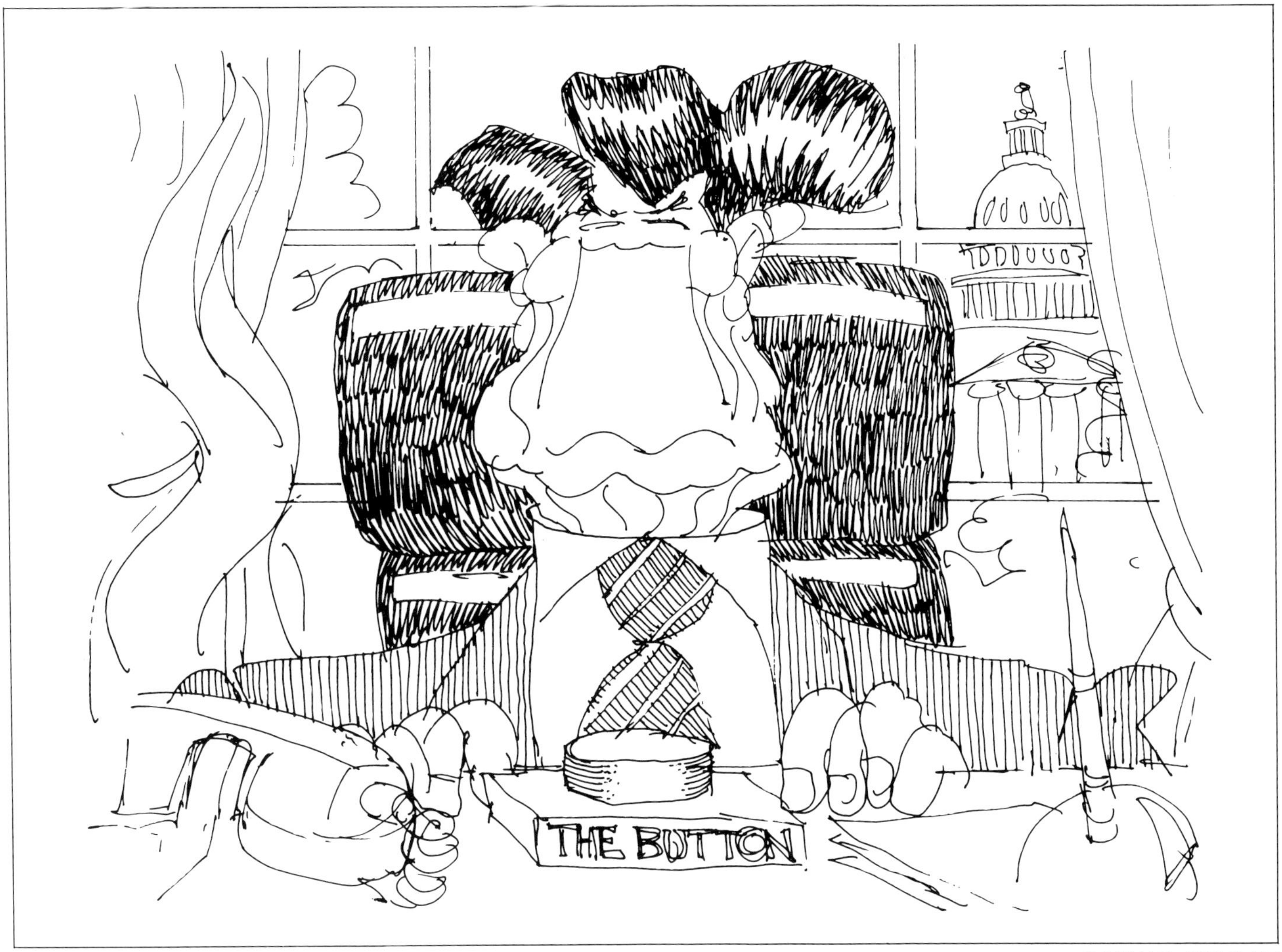
THE BUTTON

RONALD REAGAN

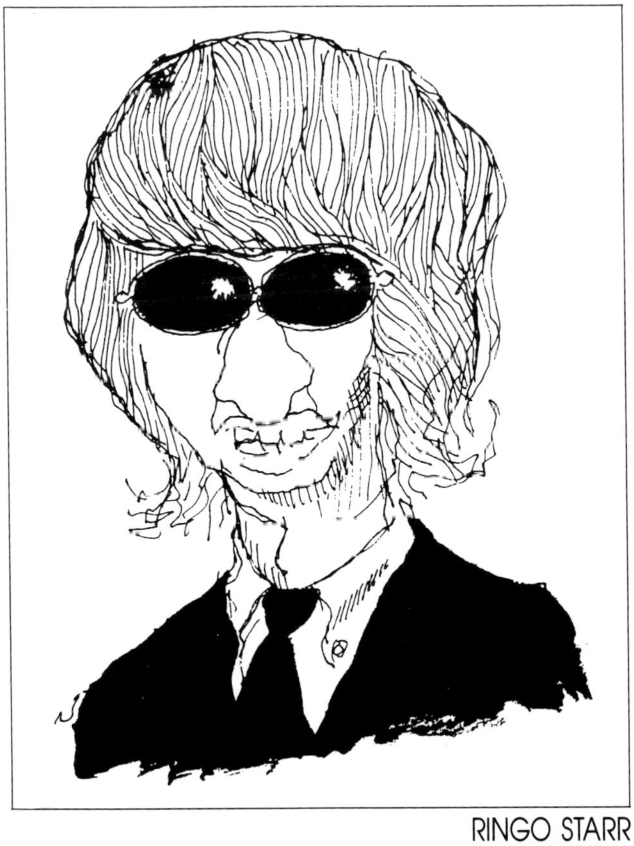

RINGO STARR

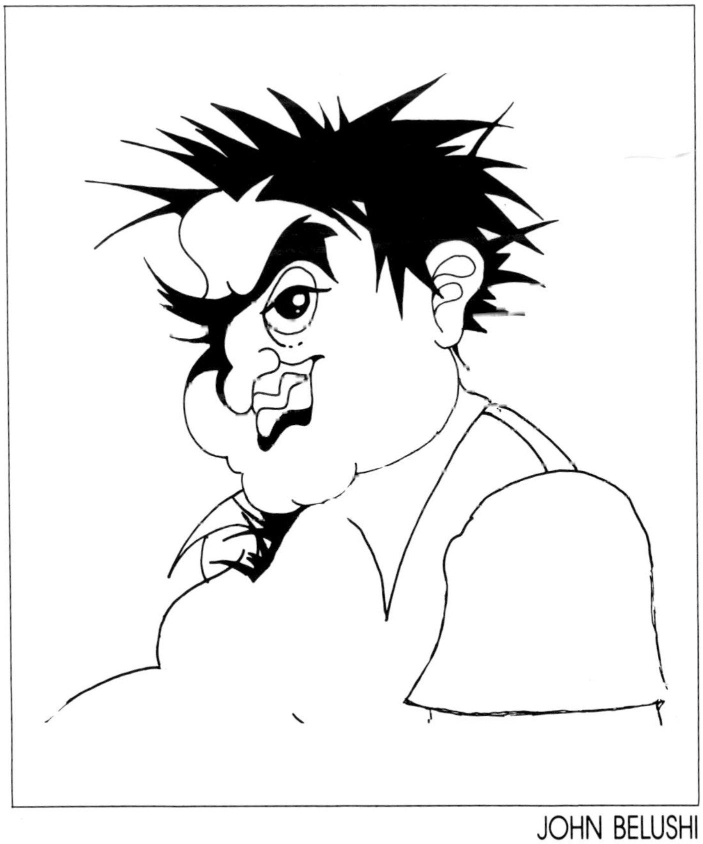

JOHN BELUSHI

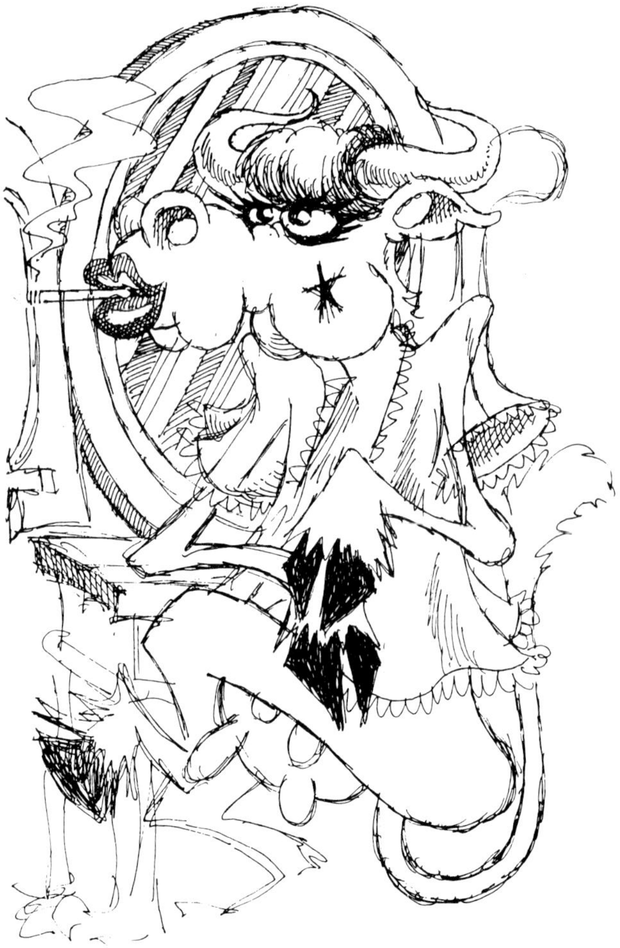
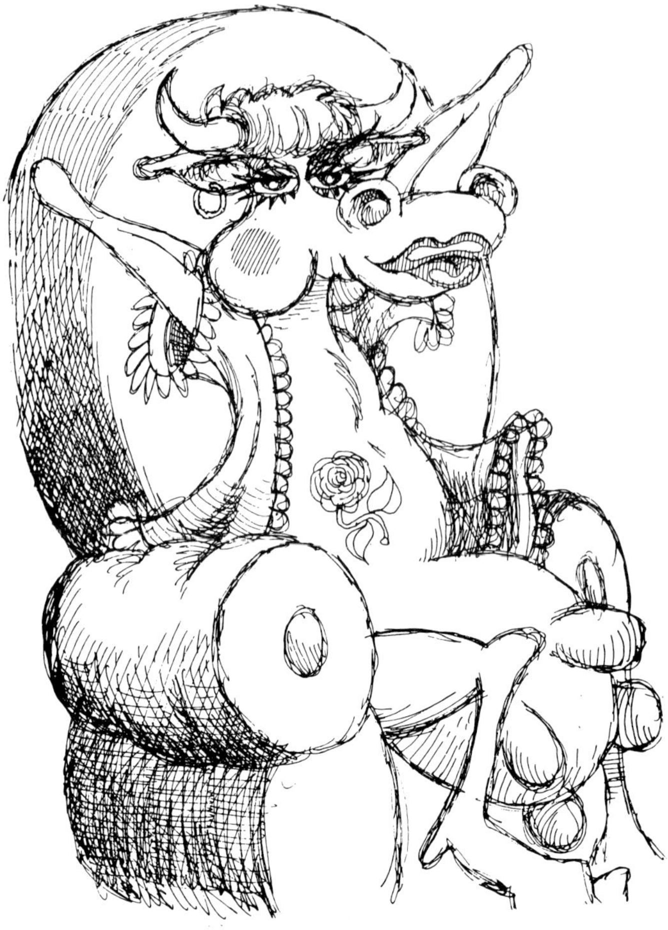
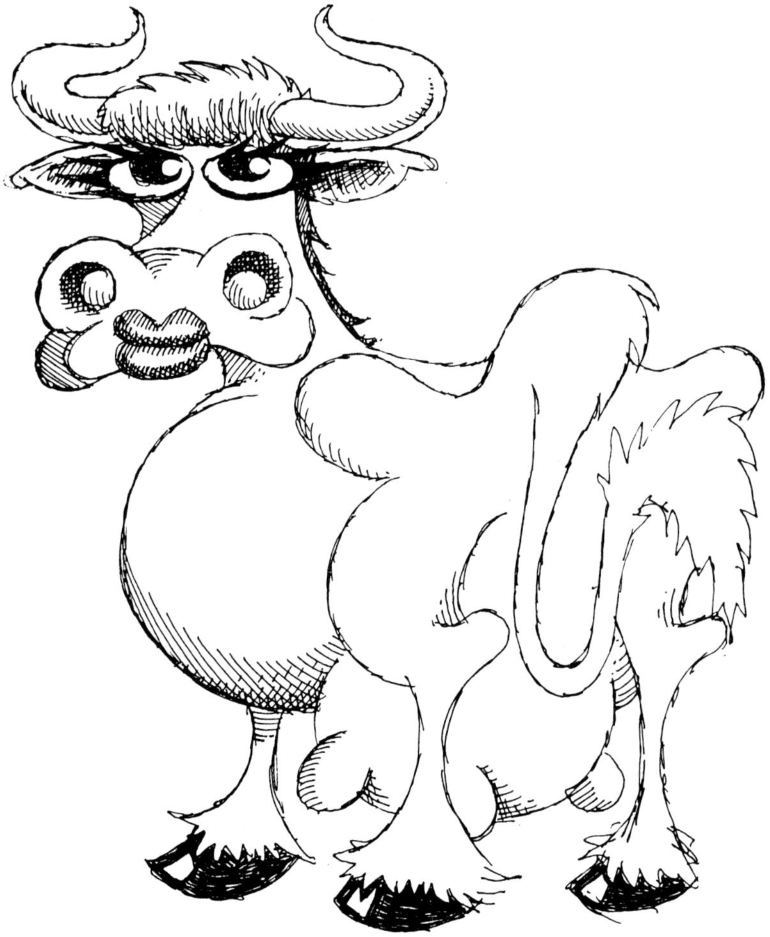

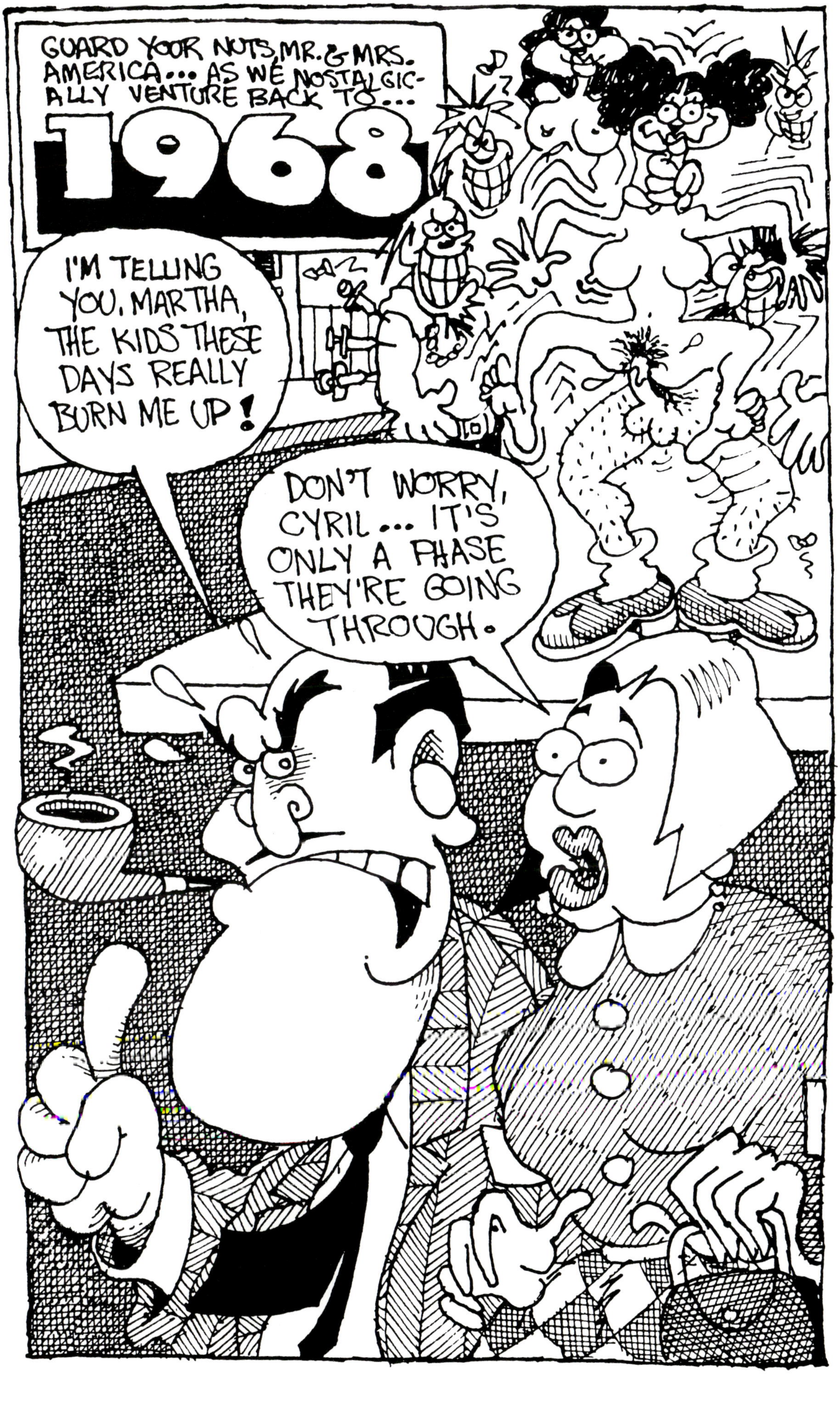
GUARD YOUR NUTS, MR. & MRS. AMERICA... AS WE NOSTALGICALLY VENTURE BACK TO...
1968
I'M TELLING YOU, MARTHA, THE KIDS THESE DAYS REALLY BURN ME UP!
DON'T WORRY, CYRIL... IT'S ONLY A PHASE THEY'RE GOING THROUGH.

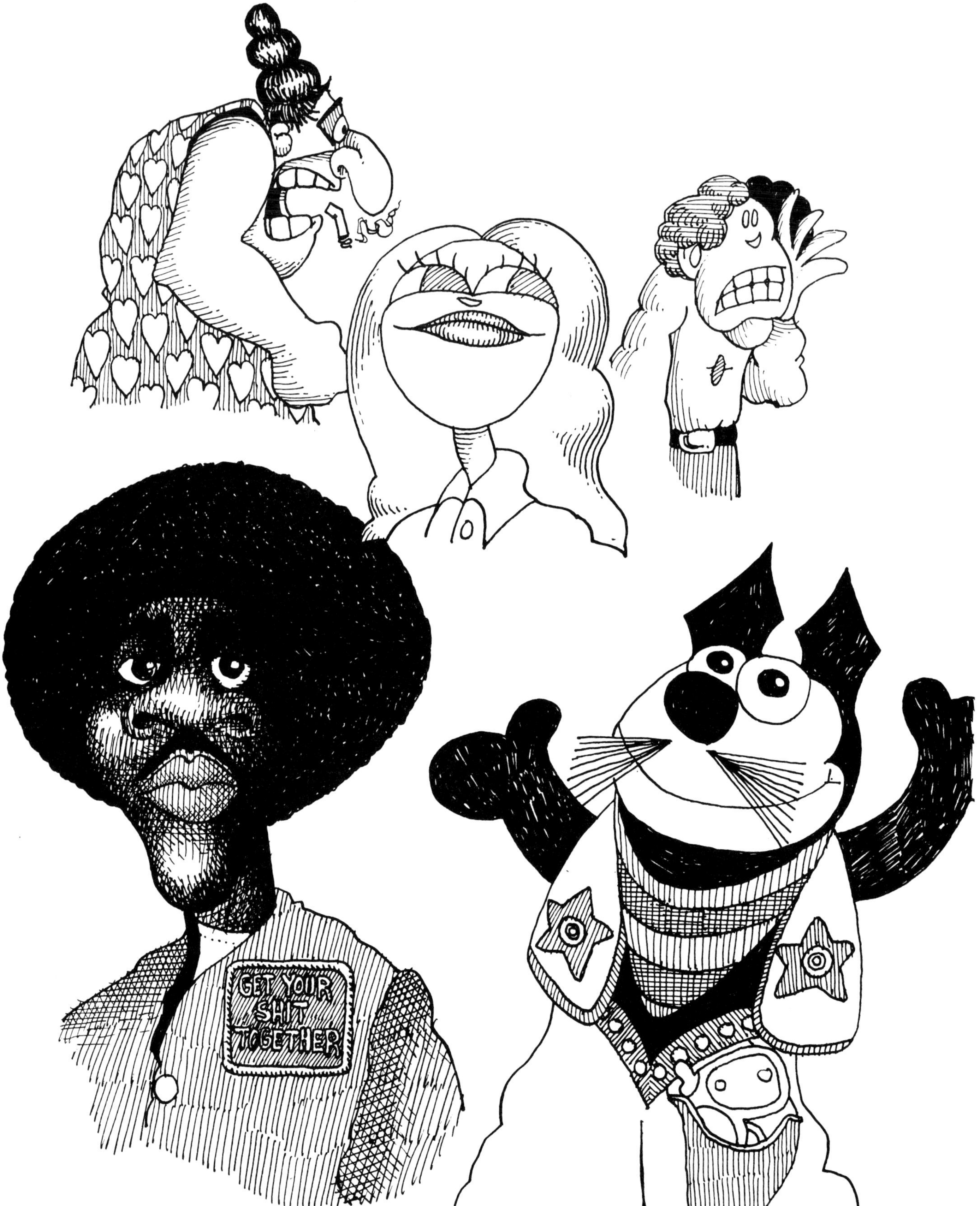
GET YOUR SHIT TOGETHER

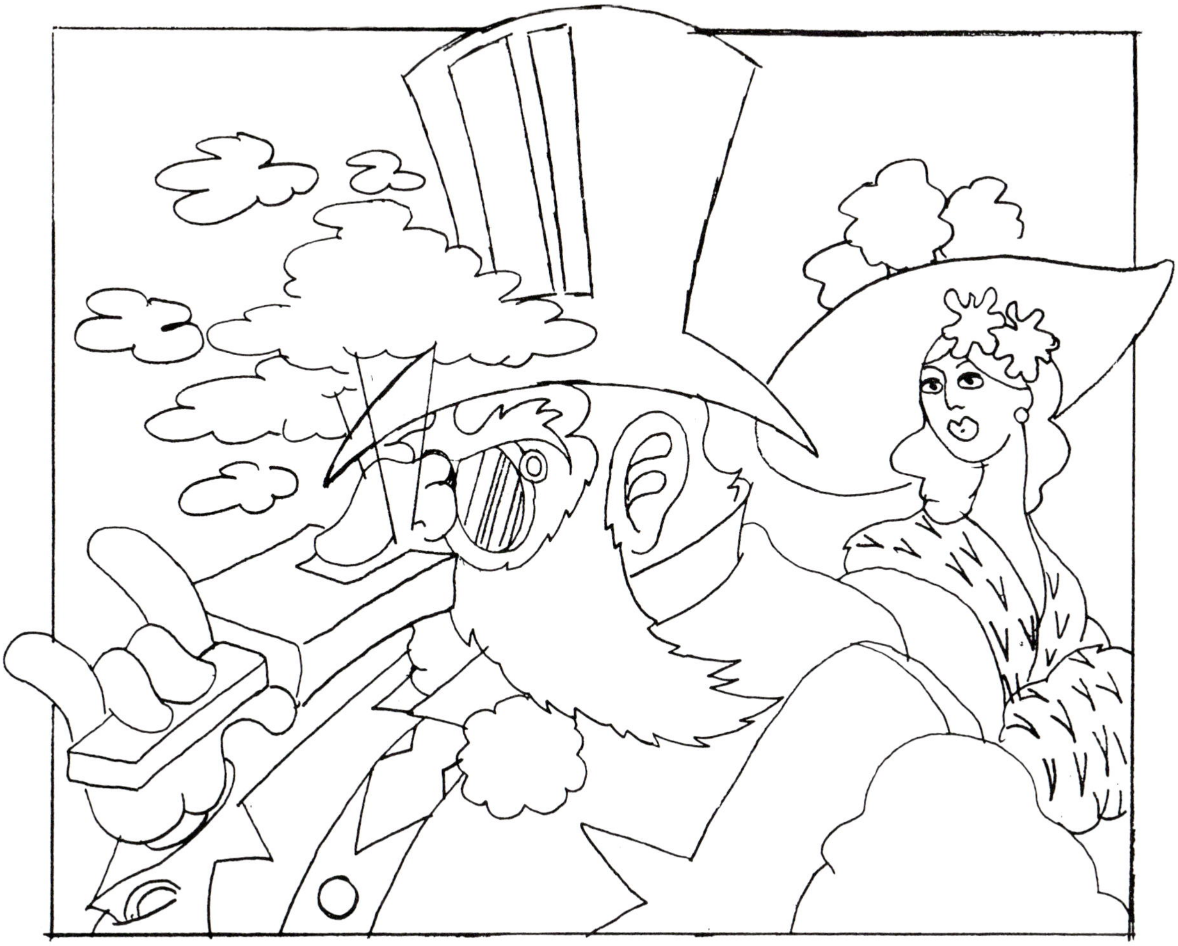

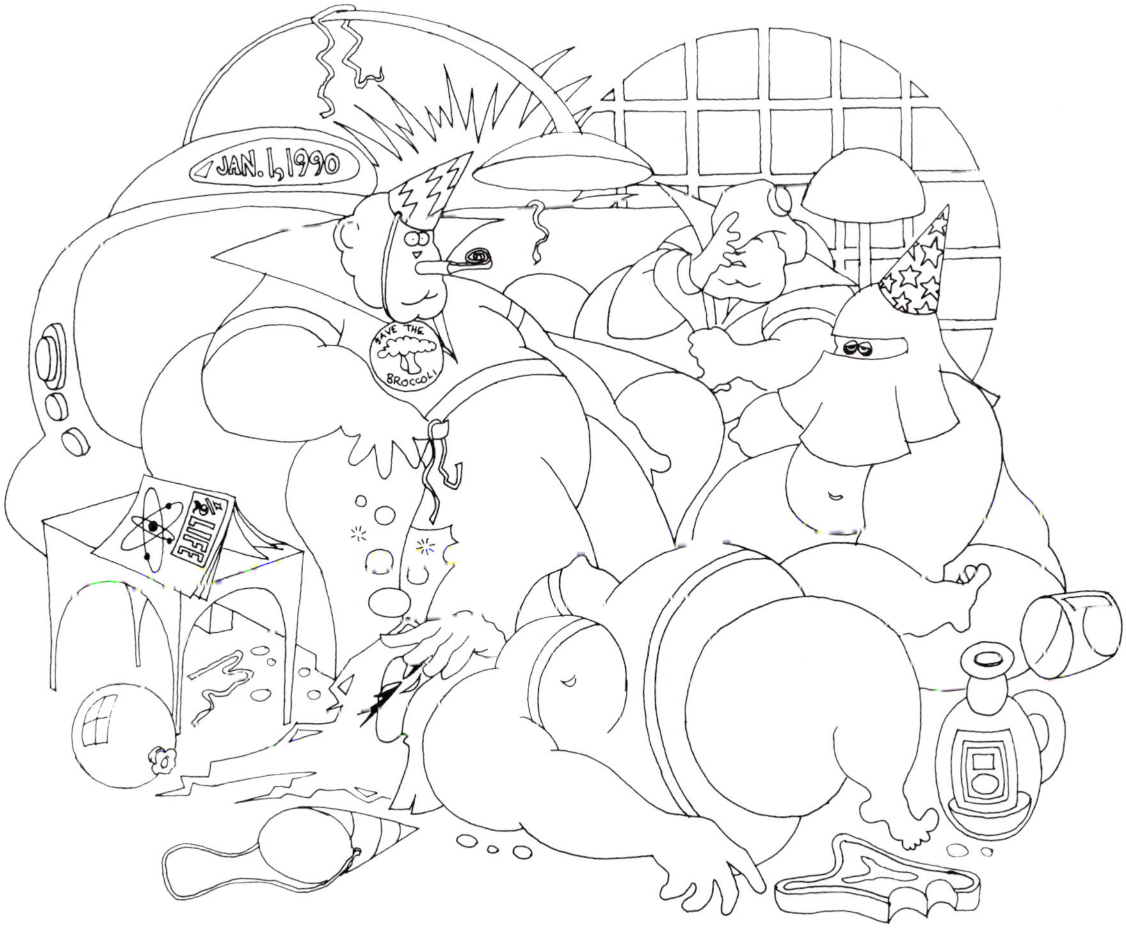
JAN. 1, 1990
SAVE THE BROCCOLI
LIFE

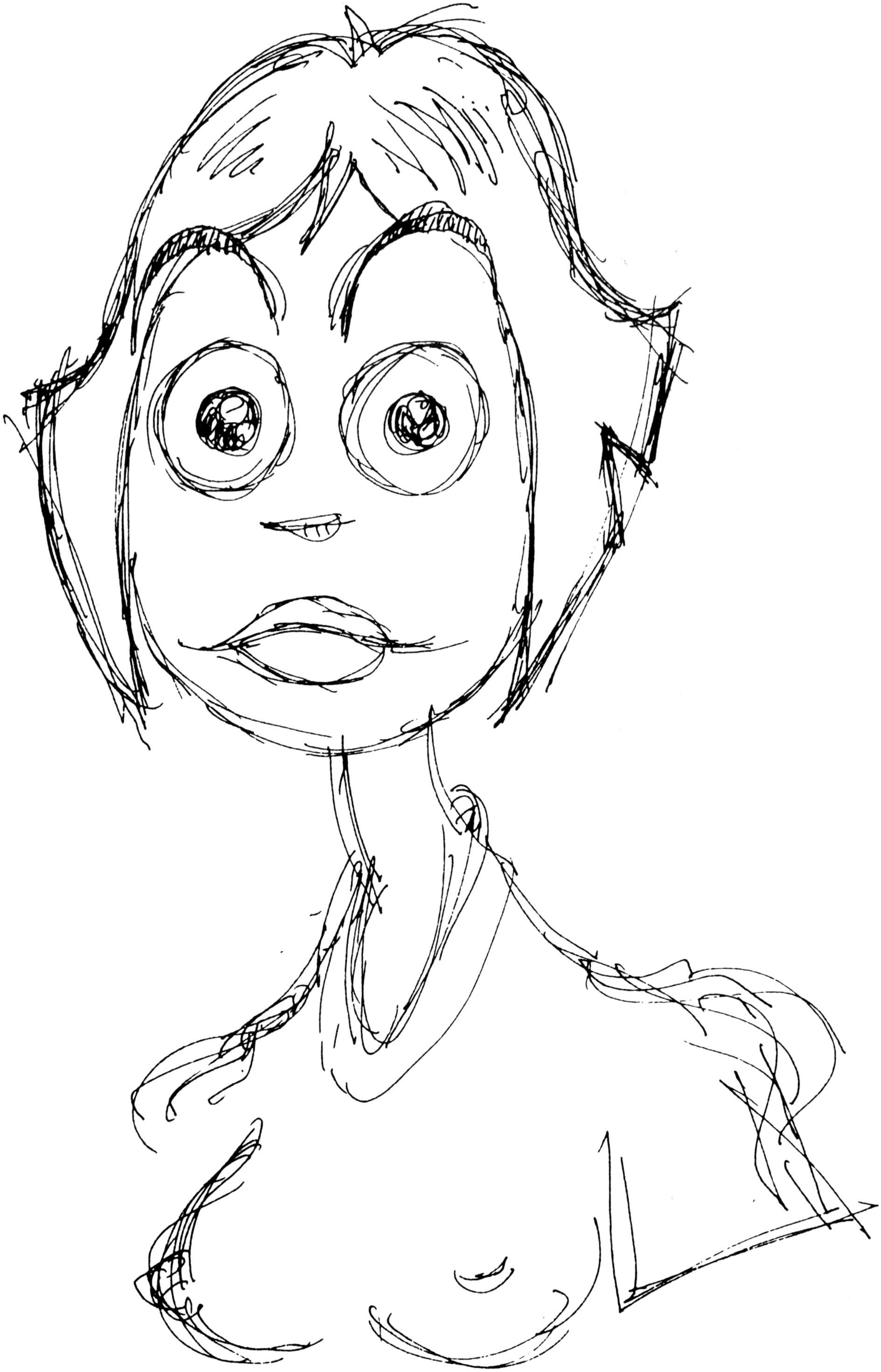

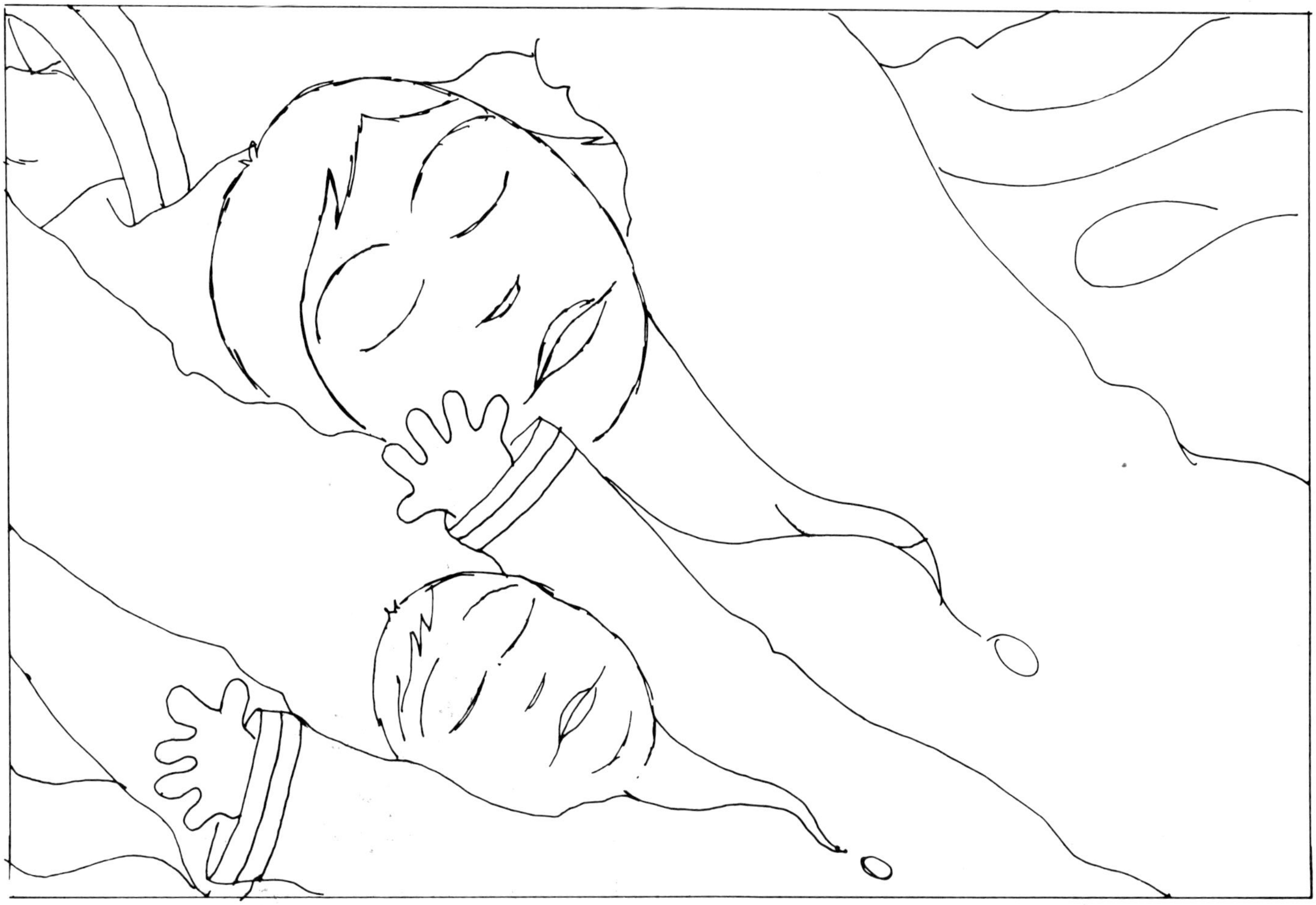

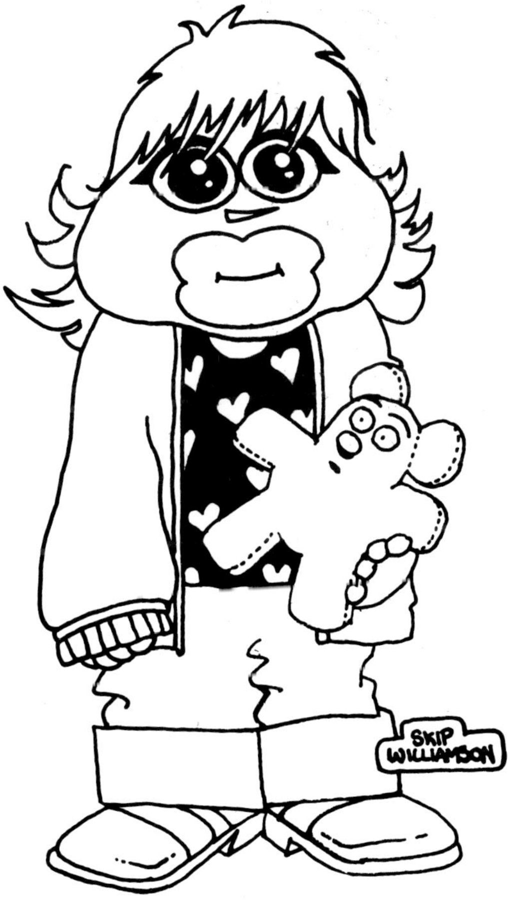
SKIP
WILLIAMSON

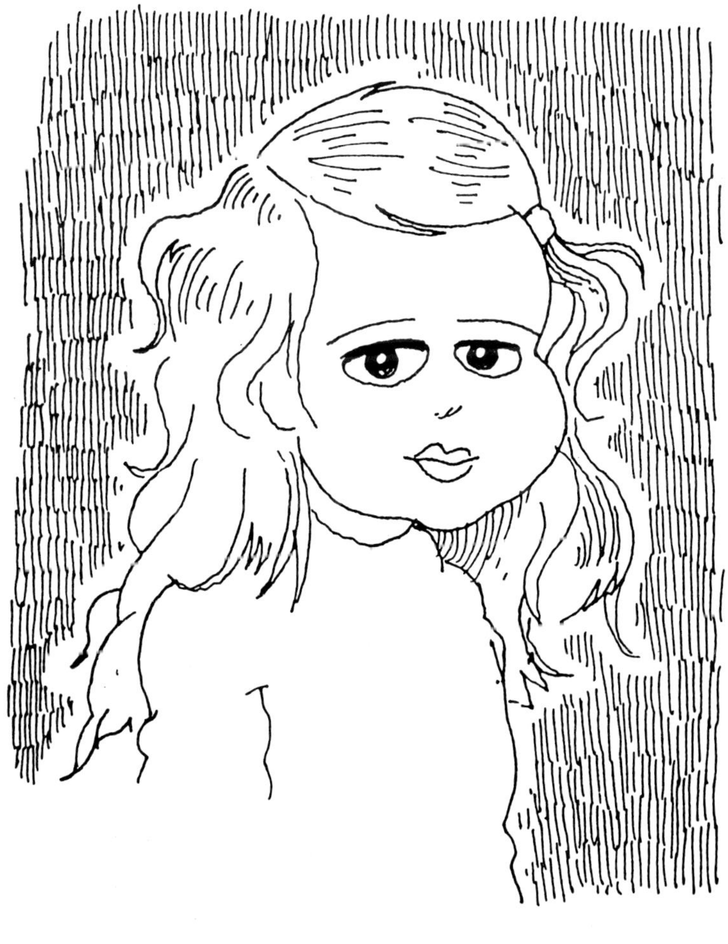

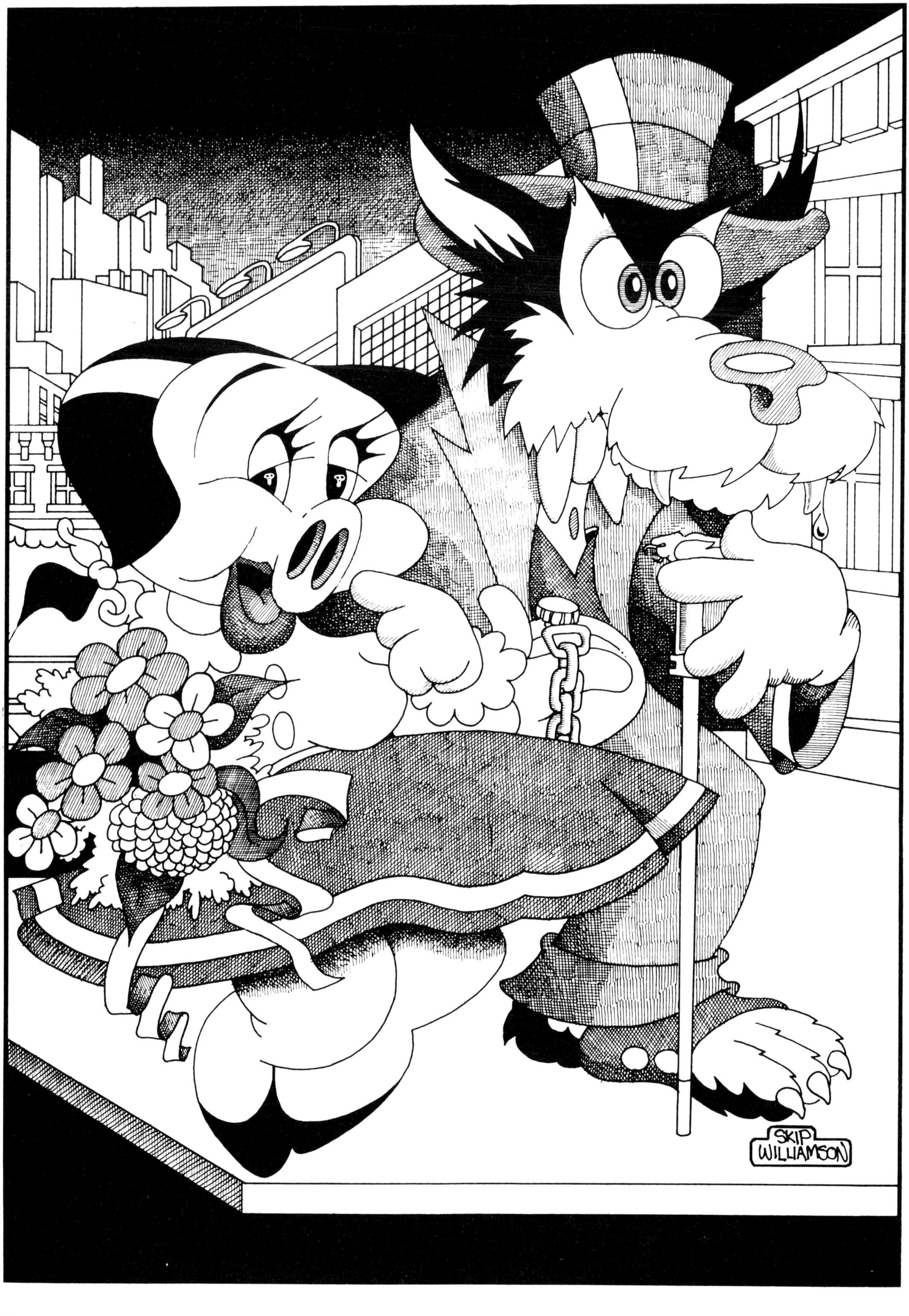
SKIP
WILLIAMSON

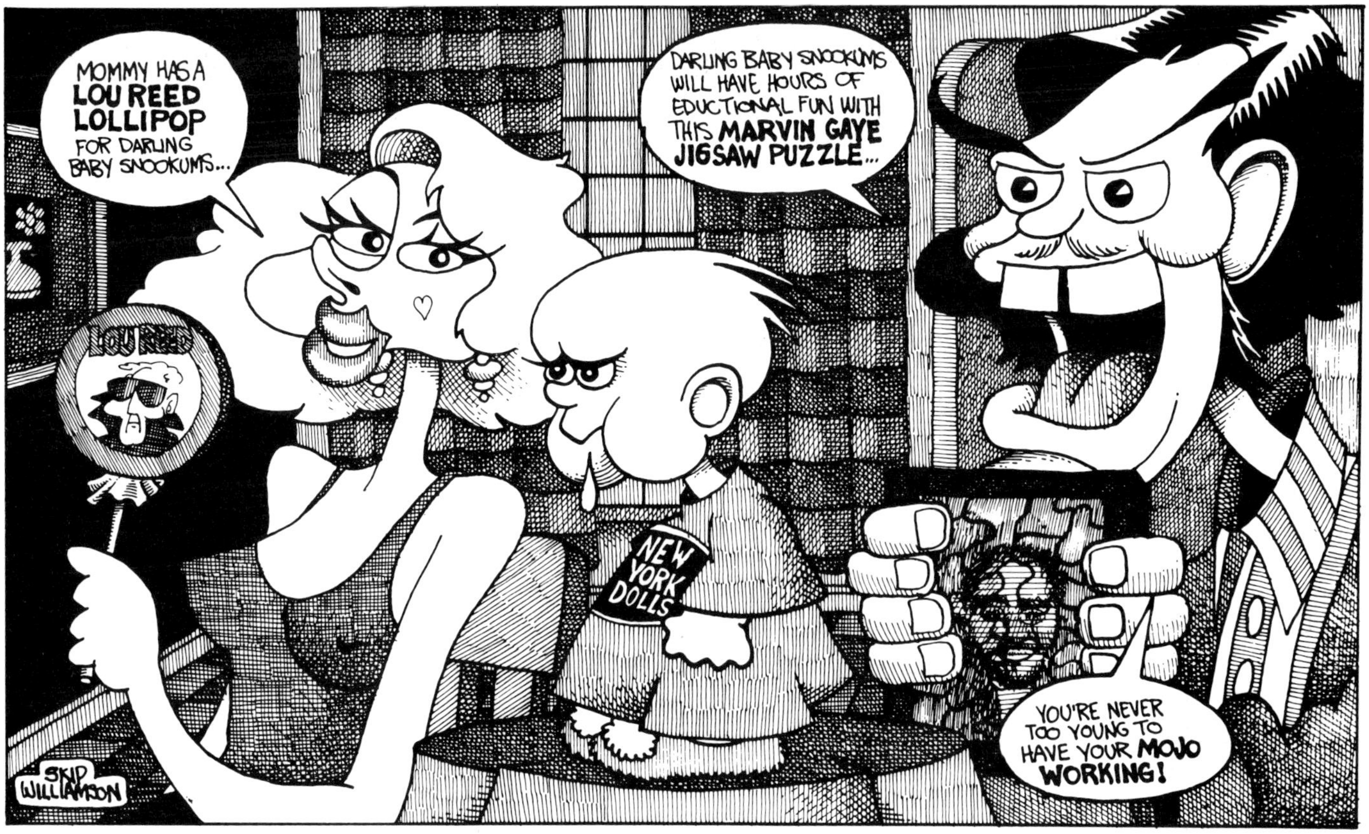
MOMMY HAS A LOU REED LOLLIPOP FOR DARLING BABY SNOOKUMS...
LOU REED
DARLING BABY SNOOKUMS WILL HAVE HOURS OF EDUCTIONAL FUN WITH THIS MARVIN GAYE JIGSAW PUZZLE...
NEW YORK DOLLS
YOU'RE NEVER TOO YOUNG TO HAVE YOUR MOJO WORKING!
SKIP WILLIAMSON

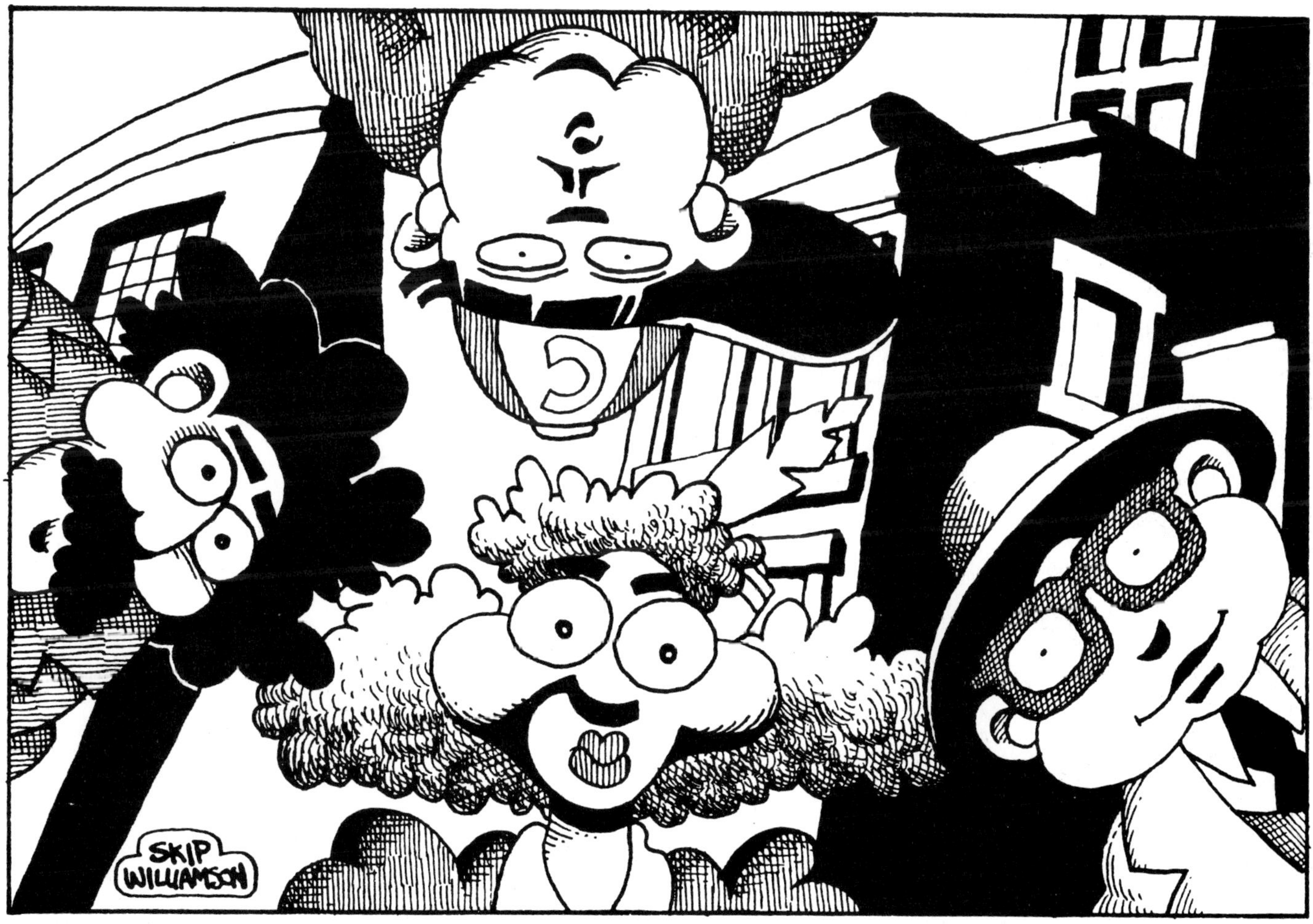
SKIP WILLIAMSON

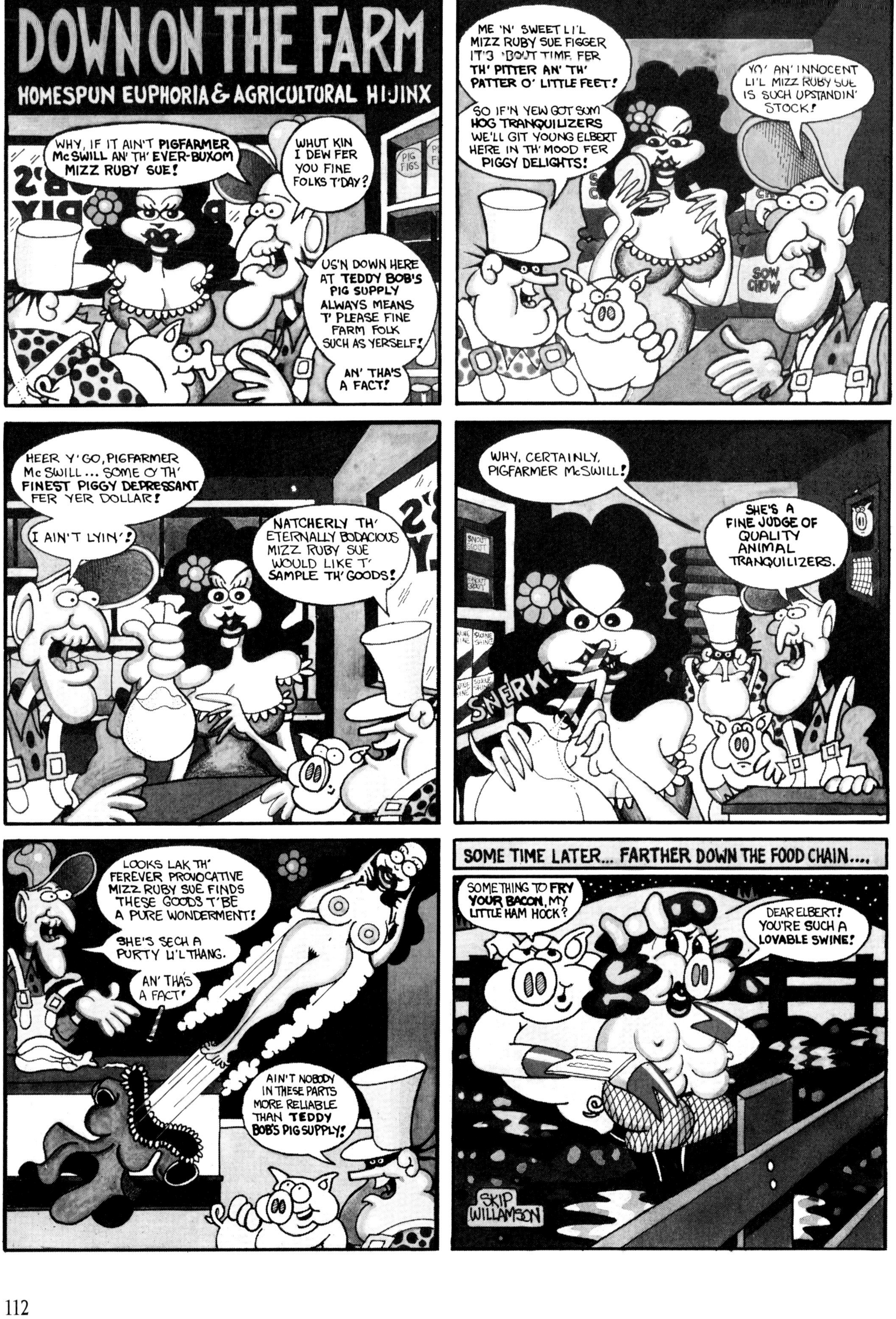
DOWN ON THE FARM
HOMESPUN EUPHORIA & AGRICULTURAL HI-JINX
WHY, IF IT AIN'T PIGFARMER McSWILL AN' TH' EVER-BUXOM MIZZ RUBY SUE!
WHUT KIN I DEW FER YOU FINE FOLKS T'DAY?
US'N DOWN HERE AT TEDDY BOB'S PIG SUPPLY ALWAYS MEANS T' PLEASE FINE FARM FOLK SUCH AS YERSELF!
AN' THA'S A FACT!
ME 'N' SWEET LI'L MIZZ RUBY SUE FIGGER IT'S 'BOUT TIME FER TH' PITTER AN' TH' PATTER O' LITTLE FEET!
SO IF'N YEW GOT SOM HOG TRANQUILIZERS WE'LL GIT YOUNG ELBERT HERE IN TH' MOOD FER PIGGY DELIGHTS!
YO' AN' INNOCENT LI'L MIZZ RUBY SUE IS SUCH UPSTANDIN' STOCK!
SOW CHOW
HEER Y' GO, PIGFARMER McSWILL ... SOME O' TH' FINEST PIGGY DEPRESSANT FER YER DOLLAR!
I AIN'T LYIN'!
NATCHERLY TH' ETERNALLY BODACIOUS MIZZ RUBY SUE WOULD LIKE T' SAMPLE TH' GOODS!
WHY, CERTAINLY, PIGFARMER McSWILL!
SHE'S A FINE JUDGE OF QUALITY ANIMAL TRANQUILIZERS.
SNERK!
LOOKS LAK TH' FEREVER PROVOCATIVE MIZZ RUBY SUE FINDS THESE GOODS T' BE A PURE WONDERMENT!
SHE'S SECH A PURTY LI'L THANG.
AN' THA'S A FACT!
AIN'T NOBODY IN THESE PARTS MORE RELIABLE THAN TEDDY BOB'S PIG SUPPLY!
SOME TIME LATER... FARTHER DOWN THE FOOD CHAIN....
SOMETHING TO FRY YOUR BACON, MY LITTLE HAM HOCK?
DEAR ELBERT! YOU'RE SUCH A LOVABLE SWINE!
SKIP WILLAMSON

SKIP WILLIAMSON'S **TOMORROW'S VENERY TODAY!**

HELLO, THERE... JUST PUTTING THE FINISHING TOUCHES ON MY LATEST INVENTION.

THE BRIGHT PROMISE OF THE FUTURE LOOMS TUMESCENT IN THE RESOURCEFUL INVENTOR'S PATH!

USE T'BE, I WOULD BE SATISFIED BY A FEW CLOSE FRIENDS, AN OUNCE OF REMARKABLE HERB AND A SUPER-8 PRINT OF 'NAZI RECTAL ROUNDUP'!...

...BUT NO MORE!

THESE ARE MODERN TIMES AND REQUIRE MODERN SOLUTIONS TO OUR PRIMAL DILEMMA!

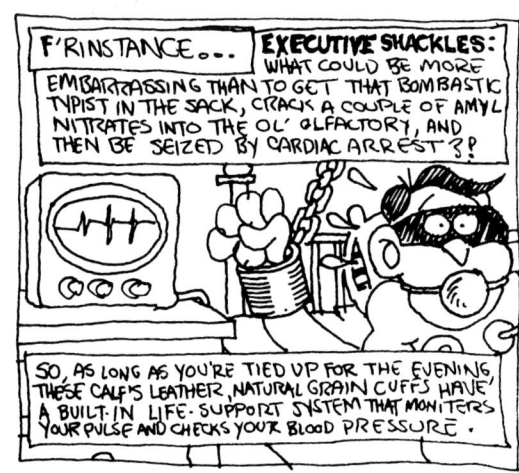

F'RINSTANCE... **EXECUTIVE SHACKLES:** WHAT COULD BE MORE EMBARRASSING THAN TO GET THAT BOMBASTIC TYPIST IN THE SACK, CRACK A COUPLE OF AMYL NITRATES INTO THE OL' OLFACTORY, AND THEN BE SEIZED BY CARDIAC ARREST?!

SO, AS LONG AS YOU'RE TIED UP FOR THE EVENING, THESE CALF'S LEATHER, NATURAL GRAIN CUFFS HAVE A BUILT-IN LIFE-SUPPORT SYSTEM THAT MONITERS YOUR PULSE AND CHECKS YOUR BLOOD PRESSURE.

PERSONALITY DILDOS: SCULPTED LIKENESSES OF YOUR FAVORITE MEDIA PRICK.

THE AYATOLLAH KHOMEINE — TENG HSIAO-P'ING — STEVE MARTIN

FOR YOU ANAL COMPULSIVES RECTAL STIMULATORS IN THE LIKENESSES OF THE VILLAGE PEOPLE, AVAILABLE IN A LEATHER-STUDDED BOXED SET.

COMBINATION ROACH CLIP AND BIRTH CONTROL DEVICE:

AVAILABLE IN DURABLE THREE-PLY CONDOM OR IUD COIL, DEPENDING ON PREFERENCE.

OBSCENE TELEPHONE ANSWERING MACHINE: SUGGEST THAT COLLECTION AGENCIES EAT YOUR SHORTS. GRAPHICALLY DESCRIBE YOUR THROBBING MANHOOD UNTIL THE 'BEEP'.

I'M SORRY I'M OUT OF THE OFFICE AT THE MOMENT... HOWEVER, BE REST ASSURED THAT IT WOULD GIVE ME VENT TO STUFF A RIDGID APPENDAGE INTO YOUR PENNY LOAFERS!

THE QUAZAR COCK RING:

HAVE A NICE DAY

WITH CHOICE OF ENDEARING READ-OUT: "HAVE A NICE DAY", "I LOVE YOU", AND "WHAT'S YOUR SIGN?".

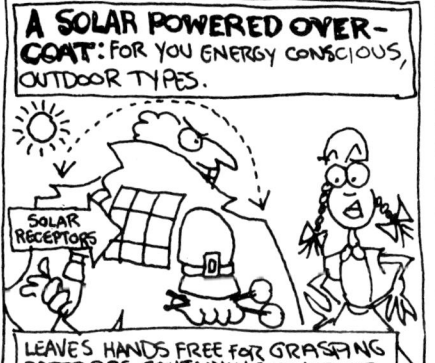

A SOLAR POWERED OVERCOAT: FOR YOU ENERGY CONSCIOUS, OUTDOOR TYPES.

SOLAR RECEPTORS

LEAVES HANDS FREE FOR GRASPING PAPER BAG CONTAINING FAVORITE BEVERAGE OR LOLLIPOPS FOR THE YOUNGSTERS.

INDESTRUCTIBLE CROTCHLESS PANTIES: EMBARRASSED BY DACRON THREAD BETWEEN YOUR MOLARS WHEN YOU HAVE YOUR TEETH CLEANED?

THESE SCANTIES WILL HOLD UP TO ALL MANNER OF LASCIVIOUS EXCESS. LIGHTWEIGHT DURABLE FABRIC DESIGNED BY NASA SCIENTISTS. SAME AS WORN BY OUR MEN IN SPACE.

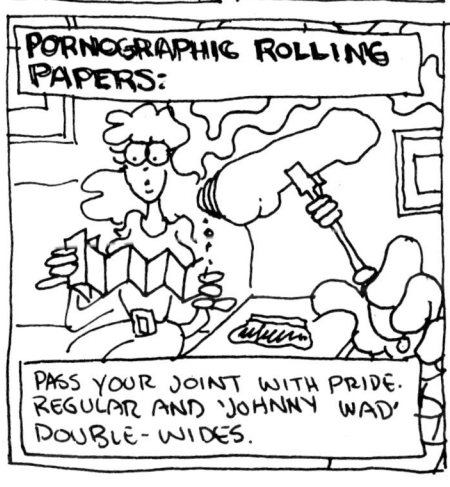

PORNOGRAPHIC ROLLING PAPERS:

PASS YOUR JOINT WITH PRIDE. REGULAR AND 'JOHNNY WAD' DOUBLE-WIDES.

COMBINATION QUAALUDE AND BIRTH CONTROL PILL:

BETTER LOVING THROUGH CHEMISTRY. KILL TWO BIRDS WITH ONE STONE.

DIRTY WORD PROCESSOR: TURN ON THE JUICE AND STEAM UP YOUR CIRCUITS WHILE EXERCISING YOUR FIRST AMENDMENT RIGHTS.

BEAT ME.... FUCK ME... EAT MY MICROCHIPS

AND YOU CALVINISTS OUT THERE SHOULD REMEMBER...

...YOU DON'T VIOLATE THE LAWS OF PHYSICS BY HAVING A SOMNOLENT SHEEP AND VIDEO TAPING EQUIPMENT IN YOUR MOTEL ROOM...

...ONLY A COUPLE OF CITY ORDINANCES IN CLEVELAND!

113

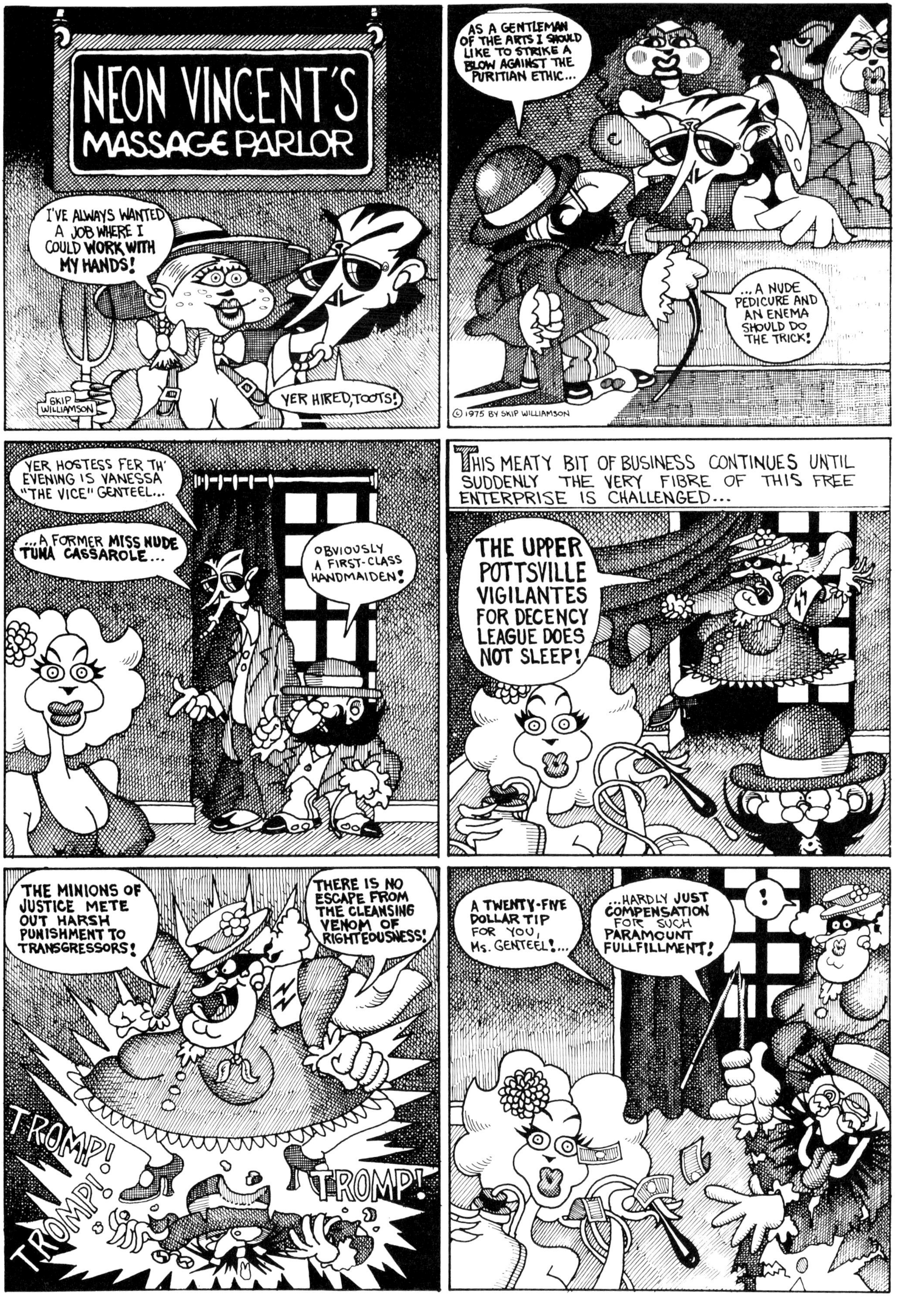
NEON VINCENT'S MASSAGE PARLOR
I'VE ALWAYS WANTED A JOB WHERE I COULD WORK WITH MY HANDS!
YER HIRED, TOOTS!
SKIP WILLIAMSON
AS A GENTLEMAN OF THE ARTS I SHOULD LIKE TO STRIKE A BLOW AGAINST THE PURITIAN ETHIC...
...A NUDE PEDICURE AND AN ENEMA SHOULD DO THE TRICK!
© 1975 BY SKIP WILLIAMSON
YER HOSTESS FER TH' EVENING IS VANESSA "THE VICE" GENTEEL...
...A FORMER MISS NUDE TUNA CASSAROLE...
OBVIOUSLY A FIRST-CLASS HANDMAIDEN!
THIS MEATY BIT OF BUSINESS CONTINUES UNTIL SUDDENLY THE VERY FIBRE OF THIS FREE ENTERPRISE IS CHALLENGED...
THE UPPER POTTSVILLE VIGILANTES FOR DECENCY LEAGUE DOES NOT SLEEP!
THE MINIONS OF JUSTICE METE OUT HARSH PUNISHMENT TO TRANSGRESSORS!
THERE IS NO ESCAPE FROM THE CLEANSING VENOM OF RIGHTEOUSNESS!
TROMP! TROMP! TROMP!
A TWENTY-FIVE DOLLAR TIP FOR YOU, Ms. GENTEEL!...
...HARDLY JUST COMPENSATION FOR SUCH PARAMOUNT FULLFILLMENT!
!

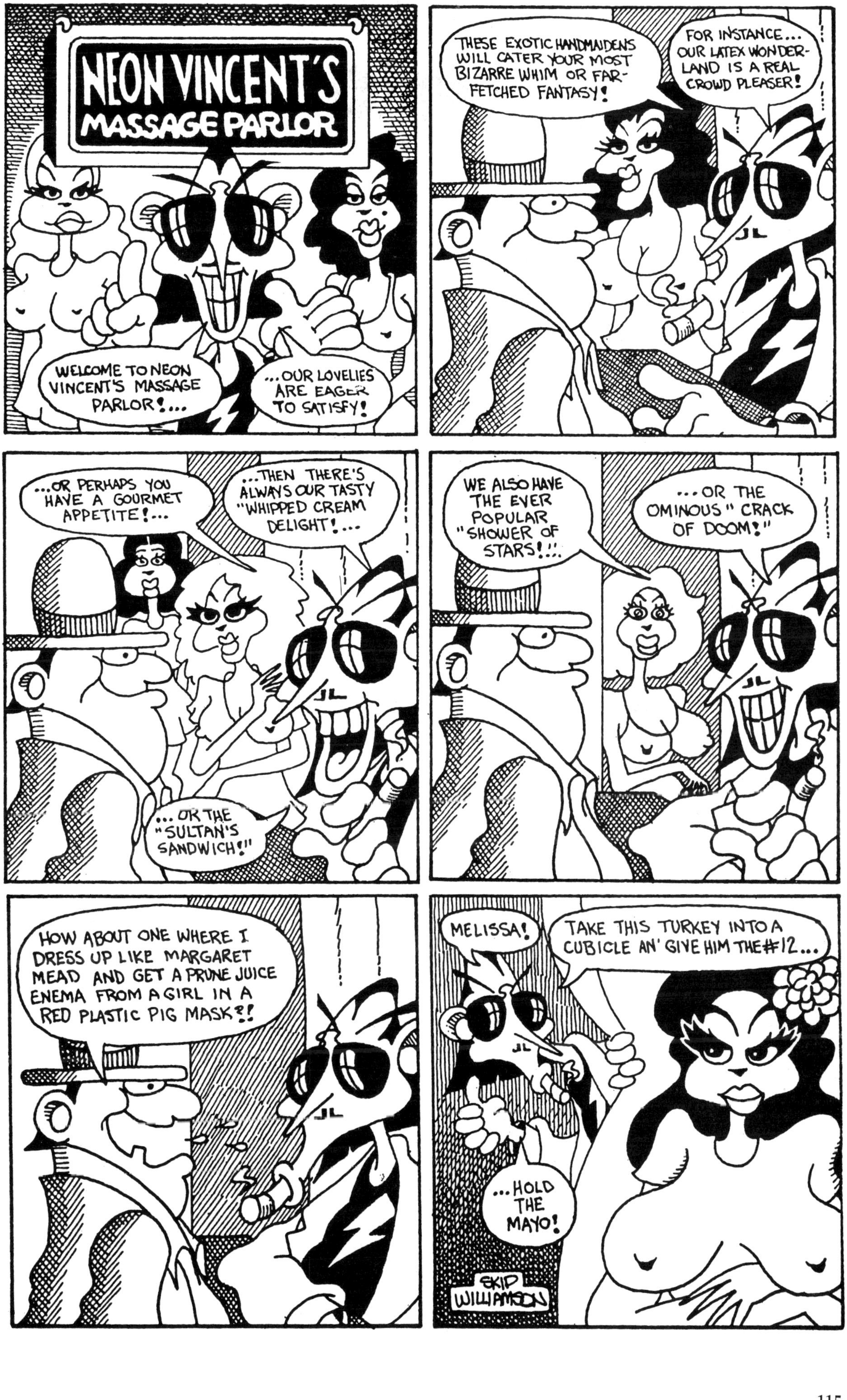
NEON VINCENT'S MASSAGE PARLOR
WELCOME TO NEON VINCENT'S MASSAGE PARLOR!...
...OUR LOVELIES ARE EAGER TO SATISFY!
THESE EXOTIC HANDMAIDENS WILL CATER YOUR MOST BIZARRE WHIM OR FAR-FETCHED FANTASY!
FOR INSTANCE... OUR LATEX WONDERLAND IS A REAL CROWD PLEASER!
...OR PERHAPS YOU HAVE A GOURMET APPETITE!...
...THEN THERE'S ALWAYS OUR TASTY "WHIPPED CREAM DELIGHT!...
...OR THE "SULTAN'S SANDWICH!"
WE ALSO HAVE THE EVER POPULAR "SHOWER OF STARS!!"
...OR THE OMINOUS "CRACK OF DOOM!"
HOW ABOUT ONE WHERE I DRESS UP LIKE MARGARET MEAD AND GET A PRUNE JUICE ENEMA FROM A GIRL IN A RED PLASTIC PIG MASK?!
MELISSA!
TAKE THIS TURKEY INTO A CUBICLE AN' GIVE HIM THE #12...
...HOLD THE MAYO!
SKIP WILLIAMSON

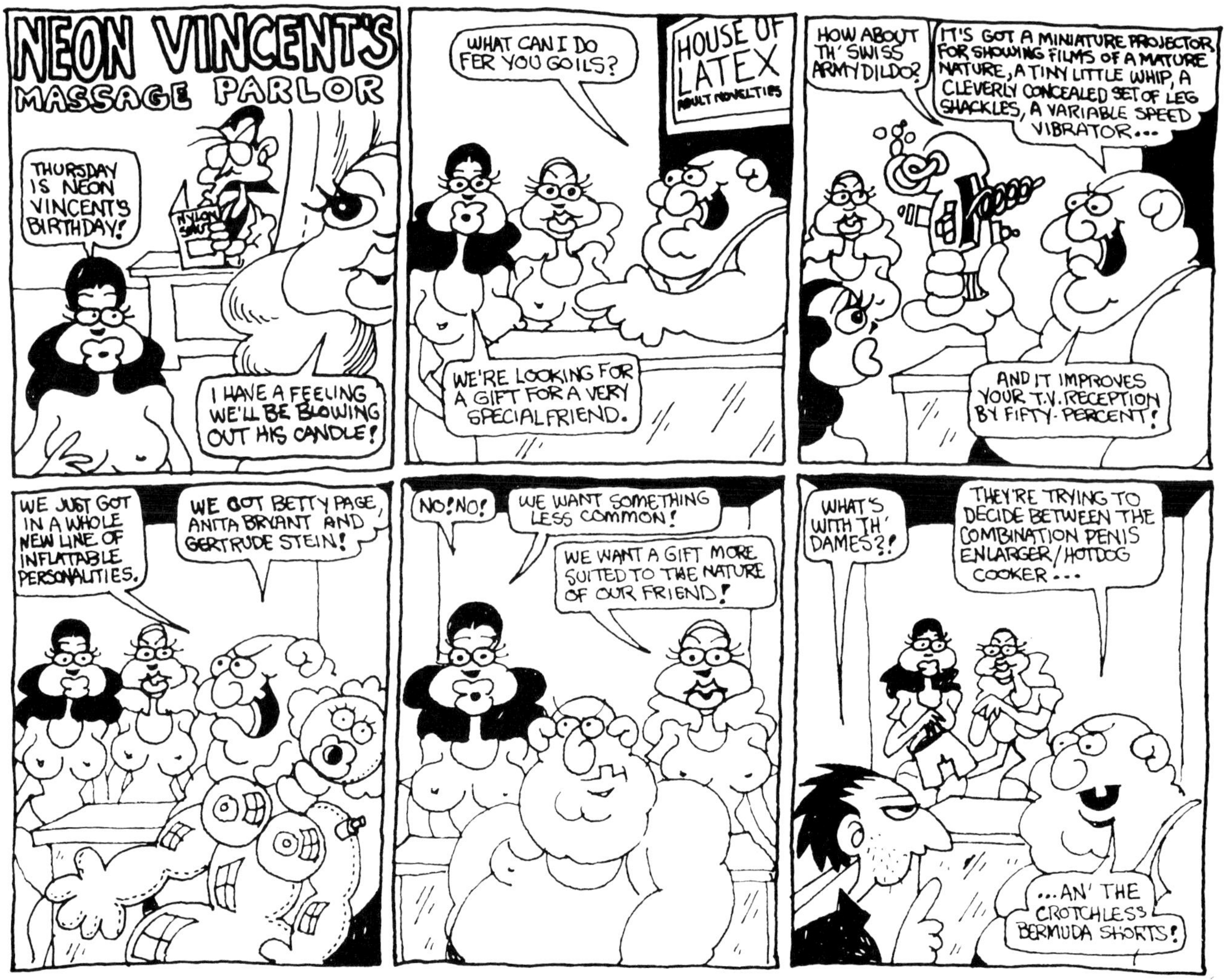
NEON VINCENT'S MASSAGE PARLOR
THURSDAY IS NEON VINCENT'S BIRTHDAY!
I HAVE A FEELING WE'LL BE BLOWING OUT HIS CANDLE!
HOUSE OF LATEX ADULT NOVELTIES
WHAT CAN I DO FER YOU GOILS?
WE'RE LOOKING FOR A GIFT FOR A VERY SPECIAL FRIEND.
HOW ABOUT TH' SWISS ARMY DILDO?
IT'S GOT A MINIATURE PROJECTOR FOR SHOWING FILMS OF A MATURE NATURE, A TINY LITTLE WHIP, A CLEVERLY CONCEALED SET OF LEG SHACKLES, A VARIABLE SPEED VIBRATOR...
AND IT IMPROVES YOUR T.V. RECEPTION BY FIFTY-PERCENT!
WE JUST GOT IN A WHOLE NEW LINE OF INFLATABLE PERSONALITIES.
WE GOT BETTY PAGE, ANITA BRYANT AND GERTRUDE STEIN!
NO! NO!
WE WANT SOMETHING LESS COMMON!
WE WANT A GIFT MORE SUITED TO THE NATURE OF OUR FRIEND!
WHAT'S WITH TH' DAMES?!
THEY'RE TRYING TO DECIDE BETWEEN THE COMBINATION PENIS ENLARGER/HOTDOG COOKER...
...AN' THE CROTCHLESS BERMUDA SHORTS!

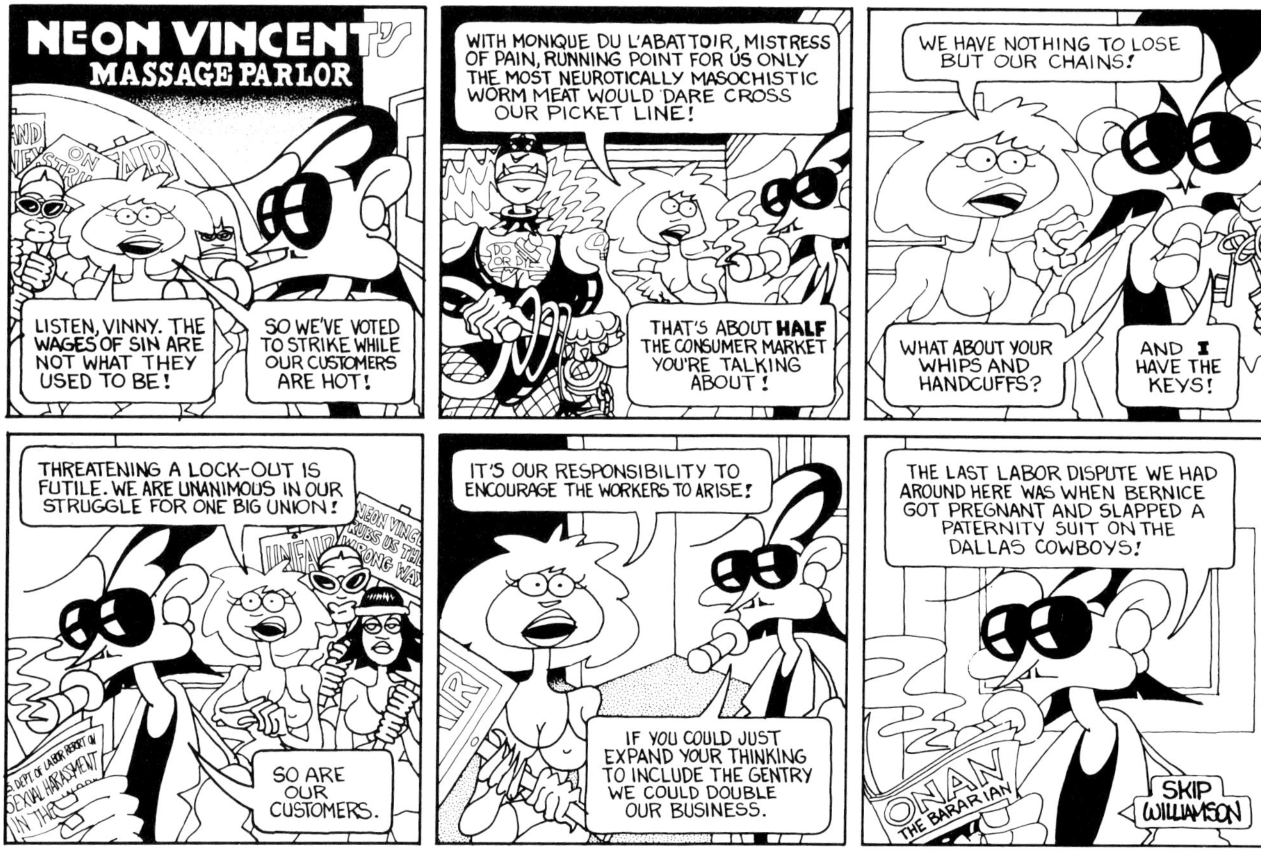
NEON VINCENT'S MASSAGE PARLOR
LISTEN, VINNY. THE WAGES OF SIN ARE NOT WHAT THEY USED TO BE!
SO WE'VE VOTED TO STRIKE WHILE OUR CUSTOMERS ARE HOT!
WITH MONIQUE DU L'ABATTOIR, MISTRESS OF PAIN, RUNNING POINT FOR US ONLY THE MOST NEUROTICALLY MASOCHISTIC WORM MEAT WOULD DARE CROSS OUR PICKET LINE!
DO OR DIE
THAT'S ABOUT HALF THE CONSUMER MARKET YOU'RE TALKING ABOUT!
WE HAVE NOTHING TO LOSE BUT OUR CHAINS!
WHAT ABOUT YOUR WHIPS AND HANDCUFFS?
AND I HAVE THE KEYS!
THREATENING A LOCK-OUT IS FUTILE. WE ARE UNANIMOUS IN OUR STRUGGLE FOR ONE BIG UNION!
SO ARE OUR CUSTOMERS.
IT'S OUR RESPONSIBILITY TO ENCOURAGE THE WORKERS TO ARISE!
IF YOU COULD JUST EXPAND YOUR THINKING TO INCLUDE THE GENTRY WE COULD DOUBLE OUR BUSINESS.
THE LAST LABOR DISPUTE WE HAD AROUND HERE WAS WHEN BERNICE GOT PREGNANT AND SLAPPED A PATERNITY SUIT ON THE DALLAS COWBOYS!
ONAN THE BARARIAN
SKIP WILLIAMSON

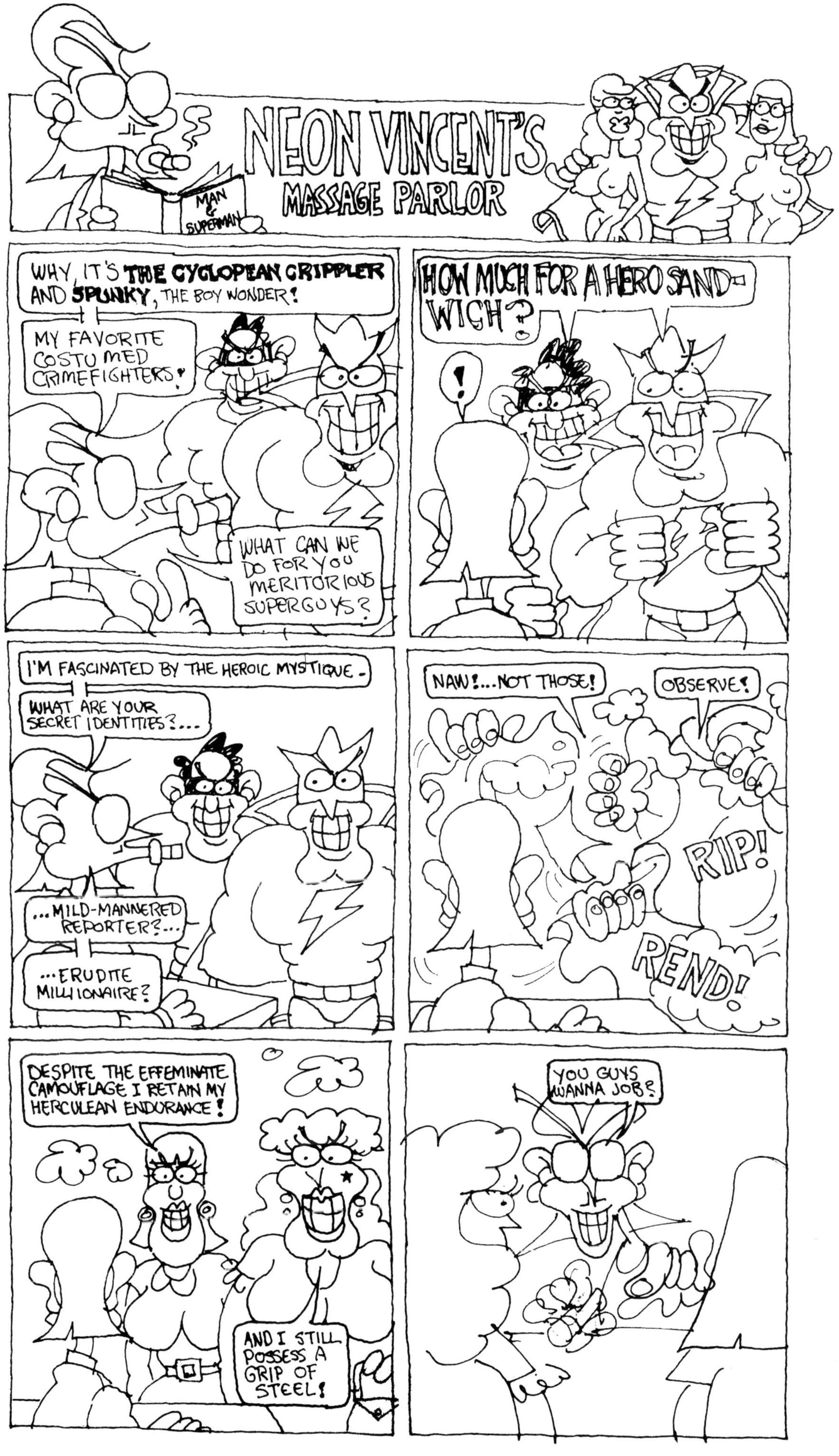
NEON VINCENT'S
MASSAGE PARLOR
MAN & SUPERMAN
WHY, IT'S THE CYCLOPEAN CRIPPLER AND SPUNKY, THE BOY WONDER!
MY FAVORITE COSTUMED CRIMEFIGHTERS!
WHAT CAN WE DO FOR YOU MERITORIOUS SUPERGUYS?
HOW MUCH FOR A HERO SAND-WICH?
!
I'M FASCINATED BY THE HEROIC MYSTIQUE -
WHAT ARE YOUR SECRET IDENTITIES?...
...MILD-MANNERED REPORTER?...
...ERUDITE MILLIONAIRE?
NAW!...NOT THOSE!
OBSERVE!
RIP!
REND!
DESPITE THE EFFEMINATE CAMOUFLAGE I RETAIN MY HERCULEAN ENDURANCE!
AND I STILL POSSESS A GRIP OF STEEL!
YOU GUYS WANNA JOB?

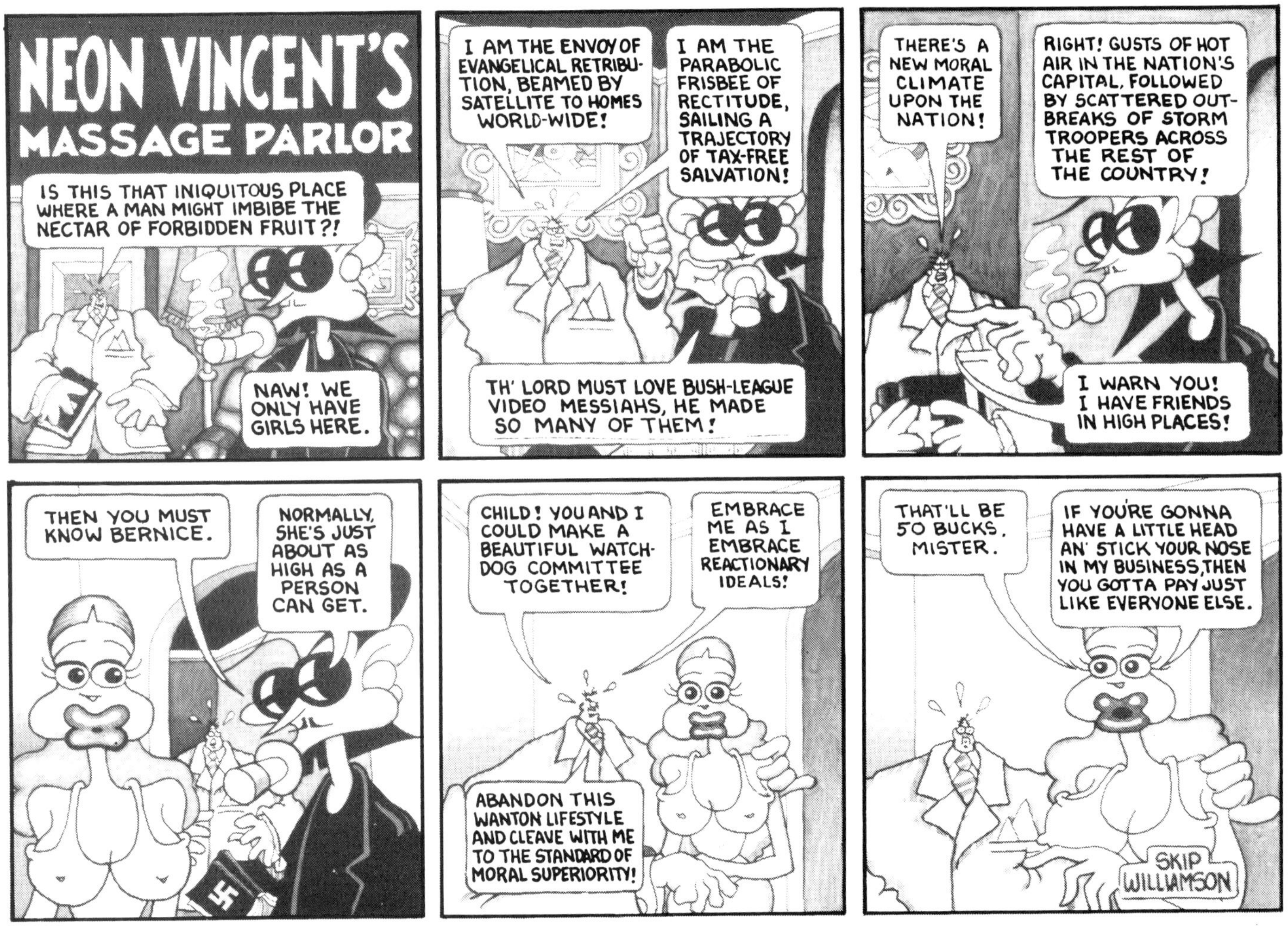
NEON VINCENT'S MASSAGE PARLOR
IS THIS THAT INIQUITOUS PLACE WHERE A MAN MIGHT IMBIBE THE NECTAR OF FORBIDDEN FRUIT?!
NAW! WE ONLY HAVE GIRLS HERE.
I AM THE ENVOY OF EVANGELICAL RETRIBUTION, BEAMED BY SATELLITE TO HOMES WORLD-WIDE!
I AM THE PARABOLIC FRISBEE OF RECTITUDE, SAILING A TRAJECTORY OF TAX-FREE SALVATION!
TH' LORD MUST LOVE BUSH-LEAGUE VIDEO MESSIAHS, HE MADE SO MANY OF THEM!
THERE'S A NEW MORAL CLIMATE UPON THE NATION!
RIGHT! GUSTS OF HOT AIR IN THE NATION'S CAPITAL, FOLLOWED BY SCATTERED OUTBREAKS OF STORM TROOPERS ACROSS THE REST OF THE COUNTRY!
I WARN YOU! I HAVE FRIENDS IN HIGH PLACES!
THEN YOU MUST KNOW BERNICE.
NORMALLY, SHE'S JUST ABOUT AS HIGH AS A PERSON CAN GET.
CHILD! YOU AND I COULD MAKE A BEAUTIFUL WATCHDOG COMMITTEE TOGETHER!
EMBRACE ME AS I EMBRACE REACTIONARY IDEALS!
ABANDON THIS WANTON LIFESTYLE AND CLEAVE WITH ME TO THE STANDARD OF MORAL SUPERIORITY!
THAT'LL BE 50 BUCKS, MISTER.
IF YOU'RE GONNA HAVE A LITTLE HEAD AN' STICK YOUR NOSE IN MY BUSINESS, THEN YOU GOTTA PAY JUST LIKE EVERYONE ELSE.
SKIP WILLIAMSON

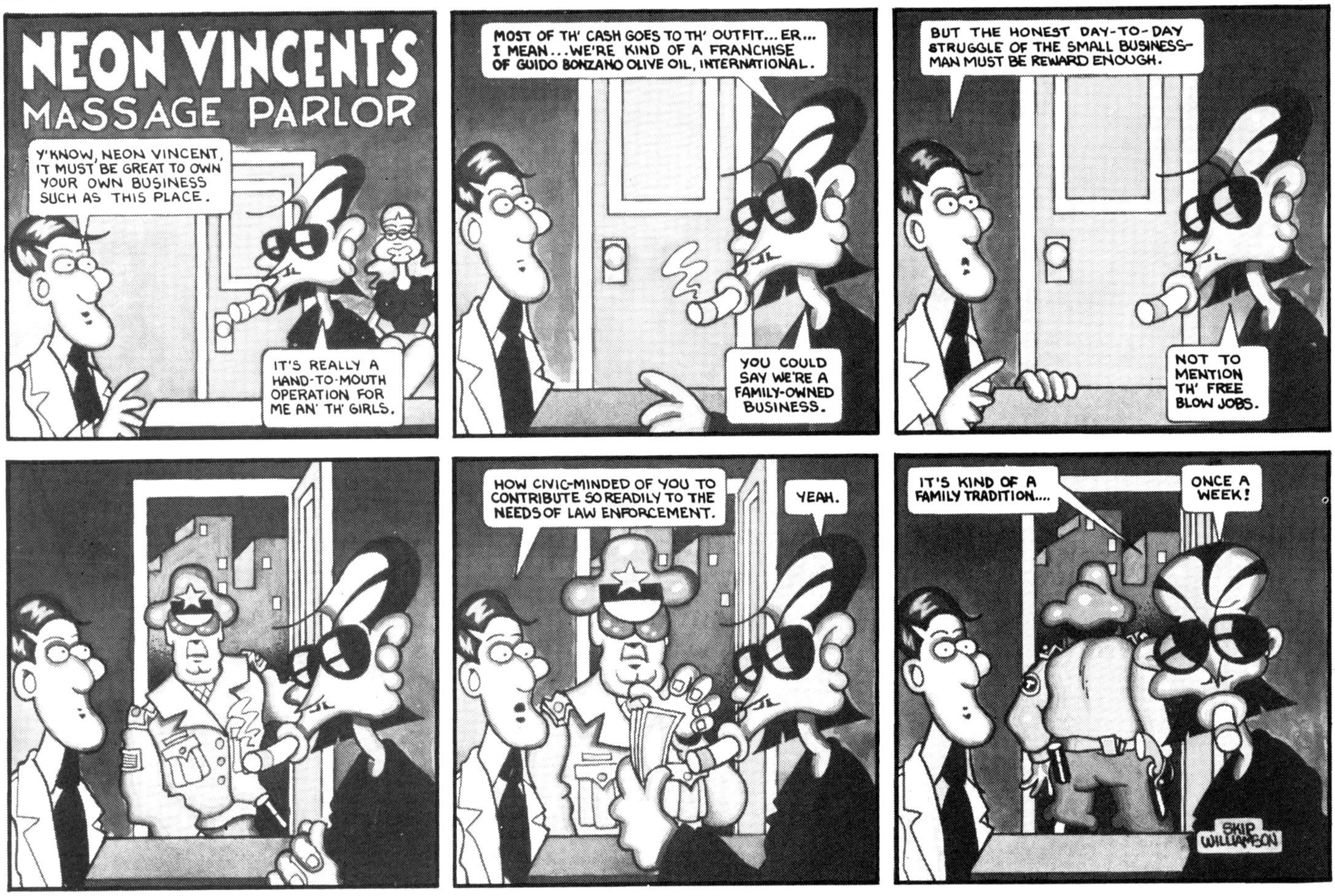
NEON VINCENT'S MASSAGE PARLOR
Y'KNOW, NEON VINCENT, IT MUST BE GREAT TO OWN YOUR OWN BUSINESS SUCH AS THIS PLACE.
IT'S REALLY A HAND-TO-MOUTH OPERATION FOR ME AN' TH' GIRLS.
MOST OF TH' CASH GOES TO TH' OUTFIT... ER... I MEAN... WE'RE KIND OF A FRANCHISE OF GUIDO BONZANO OLIVE OIL, INTERNATIONAL.
YOU COULD SAY WE'RE A FAMILY-OWNED BUSINESS.
BUT THE HONEST DAY-TO-DAY STRUGGLE OF THE SMALL BUSINESSMAN MUST BE REWARD ENOUGH.
NOT TO MENTION TH' FREE BLOW JOBS.
HOW CIVIC-MINDED OF YOU TO CONTRIBUTE SO READILY TO THE NEEDS OF LAW ENFORCEMENT.
YEAH.
IT'S KIND OF A FAMILY TRADITION....
ONCE A WEEK!
SKIP WILLIAMSON

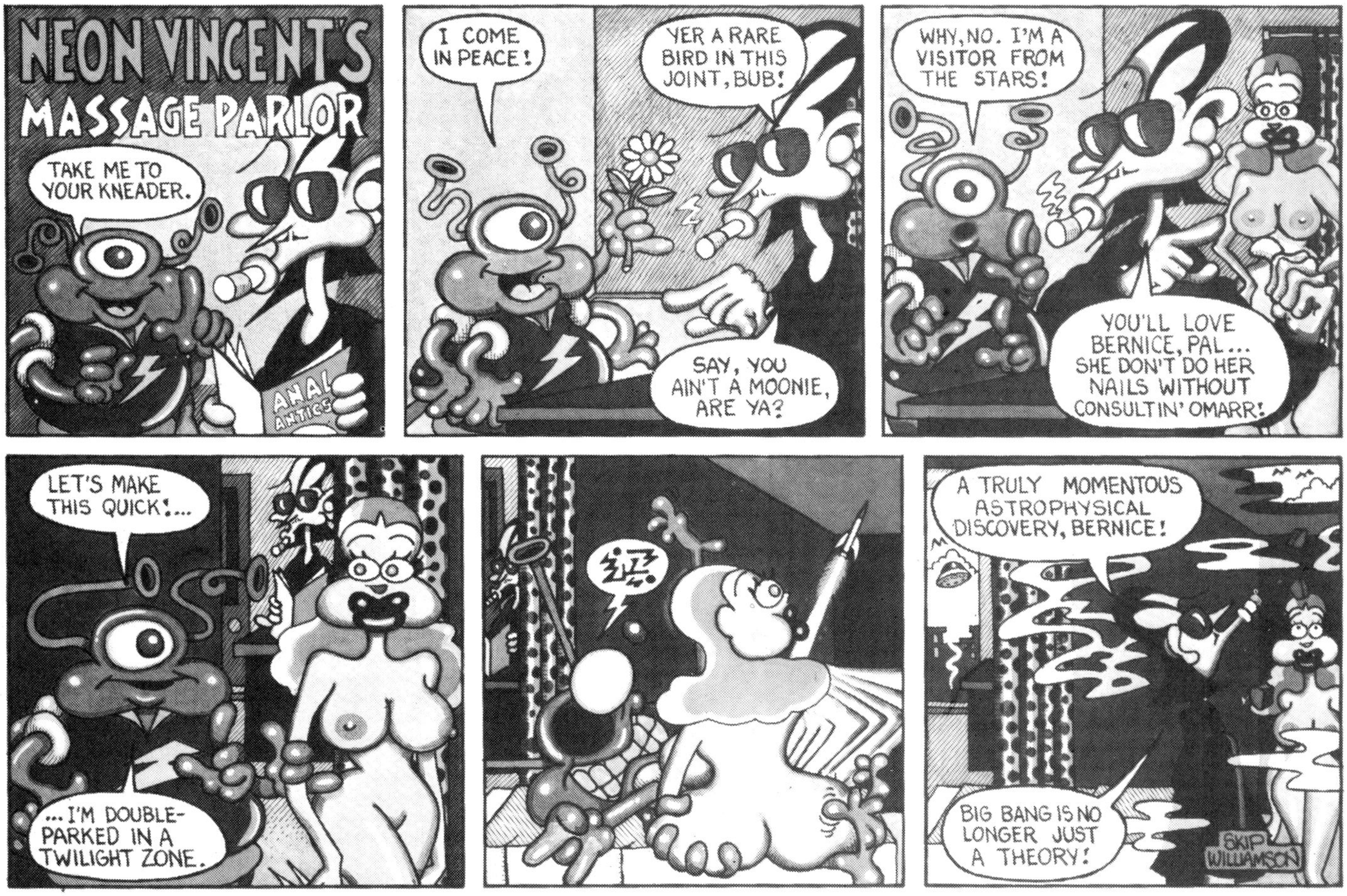
NEON VINCENT'S
MASSAGE PARLOR
TAKE ME TO YOUR KNEADER.
ANAL ANTICS
I COME IN PEACE!
YER A RARE BIRD IN THIS JOINT, BUB!
SAY, YOU AIN'T A MOONIE, ARE YA?
WHY, NO. I'M A VISITOR FROM THE STARS!
YOU'LL LOVE BERNICE, PAL... SHE DON'T DO HER NAILS WITHOUT CONSULTIN' OMARR!
LET'S MAKE THIS QUICK!...
...I'M DOUBLE-PARKED IN A TWILIGHT ZONE.
A TRULY MOMENTOUS ASTROPHYSICAL DISCOVERY, BERNICE!
BIG BANG IS NO LONGER JUST A THEORY!
SKIP WILLIAMSON

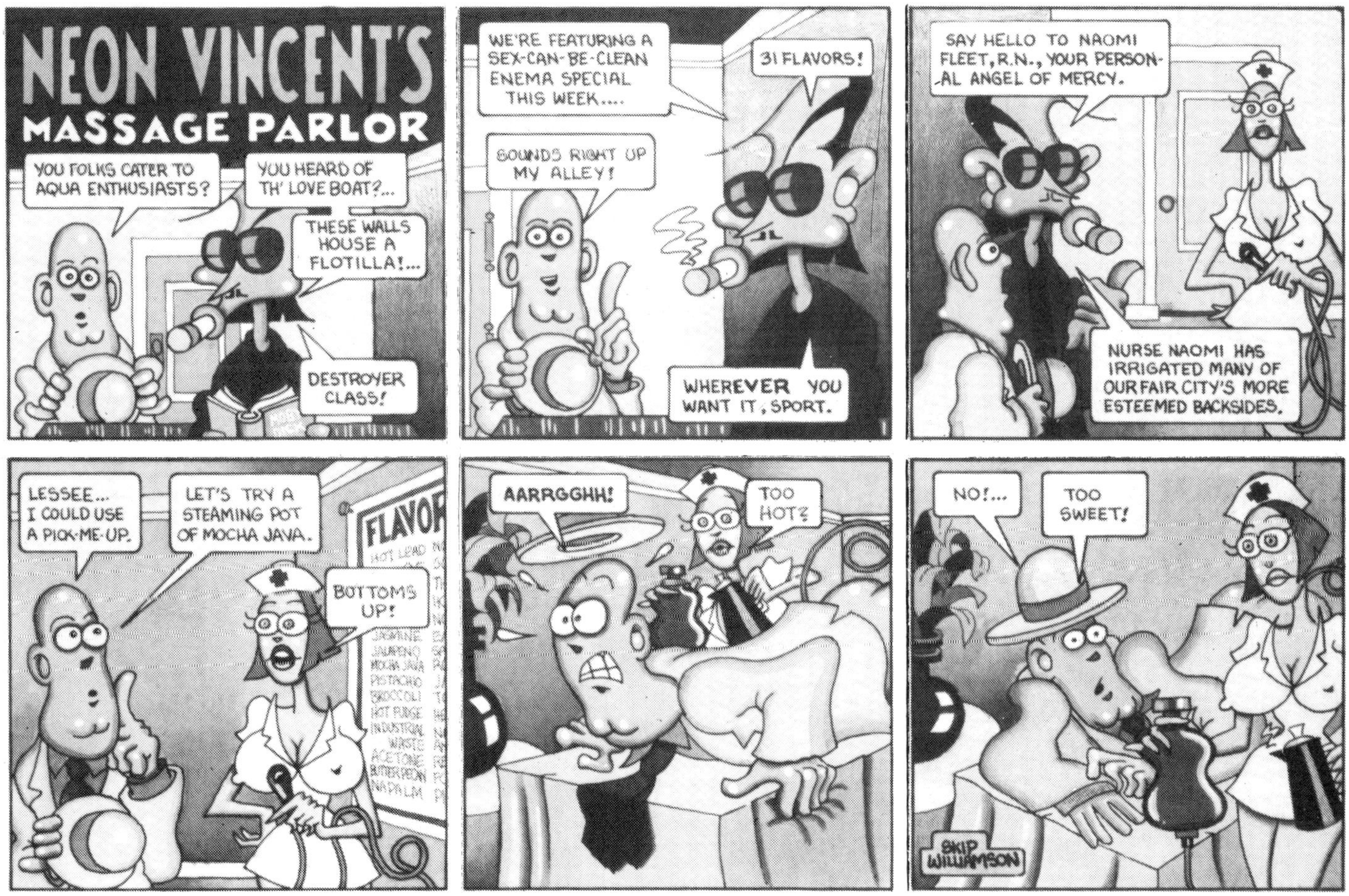
NEON VINCENT'S
MASSAGE PARLOR
YOU FOLKS CATER TO AQUA ENTHUSIASTS?
YOU HEARD OF TH' LOVE BOAT?...
THESE WALLS HOUSE A FLOTILLA!...
DESTROYER CLASS!
WE'RE FEATURING A SEX-CAN-BE-CLEAN ENEMA SPECIAL THIS WEEK....
31 FLAVORS!
SOUNDS RIGHT UP MY ALLEY!
WHEREVER YOU WANT IT, SPORT.
SAY HELLO TO NAOMI FLEET, R.N., YOUR PERSONAL ANGEL OF MERCY.
NURSE NAOMI HAS IRRIGATED MANY OF OUR FAIR CITY'S MORE ESTEEMED BACKSIDES.
LESSEE... I COULD USE A PICK-ME-UP.
LET'S TRY A STEAMING POT OF MOCHA JAVA.
BOTTOMS UP!
FLAVOR
JASMINE
JALAPENO
MOCHA JAVA
PISTACHIO
BROCCOLI
HOT FUDGE
INDUSTRIAL WASTE
ACETONE
BUTTER PECAN
NAPALM
AARRGGHH!
TOO HOT?
NO!...
TOO SWEET!
SKIP WILLIAMSON

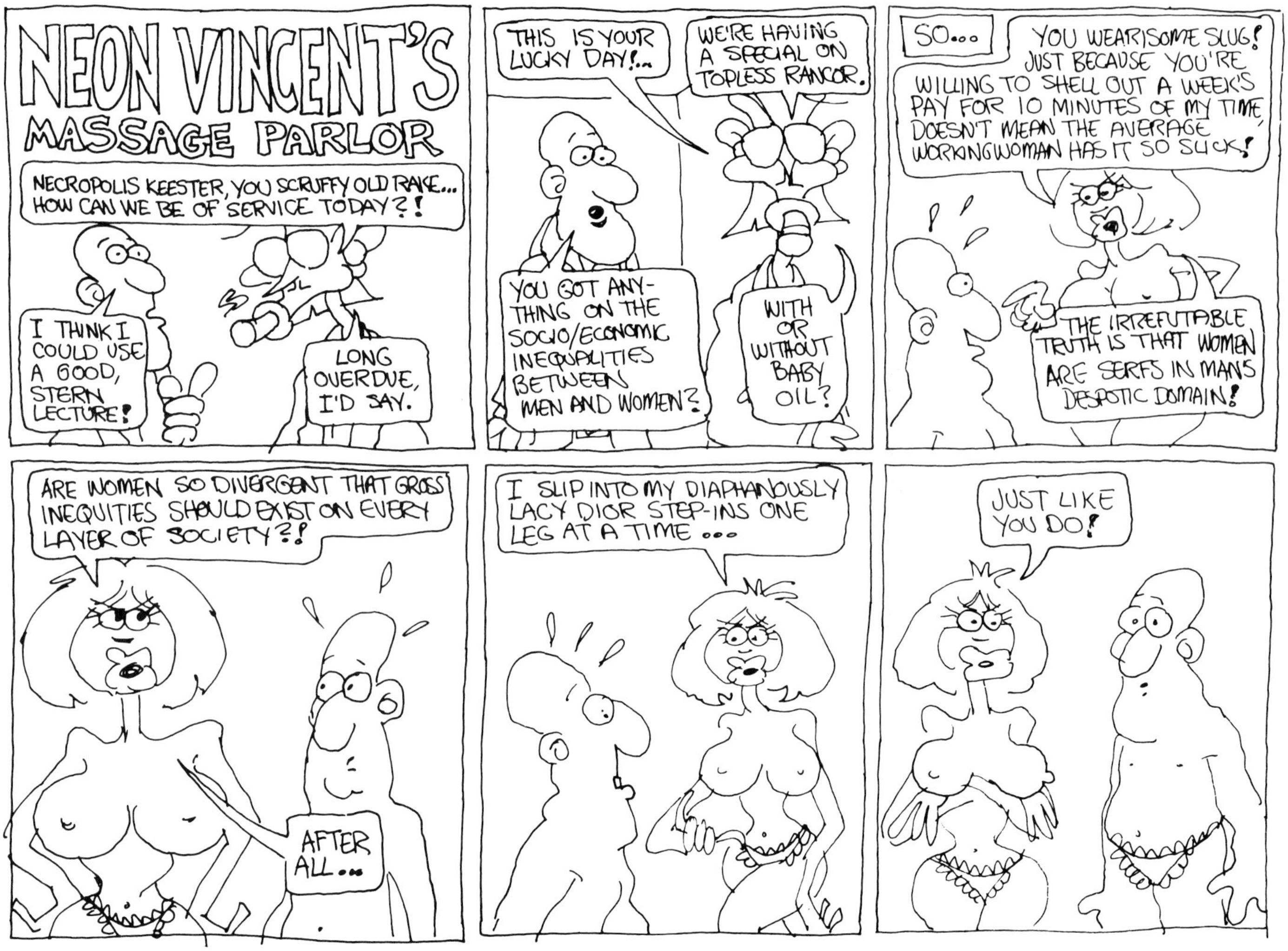
NEON VINCENT'S MASSAGE PARLOR
NECROPOLIS KEESTER, YOU SCRUFFY OLD RAKE... HOW CAN WE BE OF SERVICE TODAY?!
I THINK I COULD USE A GOOD, STERN LECTURE!
LONG OVERDUE, I'D SAY.
THIS IS YOUR LUCKY DAY!...
WE'RE HAVING A SPECIAL ON TOPLESS RANCOR.
YOU GOT ANYTHING ON THE SOCIO/ECONOMIC INEQUALITIES BETWEEN MEN AND WOMEN?
WITH OR WITHOUT BABY OIL?
SO...
YOU WEARISOME SLUG! JUST BECAUSE YOU'RE WILLING TO SHELL OUT A WEEK'S PAY FOR 10 MINUTES OF MY TIME, DOESN'T MEAN THE AVERAGE WORKINGWOMAN HAS IT SO SLICK!
THE IRREFUTABLE TRUTH IS THAT WOMEN ARE SERFS IN MAN'S DESPOTIC DOMAIN!
ARE WOMEN SO DIVERGENT THAT GROSS INEQUITIES SHOULD EXIST ON EVERY LAYER OF SOCIETY?!
AFTER ALL...
I SLIP INTO MY DIAPHANOUSLY LACY DIOR STEP-INS ONE LEG AT A TIME...
JUST LIKE YOU DO!

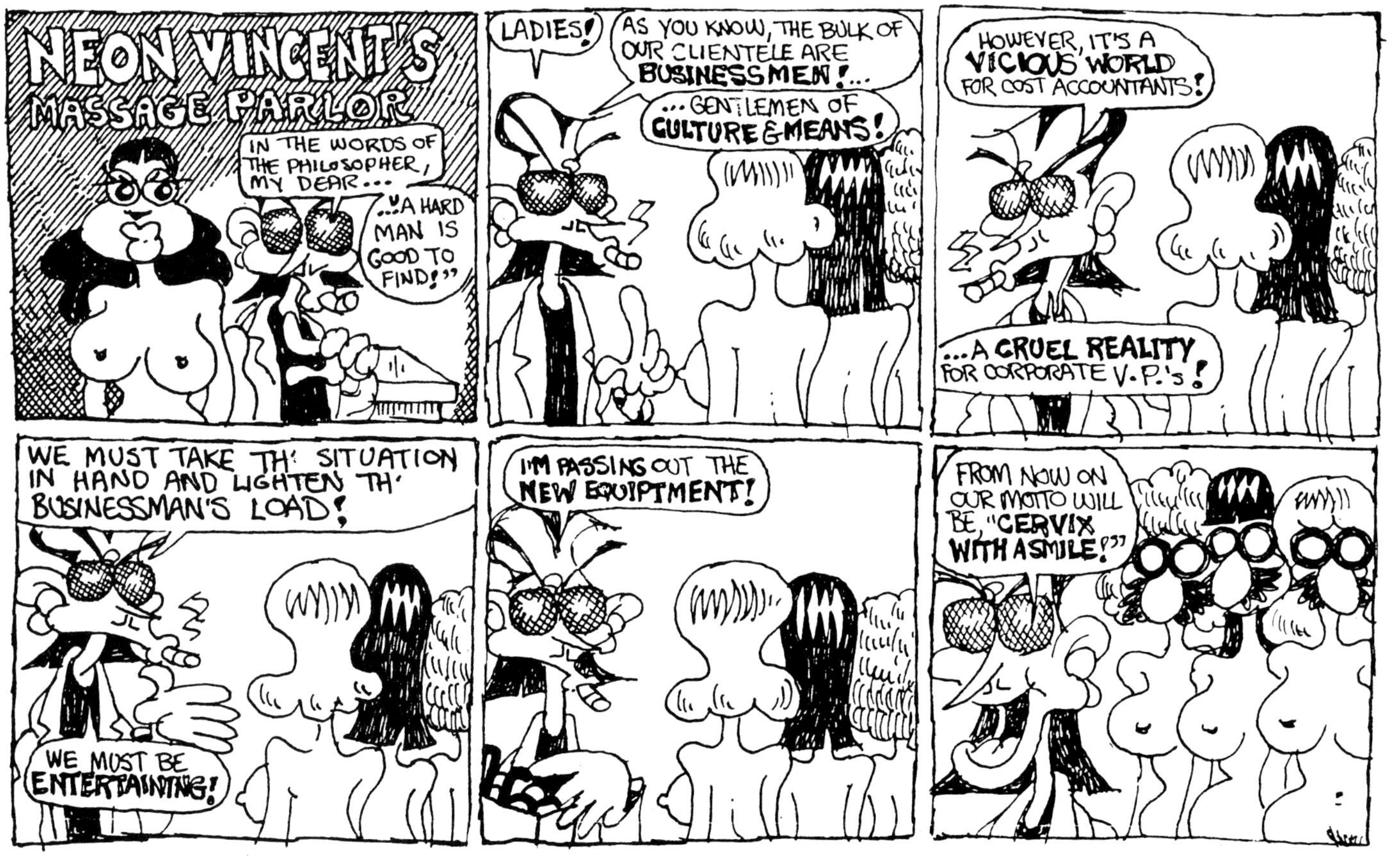
NEON VINCENT'S MASSAGE PARLOR
IN THE WORDS OF THE PHILOSOPHER, MY DEAR...
"...A HARD MAN IS GOOD TO FIND!"
LADIES!
AS YOU KNOW, THE BULK OF OUR CLIENTELE ARE BUSINESSMEN!...
...GENTLEMEN OF CULTURE & MEANS!
HOWEVER, IT'S A VICIOUS WORLD FOR COST ACCOUNTANTS!
...A CRUEL REALITY FOR CORPORATE V.P.'s!
WE MUST TAKE TH' SITUATION IN HAND AND LIGHTEN TH' BUSINESSMAN'S LOAD!
WE MUST BE ENTERTAINING!
I'M PASSING OUT THE NEW EQUIPTMENT!
FROM NOW ON OUR MOTTO WILL BE, "CERVIX WITH A SMILE!"

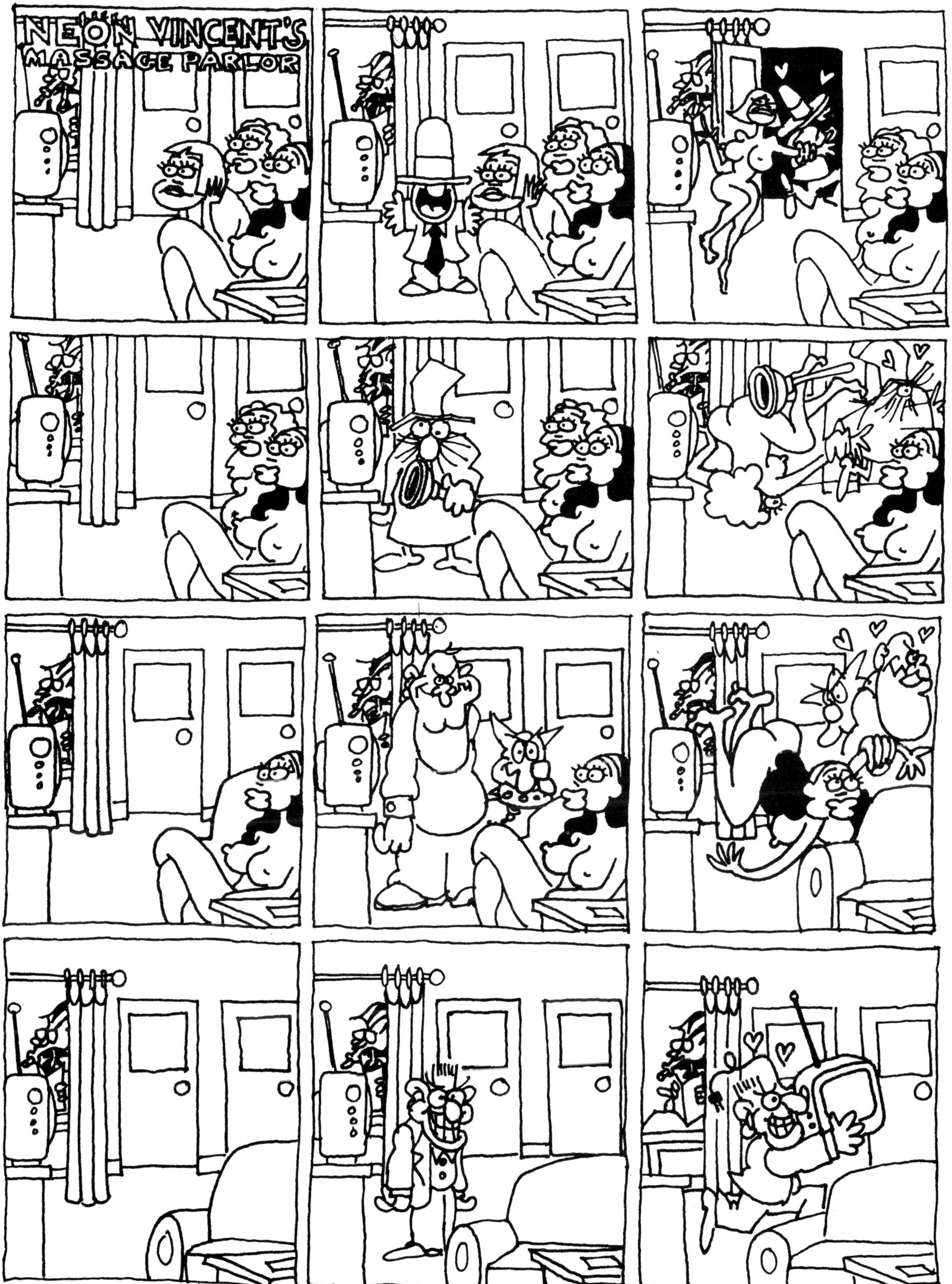
NEON VINCENT'S
MASSAGE PARLOR

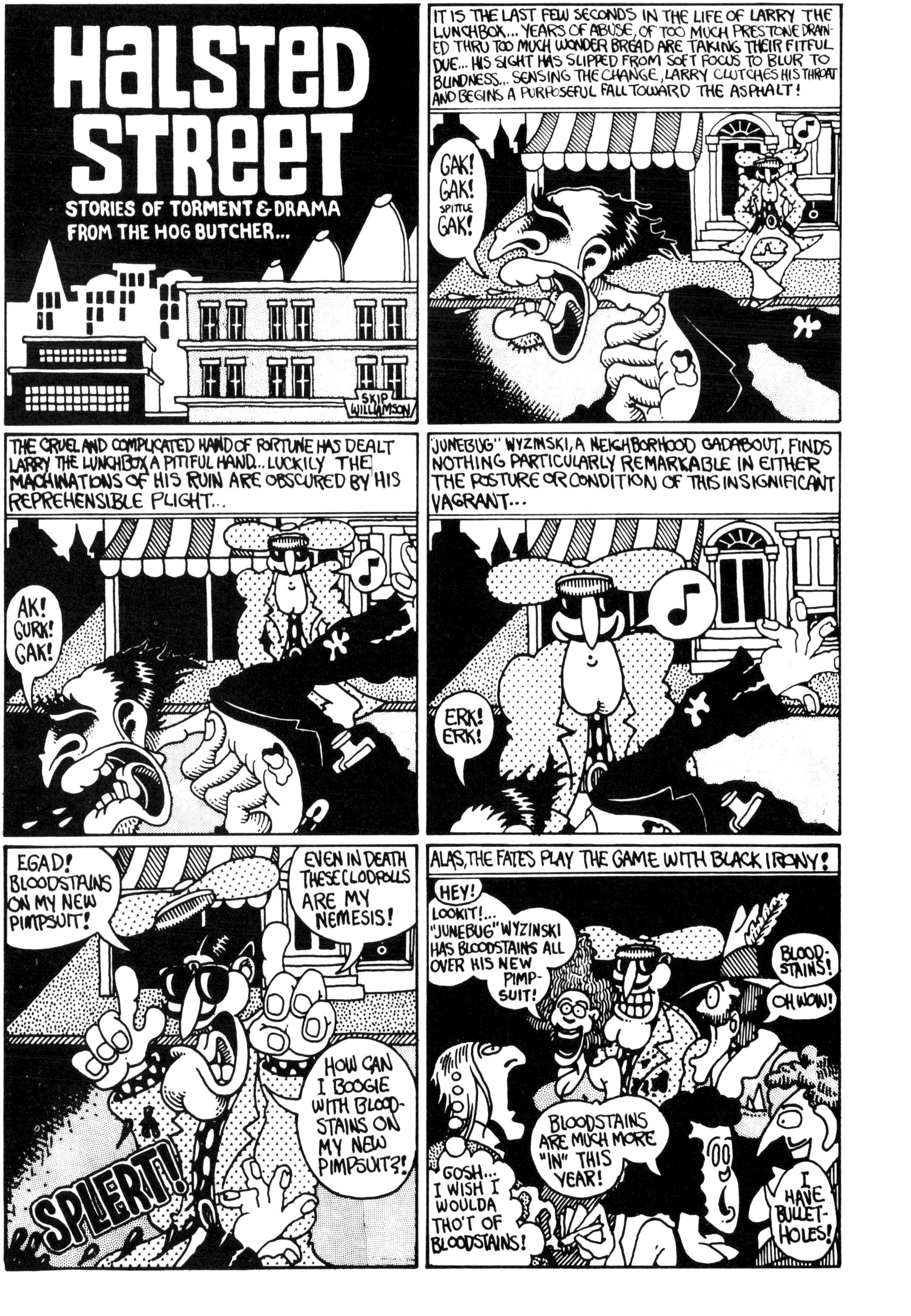
HALSTED STREET
STORIES OF TORMENT & DRAMA FROM THE HOG BUTCHER...
SKIP WILLIAMSON
IT IS THE LAST FEW SECONDS IN THE LIFE OF LARRY THE LUNCHBOX... YEARS OF ABUSE, OF TOO MUCH PRESTONE DRAINED THRU TOO MUCH WONDER BREAD ARE TAKING THEIR FITFUL DUE... HIS SIGHT HAS SLIPPED FROM SOFT FOCUS TO BLUR TO BLINDNESS... SENSING THE CHANGE, LARRY CLUTCHES HIS THROAT AND BEGINS A PURPOSEFUL FALL TOWARD THE ASPHALT!
GAK! GAK! SPITTLE GAK!
THE CRUEL AND COMPLICATED HAND OF FORTUNE HAS DEALT LARRY THE LUNCHBOX A PITIFUL HAND... LUCKILY THE MACHINATIONS OF HIS RUIN ARE OBSCURED BY HIS REPREHENSIBLE PLIGHT...
AK! GURK! GAK!
"JUNEBUG" WYZINSKI, A NEIGHBORHOOD GADABOUT, FINDS NOTHING PARTICULARLY REMARKABLE IN EITHER THE POSTURE OR CONDITION OF THIS INSIGNIFICANT VAGRANT...
ERK! ERK!
EGAD! BLOODSTAINS ON MY NEW PIMPSUIT!
EVEN IN DEATH THESE CLODPOLLS ARE MY NEMESIS!
HOW CAN I BOOGIE WITH BLOODSTAINS ON MY NEW PIMPSUIT?!
SPLERT!
ALAS, THE FATES PLAY THE GAME WITH BLACK IRONY!
HEY! LOOKIT!... "JUNEBUG" WYZINSKI HAS BLOODSTAINS ALL OVER HIS NEW PIMPSUIT!
BLOODSTAINS!
OH WOW!
BLOODSTAINS ARE MUCH MORE "IN" THIS YEAR!
GOSH... I WISH I WOULDA THO'T OF BLOODSTAINS!
I HAVE BULLET-HOLES!

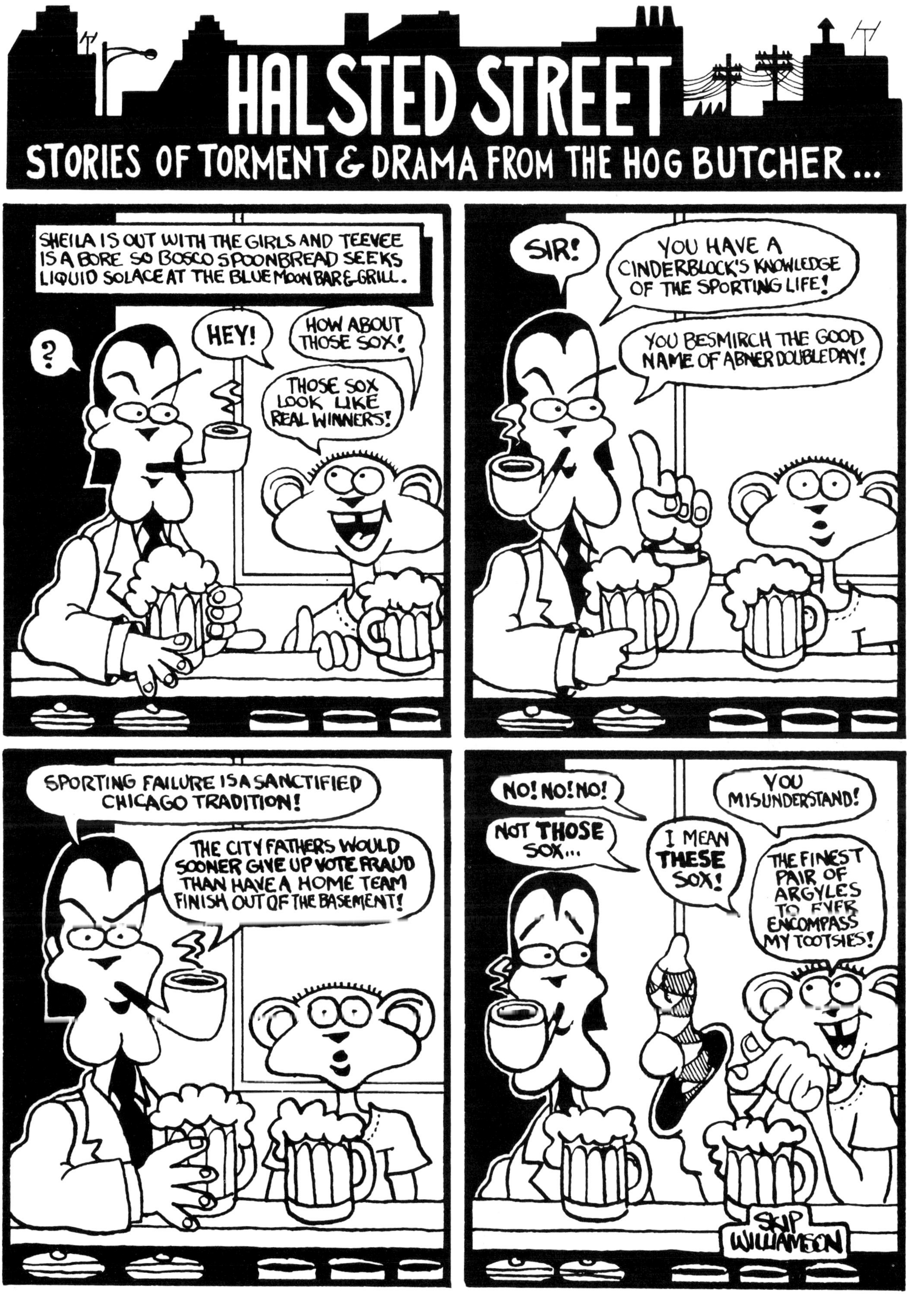
HALSTED STREET
STORIES OF TORMENT & DRAMA FROM THE HOG BUTCHER...
SHEILA IS OUT WITH THE GIRLS AND TEEVEE IS A BORE SO BOSCO SPOONBREAD SEEKS LIQUID SOLACE AT THE BLUE MOON BAR & GRILL.
?
HEY!
HOW ABOUT THOSE SOX!
THOSE SOX LOOK LIKE REAL WINNERS!
SIR!
YOU HAVE A CINDERBLOCK'S KNOWLEDGE OF THE SPORTING LIFE!
YOU BESMIRCH THE GOOD NAME OF ABNER DOUBLEDAY!
SPORTING FAILURE IS A SANCTIFIED CHICAGO TRADITION!
THE CITY FATHERS WOULD SOONER GIVE UP VOTE FRAUD THAN HAVE A HOME TEAM FINISH OUT OF THE BASEMENT!
NO! NO! NO!
NOT THOSE SOX...
YOU MISUNDERSTAND!
I MEAN THESE SOX!
THE FINEST PAIR OF ARGYLES TO EVER ENCOMPASS MY TOOTSIES!
SKIP WILLIAMSON

HALSTED STREET

STORIES OF TORMENT & DRAMA FROM THE HOG BUTCHER...

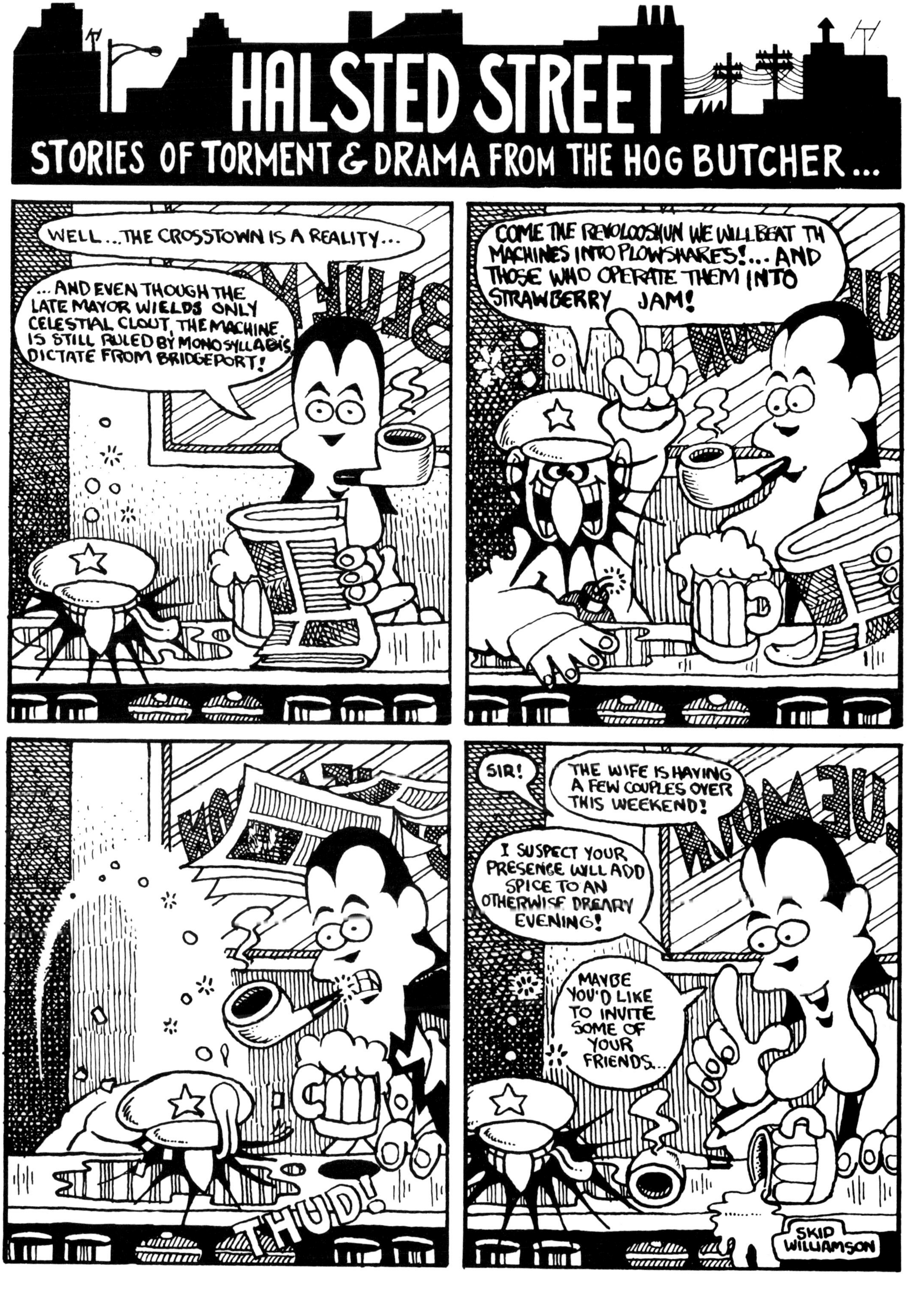
HALSTED STREET
STORIES OF TORMENT & DRAMA FROM THE HOG BUTCHER...
WELL... THE CROSSTOWN IS A REALITY...
... AND EVEN THOUGH THE LATE MAYOR WIELDS ONLY CELESTIAL CLOUT, THE MACHINE IS STILL RULED BY MONOSYLLABIC DICTATE FROM BRIDGEPORT!
COME THE REVOLOOSHUN WE WILL BEAT TH MACHINES INTO PLOWSHARES!... AND THOSE WHO OPERATE THEM INTO STRAWBERRY JAM!
THUD!
SIR!
THE WIFE IS HAVING A FEW COUPLES OVER THIS WEEKEND!
I SUSPECT YOUR PRESENCE WILL ADD SPICE TO AN OTHERWISE DREARY EVENING!
MAYBE YOU'D LIKE TO INVITE SOME OF YOUR FRIENDS...
SKID WILLIAMSON

HALSTED STREET
STORIES OF TORMENT & DRAMA FROM THE HOG BUTCHER...

SO! YOU THINK THE MEDIA BIZ IS JUST ONE THREE HOUR LUNCH AFTER ANOTHER?...JUST ONE DOUBLE JACK DANIELS' STRAIGHT UP (HOLD THE ROCKS) AFTER ANOTHER?...

WHAT WE NEED IS A STORY WITH PUNCH! WE NEED AN ISSUE WITH PAZAZZ!

HOW ABOUT KOREAN BRIBERY?

TOO TOUCHY!

HOWABOUT RACIAL STRIFE IN MARQUETTE PARK?

NAW! THAT'S OLD HAT!

OLD PRINTER'S DEVIL

...BUT SOMEWHERE IN THE BOWELS OF "THE CITY THAT WORKS" A NEWSROOM HERE, A CITY DESK THERE, MUST PUMP OUT THE MEDIA FIX WE CRAVE...

HEY, CHIEF! YOU WANT A REALLY SIGNIFICANT ISSUE?!...

...HOWABOUT "SCANDAL-RIDDEN EX-COP SHOT DOWN GANGLAND STYLE ON NORTHWEST SIDE"?

NAW! TOO PEDESTRIAN!...

WHAT WE NEED IS AN ISSUE THAT'S REALLY SIGNIFICANT THE DOMESTIC YET ALSO CATERS TO THOSE OF A VIOLENT BENT!...

WE'VE USED UP KING TUT...

CHILD PORNOGRAPHY HAS LOST ITS CHARM...

I MEAN...SOMEBODY HAS TO PICK THROUGH OUR WASTEFUL EXCESSES TO GET TO THE REALLY SIGNIFICANT ISSUES OF OUR TIME!

WHAT WE NEED IS AN ISSUE THAT SIGNIFICANTLY AFFECTS AD SALES OR NIELSEN RATINGS!

HEY! WHAT'S THIS COMING IN ON THE TELETYPE?!

HEY, BOSCO! AIN'T THIS YER OL' LADY?!

THIS WOMAN IS BEING HELD HOSTAGE BY HOMICIDAL VEGETARIANS IN A NORTH SIDE A&P!...

SKIP WILLIAMSON

...TUNE IN NEXT WEEK

HALSTED STREET
STORIES OF TORMENT & DRAMA FROM THE HOG BUTCHER...

WAFTING TO THE STRAINS OF VAN DYKE AND THE DIESEL DOGS, THE PARAMOURS OF CHICAGO PUNKDOM CONGREGATE AT DE RIGUEUR DISCO, LA MERE DISPAIR!...

HAVE A NICE DAY

THE EVENTS OF THE HOUR DO NOT ESCAPE THE BLEARY SCRUTINY OF THESE NIHILISTIC TRENDSETTERS.

HEY, LOOK!

I GOT TH' NEW TED NUGENT SINGLE, "KILL YOUR MEAT!"

TED NUGENT?!

HOW GAUCHE!

MEAT MUSIC IS OUT!

VEGTABLE MUSIC IS IN!

HERE IS TH' HOT NEW DISC, "ROOT ROT ROCK!"

?

I AM EVEN HIPPER...

I HAVE MONOSODIUM-GLUTAMATE MUSIC!

SKIP WILLIAMSON

127

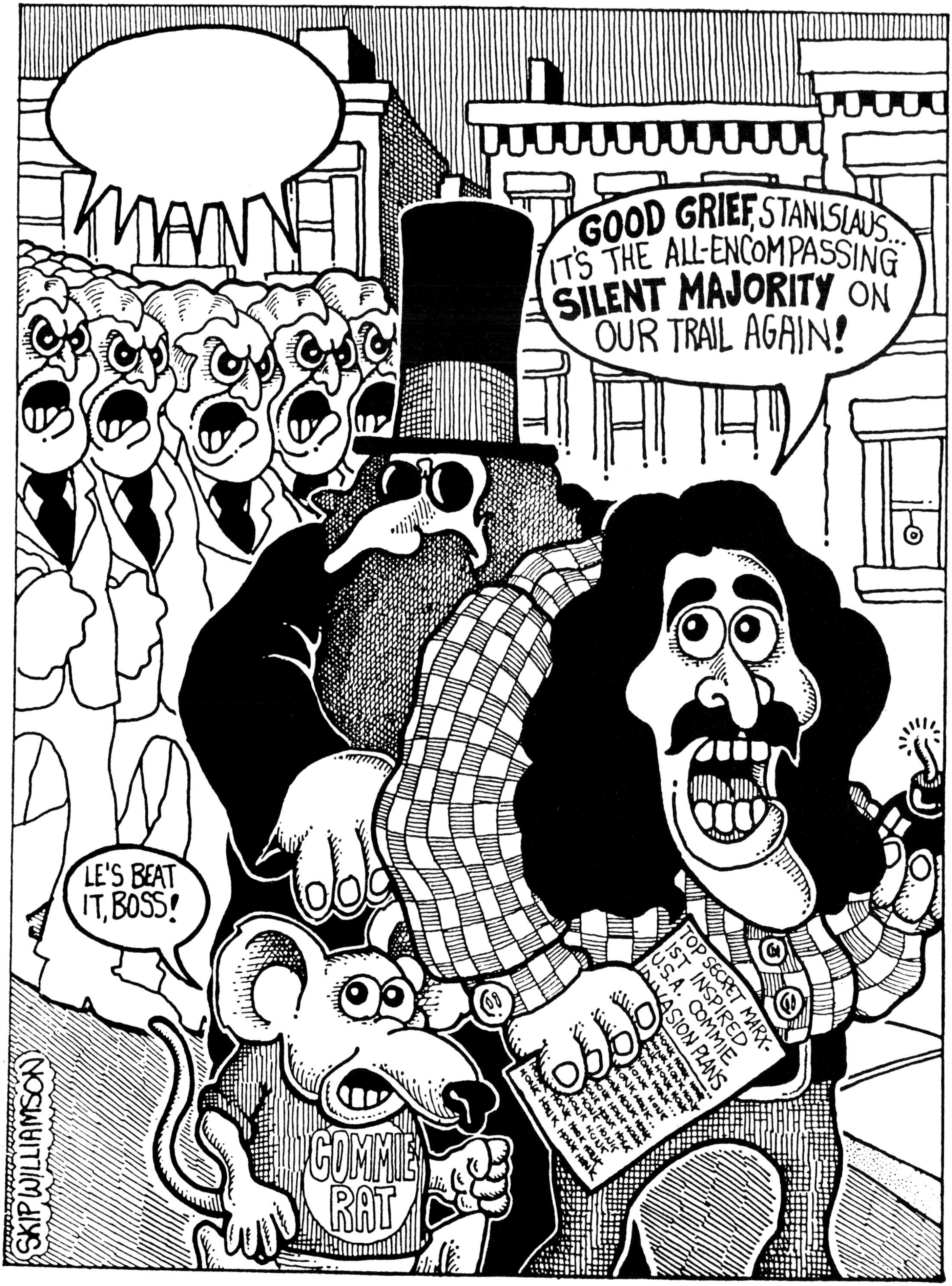
GOOD GRIEF, STANISLAUS... IT'S THE ALL-ENCOMPASSING SILENT MAJORITY ON OUR TRAIL AGAIN!
LE'S BEAT IT, BOSS!
TOP SECRET MARX-IST INSPIRED U.S.A. COMMIE INVASION PLANS
COMMIE RAT
SKIP WILLIAMSON